The Grand Tour of Galway

The Grand Tour
of Galway

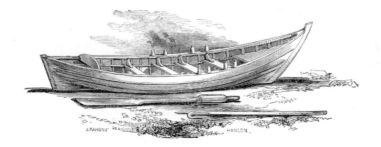

Compiled by

CORNELIUS KELLY

CAILLEACH BOOKS

Published by
CAILLEACH BOOKS
Allihies, Beara, County Cork
email: grandtourbooks@eircom.net

ISBN 0–9537823–2–8

Cover design by Anissa Fox
Cover illustration Galway Harbour in 1830 (front) and Chancel Arch, Tuam Cathedral by Daniel Grose (back).
Typesetting by Carrigboy Typesetting Services, Durrus, County Cork
Printed by ColourBooks Ltd., Baldoyle, Dublin

Contents

Galway Fisherwoman

Introduction

'And yet, in the Middle Ages these waters were cut by thousands of foreign ships. The signs at the corners of the narrow streets record the city's connection with Latin Europe – Madeira Street, Merchant Street, Spaniards Walk, Madeira Island . . .', James Joyce wrote while visiting Galway in 1912. And like Joyce many earlier visitors left us accounts of their adventures in Galway. *The Grand Tour of Galway* brings them together– from Giraldus Cambrensis in the twelfth century to Pete McCarthy eight hundred years later.

When Giraldus Cambrensis visited Galway with Prince John, Athenry was the biggest town in the county. Galway City was still a small fishing village which, by the fifteenth century, had grown to become a centre of international commerce. The harbour bustled with foreign ships, buildings of brick and stone lined the streets, and merchants bargained and haggled under sheltering arcades. With its rich trade with Spain and the Continent dominated by the thirteen leading Norman families, Galway became known as the City of the Tribes. At the end the fifteenth century, the city fathers felt confident enough to request that the Vatican grant them complete local control of the church and its clergy. In their petition they described themselves as 'a modest and civil people' and the Gaelic Irish as 'a savage race, unpolished and illiterate.' When cartographer John Speed made his pictorial map at the beginning of the seventeenth century, Galway had grown to become a city of considerable size surrounded by walls and towers. On one of the gates a sign read: 'From the Ferocious O'Flaherties, Good Lord Deliver Us.'

But the wars of the seventeenth century caused Galway's trade to decline. Soon weeds grew between the flagstones and the courtyards filled up with refuse. Yet these upheavals also brought visitors to Galway: Ann Fanshawe and her husband Richard, Secretary of War to the Prince of Wales, fled here in 1650 to catch a ship to Spain; Edmund Ludlow followed a year later at the head of the Cromwellian Army. At century's end the desolation was still visible to John Dunton when he visited the site of the Battle of Aughrim and wrote 'the bones of the dead which lie yet to be seen would make a man take notice of the place.'

When commerce returned to Galway in the late seventeenth century it brought new waves of visitors. In 1825, the publication of a book, *Letters from the Irish Highlands* put Connemara on the tourist map for the first time. This collection of letters by the Blake family of Renvyle House helped people see these wild Irish highlands not as a savage wilderness

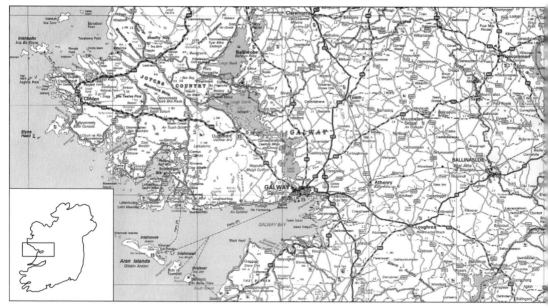

Contemporary map of the County of Galway

but as a place of beauty. For many tourists prevented from travelling on the Continent by wars, County Galway became a new romantic destination.

Though pioneering antiquarians such as Edward Lhuyd visited the Aran Islands, it was not until George Petrie's 1821 visit that their rich prehistoric and ecclesiastical heritage was brought to the public's attention. Others followed and this interest culminated in the visit of the Ethnological Society in September 1857, when seventy people – including such luminaries of Irish antiquarian research as John O'Donovan, Eugene O'Curry and William Wilde – were treated to a display of bird-nest robbing before proceeding to Dun Aengus for a picnic.

With its varied and dramatic landscapes, it is only natural that artists were drawn to County Galway. Some came to get inspiration from the dramatic scenery while others came to study the cadences of local speech. Illustrations by George Petrie and Jack Yeats, photographs by John Millington Synge, and word pictures by William Orpen, Paul Henry and Augustus John, combine to give the reader a fascinating view of the county. They bring to life the dramatic landscapes; churning ocean, endless bog, the flash of a red petticoat in a stone-grey field. Many artists too were drawn by Lady Gregory's Coole Park. Edward Martyn, Arthur Symons, George Moore, William Butler Yeats, John Millington Synge, Augustus John, and Sean O'Casey all visited – many of them to leave their initials on the Autograph Tree.

*Lynch's Castle, Galway, where James Lynch hanged his own son Walter in 1492
(Lawrence Collection R881)*

Doorway of the Church of the Saint

But whether they came to Galway to star in a film, to write articles in Italian, to renovate a Bishop's palace, or to hunt with the Galway Blazers, each person has left us a fascinating account of his or her adventure. John Wesley, the founder of Methodism, came to preach at the Court House; Maud Gonne MacBride to address a political rally near Woodford; B.N. Hedderman to serve as the first district nurse on the Aran Islands; John Huston to renovate a stately home; and perhaps the most dramatic of all, aviator Arthur Whitten Brown, of Alcock & Brown fame, to land in Connemara after completing the first Transatlantic flight ever. In every conveyance from carriage to curragh, bike to plane, on horseback or on foot, their accounts take the reader on a tour to every part of the county and on a journey back through time.

Cornelius Kelly

Giraldus Cambrensis

1185

GERALD DE BARRI, better known as Giraldus Cambrensis (1146–1220), was born in Pembrokeshire in Wales. He made several trips to France, studying and lecturing. Shortly after his return to England he was ordained a priest and became one of Henry II's chaplains. In 1185, the King sent him to Ireland to accompany his son Prince John. Cambrensis spent two years in Ireland and, on his return to England, wrote *Topographia Hiberniae* which he read publicly at Oxford over three successive days. It is one of the earliest travel descriptions of Ireland – often painting a fantastical picture of the country.

There is an island in the sea west of Connacht which is said to be consecrated by St. Brendan. In this island human corpses are not buried and do not putrefy, but are placed in the open and remain without corruption. Here men see with some wonder and recognize their grandfathers, great-grandfathers, and great-great-grandfathers and a long line of ancestors. There is another remarkable thing about this island: while the whole of Ireland is infested with mice, there is not a single mouse here. For no mouse is bred here nor does one live if it be brought here. If by chance it is brought in, it makes straight for the nearest point of the sea and throws itself in; and if it be prevented, it dies on the spot . . .

There is in Connacht a village celebrated for a church of St. Nannan. In olden times there was such a multitude of fleas there that the place was almost abandoned because of the pestilence, and was left without inhabitants, until, through the intercession of St. Nannan, the fleas were brought to a certain neighbouring meadow. The divine intervention because of the merits of the saint so cleansed the place that not a single flea could ever afterwards be found here. But the number of them in the meadow is so great, that it ever remains inaccessible not only to men but also to beasts.

From *The Topography of Ireland*

Fynes Moryson

1600

BORN AT CALDEBY, Lincolnshire, Fynes Moryson (1566–1630) received a degree from Cambridge University in 1587. He remained at the college until his desire to see foreign countries got the better of him. He

Galway City in the eighteen fifties

received a licence to travel and, after two years' preparation, embarked for the Continent in 1591. Moryson spent the next six years visiting almost every part of Europe and studying at Leyden University, in the Netherlands. After returning to England, he travelled through Scotland before coming to Ireland in November 1600. He served as private secretary to Lord Mountjoy and was with him at the Battle of Kinsale. Moryson returned to England with Mountjoy and his account of his travels was published as *An Itinerary* in 1617.

Connaght is the fourth part of Ireland, a fruitfull Prouince, but hauing many Boggs and thicke Woods, and it diuided into six Countyes, of Clare, of Leitrim, of Galloway, of Rosecomen, of Maio, and of Sligo. The County of Clare or Thowmond, hath his Earles of Thowmond, of the Family of the Obrenes the old Kings of Connaght, and Toam is the seate of an Archbishop, onely part but the greatest of this County was called Clare of Thomas Clare Earle of Glocester. The adioyning territory Clan

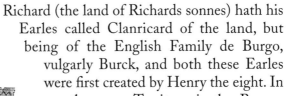

Richard (the land of Richards sonnes) hath his Earles called Clanricard of the land, but being of the English Family de Burgo, vulgarly Burck, and both these Earles were first created by Henry the eight. In the same Territory is the Barony Atterith, belonging to the Barons of the English Family Bermingham, of old very warlike: but their posteritie haue degenerated to the Irish barbarisme. The city of Galway giuing name to the County, lying vpon the Sea, is frequently inhabited with ciuill people, and fairely built. The Northern part of Connaght is inhabited by these Irish Septs, O Conor, O Rorke, and Mac Diarmod. Upon the Westerne coast lyes the Iland Arran, famous for the fabulous long life of the inhabitants.

From *The Field Day Anthology of Irish Writing*

Oliver St. John

1601

OLIVER ST. JOHN (1559–1630) was born in Wiltshire and graduated from Oxford University in 1578. He had to flee England when he killed the navigator George Best in a duel and spent several years as a soldier on the Continent. St. John came to Ireland with Lord Mountjoy and, like Fynes Moryson, he was at the Battle of Kinsale. He sat in the English Parliament for two years until his appointment as Master of the Ordnance in Ireland. In 1613 St. John was elected to the Irish Parliament and some years later was appointed Lord Deputy of Ireland. His 'intolerable severity' in dealing with dissent made him many enemies and he was eventually forced out of office.

*G*alway is small but all of fayer and stately buildings; the fronts of their howses towards the streets, being all of hewed stone, upp to the topp, and garnyshed with fayer battlements in an uniform cowrse, as if the whole towne hadd beene builte upon one modell. The merchants are riche and great adventurers at sea. They keepe goode hospitality and are kind to strangers, and in their manner of entertaynement and in fashioning and appearllinghe themselves and their wives doe most preserve the ancyent manner and state of any town that ever I sawe. The towne is built upon a rocke envyroned almost with the sea and the ryver, compassed with a strong wall, and good defences, after the auncient manner, and such as with a fewe men it may defend itself against any army.

[Athenry] Eight miles from Galway, Elder than yt, built by the English, whiles they hadd their swords in their hands, and kept themselves close in garryson. Now it hath a very small and poore habitacion and people. Yet the walls stand still large in compass and very strong and fayer.

From *The Description of Ireland in Anno 1598*

John Speed

1610

HISTORIAN AND CARTOGRAPHER John Speed (1552–1629) was born in Farringdon, Cheshire. Following in his father's footsteps, he became a tailor, and received the freedom of the Merchant Taylors' Company in 1580. Two years later he married and built a house for his family on land leased from the company and he and his wife Susanna raised twelve sons and six daughters there. Speed started making maps of the English counties during his leisure time and he presented these to Queen Elizabeth I. His maps, including his pictorial map of Galway, were collected and published in 1611 as Speed's *Theatre of the Empire of Great Britain*.

*T*he Principal City of this Province, and, which may worthily be acounted the third in *Ireland*, is *Galway*, in *Irish Galllive*, built in manner much like to a Tower. It is dignified with a Bishops See, and it is much frequented with Merchants, by reason whereof, and the benefit of the Road and Haven, it is gainful to the Inhabitants, through traffique and exchange of rich commodities, both by Sea and Land. Not far from which, near the West shoar that lies indented with small in-lets and outlets, in a row, are the Islands called Arran, about which many a foolish fable goes, as if they were the Islands of the living, wherein none died at any time, or were subject to mortality, which is as superstitous observation, as that

John Speed's pictorial map of Galway from James Hardiman's
History of the Town and Country of Galway

used in some other corners of the Country, where the people leave the right Arms of their Infant males unchristned (as they term it) to the end that at any time afterwards, they might give a more deadly and ungracious blow when they strike: which things do not only shew how palpable they are carried away by traditious obscurities, but do also intimate how full their hearts be of inveterate revenge.

From *An Epitome of Mr. John Speed's Theatre of the Empire of Great Britain*

Ann Fanshawe

1650

BORN IN HART STREET, St. Olave's, in London, Ann Harrison (1625–1680) was trained in the ladylike arts but much preferred sporting activities, such as riding and running. In 1642, her father, Sir John Harrison, was imprisoned and his property confiscated by the Parliamentarians. In 1643, Ann moved to Oxford with her family and soon after married her cousin Sir Richard Fanshawe, Secretary of War to the Prince of Wales. Although they had fourteen children together, only five survived their father. Ann Fanshawe and her husband returned to Jersey with the Prince and then went to Ireland. In 1649, Ann Fanshawe arrived in Cork and, the following January, the Fanshawes fled to Galway with the Cromwellian forces at their heels. Her account of her life, written in 1647 was first published in 1829.

Ann Fanshawe

*B*y this time my husband had received order from the King to give the Lord Inchiquin the seal to keep until further order from His Majesty. When the business was settled we went, accompanied with my Lord Inchiquin and his family four or five miles towards Galway, which we did by force and not by choice. For the plague had been so hot in that city the summer before that it was almost depopulated – and the haven as much as the town. But your father, hearing that by accident there was a great ship of Amsterdam bound for Malaga in Spain, and Cromwell pursuing his conquest at our backs, resolved to fall into the hands of God rather than into the hands of men, and with his family of about ten persons came to the town at the latter end of [January], where we found guards placed, that none should enter without certificate from whence they came. But notwithstanding that your father came to embark himself for Spain, and that there was a merchant's house took for us that was near the sea-side (and one of their best), they told us if we pleased to 'light, they would wait on us to the place. But it was long from thence and no horses

6

Old door porch in Galway

were admitted into the town. An Irish footman that heard this, and served us, said, 'I lived here some years and know every street, and I likewise know a much nearer way than these men can show you, sir. Therefore come with me, if you please.' We resolved to follow him, and sent our horses to stables in the suburbs. He led us all on the back side of the town under the walls, over which the people during the plague (which was not yet quite stopped) had flung out all their dung, dirt, and rags, and we walked up to middle of our legs in them; for being engaged, we could not get back. At last we found the house, by the master standing in the door expecting us, who said, 'You are welcome to this desolate city, where you now see the street grown over with grass, once the finest little city in

7

the world'; and, indeed, it was easy to think so, the buildings were uniformly built and a very fine market-place, and walks arched and paved by the sea-side for their merchants to walk on, and a most noble harbour. Our house was very clean, only one maid in it besides the master. We had a very good supper provided, and being very weary we went early to bed. But we could not rest very well, fancying our legs bit. The next morning, as soon as my husband had put on his gown and begun to put on his stockings, he called me, saying, 'My heart, what great spots are these on my legs? Sure, it is the plague. But I am very well and feel nothing.' At which I ran out of the bed to him, and saw my own legs in the same condition; and upon examining the cause we found that the sheets being short and the blankets full of fleas, we had those spots made by them.

From *The Memoirs of Ann, Lady Fanshawe*

Edmund Ludlow

1651

EDMUND LUDLOW (1617–1691) was born in Wiltshire, the son of a radical Republican. After graduating from Oxford University at 19, he joined the bodyguard of the Earl of Essex and became active in the military leadership of the rebellion. Ludlow was one of the judges of King Charles I and signed the King's death warrant. In 1646, he was appointed second-in-command of the army in Ireland and took over command when Ireton died. Ludlow had almost completed the conquest of Ireland by the time the new commander arrived. On his return to England he was arrested for his anti-Cromwellian activities but later released. After the Restoration, Ludlow went into exile and lived in Switzerland for the remainder of his life and his *Memoirs* were published in Vevey in 1689.

Edmund Ludlow

The home of the Marquis of Clanricarde drawn by
Paul Gauci in the early nineteenth century

We began our march about five in the afternoon, and by twelve at night, having marched between sixteen and seventeen miles, we dismounted, to forage our horses, and rest ourselves. Before day we mounted, and continued our march through a desolate country, the people being fled, and no provisions to be had but what we carried with us. About ten in the morning our forlorn perceived a creaght, as the country people call it, where half a dozen families, with their cattle, were got together. Some of those who saw them first, presuming all the Irish in that country to be enemies, began to kill them; of which having notice, I put a stop to it, and took a share with them of a pot of sour milk, which seemed to me the most pleasant liquor that ever I drank. In the afternoon we found the ways exceeding bad, and almost impassable, many of the hurdles which had been laid upon them being drawn away, as we supposed, by the enemy: yet, in a little more than twenty-four hours, we had marched about forty miles, and were informed that Sir Charles Coote was besieging Portumna, a house of the earl of Clanrickard, and that the enemy were about Athenree. Upon this notice, leaving my party advantageously posted, in a place furnished with provisions for themselves

Thomas Phillip's drawing of Galway in 1685

and horses, I took with me sixty horse and went to Portumna, to be informed more particularly concerning the state of affairs. At my arrival I understood that an attempt had been made upon the place, wherein our men had become repulsed; but that the enemy, having a large line to keep, and many poor people within, fearing to hazard another assault, had agreed to surrender upon articles next morning; which was done accordingly. And now having found Sir Charles Coote's party in good condition, and able to deal with the enemy on that side, I returned to my body of horse, with which, and five hundred more that joined me, commanded by commissary-general Reynolds, I followed, and endeavoured to find out the enemy; but they removed from one place to another with such expedition, that we could not overtake them, having left their carriages, in order to march the lighter, at a castle belonging to one Mr. Brabston, situated upon a considerable pass. This place I endeavoured to reduce; and though it was indifferently strong, and we were very ill provided for such an attempt, yet after some resistance the enemy delivered it upon articles, whereby they were permitted to carry off whatsoever belonged properly to them; the tents and draught-oxen remaining in our possession, with several other things belonging to the earl of Clanrickard, whom the earl of Ormond had constituted his deputy in those parts. Having put a garrison into this place, and sent back commissary-general Reynolds with his party to Portumna, I marched with my horse towards Limerick, and came to Gourtenshegore, a castle belonging to Sir Dermot O'Shortness, who was then gone to Galway, but had left his tenants with some soldiers, and one Foliot, an Englishman, to command them in the castle.

From *The Memoirs of Edmund Ludlow*

John Dunton
1698

JOHN DUNTON (1659–1733) was born in Graddham, Huntingdonshire. His mother died when he was less than one year old and his clergyman father moved to Ireland, leaving his son behind. He returned eight years later determined to educate his son for the clergy. But the younger Dunton had other ideas. At fourteen he was apprenticed to a bookseller in London and soon started his own venture. In 1698 Dunton came to Ireland. In Dublin he sold his books at auction and got involved in a dispute with a local bookseller which became the subject of *The Dublin Scuffle*, published in 1699. He also travelled to County Galway, visiting the site of the Battle of Aughrim.

From hence I continued my journey through an uneven rough country towards Galway, here the miles lengthen very much as the country grew worse, as if the badness of the commodity made the inhabitants there afford better measure. At the end of ten miles I came to a place called Ballinasloe, which has nothing remarkable in it. Here the River Suck divides the counties of Galway and Roscommon, three miles beyond this town is Aghrim, an obscure village consisting of few cabins and an old castle, but now made famous by the defeat of St. Ruth and the Irish army; the bones of the dead which lie yet to be seen would make a man take notice of the place. Tis said the Irish here lost 7000 men with their whole camp and all their cannon, whilst the whole loss of the English did not exceed 1000. This which I am very well assured of is very strange. After the battle the English did not tarry to bury any of the dead but their own, and left those of the enemy exposed to the fowls of the air, for the country was then so uninhabited that there were not hands to inter them. Many dogs resorted to this aceldama where for want of other food they fed on man's flesh, and thereby became so dangerous and fierce that a single person could not pass that way without manifest hazard. But a greyhound kept close by the dead body of one who was supposed to have been his master night and day, and though he fed upon other corpses with the rest of the dogs, yet he would not allow them nor anything else to touch that which he guarded. When the corpses were all consumed the other dogs departed, but this used to go every night to adjacent villages for food and return presently to the place where the beloved bones lay, for all the flesh was consumed by putrefaction, and thus he continued from July till January following, when a soldier passing that way near the dog, who perhaps feared a disturbance of what he so carefully watched, he flew upon the soldier, who shot him with his piece.

From hence to Athenry are fifteen miles through no very delightful country; in it is a wood through which the road lies which affords one remarkable story of the cunning of a fox as that I now acquainted you with the love of a dog. A country fellow who used to carry fresh herrings from Galway to Athlone and those parts of the country had made this his constant road, his fish he used to carry in two wicker baskets without covers, hanging on each side of his horse; one day as he had entered a little into the wood he found a fox lying in the way as if he were dead, and as such he took him by the legs and threw across his horses back with his head in one basket and his hinder legs in the other, secure enough of his skin in the evening, thus he trudged on leading his horse until he had almost gone through the wood, when on some occasion or other, he turned back and missed his fox, which he thought had slipped off, but looking into the baskets they were almost emptied of the fish, the poor fellow surprised searched the bottoms of them and found they were whole and unbroken he then tied his beast to a bush and went hastily back where he saw herrings scattered up and down in the highway but he never recovered them all, for Mr. Reynard had conveyed several into some of his own privacies; so various are the undoubted instances of the sagacity of beasts, that I can almost believe such a thing as this might have been, and because many of them are endowed with something very like reason, though some people would be very angry at giving it that name, which they suppose the effect only of the immortal soul.

When King John came into Ireland to reduce some of his rebellious people here, he built the town of Athenry, and environed it with a good stone wall to be a curb upon them in those parts. A mile or two from you it makes a great figure, but like most other ill things it shows best at a distance, for when you are in it 'tis a poor pitiful miserable place, full of cabins and several ruined stone houses and castles; I guess it was once a considerable place, for it has a Tholsel or Town house. This town gives the title of Baron to one Bermingham who is the first of that degree of nobility in Ireland.

Galway is eight miles from hence; about Athenry are delicate sheep walks for near two miles, but all the rest of the way is rocky and barren; Galway is an ancient town and has been of very considerable trade with Spain and France, but now there are not so many merchants among them. I do not take upon me to give you any military account of the place and its fortifications, but this I can tell you, the inhabitants are generally Irish papists, but few protestants besides the soldiery quartered there which commonly are one regiment.

From *Irish Life in the Seventeenth Century*

Edward Lhuyd

1700

CELTIC SCHOLAR and linguist Edward Lhuyd (1660–1709) was born in Wales and educated at Jesus College, Oxford. In 1690 he became Keeper of the Ashmolean Museum and thereafter devoted his efforts to researching the language and antiquities of the Celtic countries. In 1699 and 1700, he travelled through Ireland collecting material and compiling the first Irish-English dictionary. When Lhuyd died, the University sold his collection of manuscripts to pay off his debts. Some of these, including the *Book of Leinster* and the *Yellow Book of Leacan* were eventually donated to the Library of Trinity College Dublin.

For antiquities, Ireland affords no great variety; at least it was not our fortune to be much diverted that way. I have in divers parts of the kingdom picked up about 20 or 30 Irish manuscripts on parchment: but the ignorance of their criticks is such, that tho' I consulted the chiefest of them, as O Flaherty (author of *Ogygia*) and several others, they could scarce interpret one page of all my manuscripts; and this is occasioned by the want of a Dictionary, which it seems none of their Nation ever took the trouble to compose.

In the Isle of Arran (near Galloway) we found great plenty of the *Adianthum verum*, and a sort of matted Campion with a white flower, which I bewail the loss of; for an imperfect sprig of it was only brought me; and I waited afterwards in rain almost a whole week for fair weather, to have gone in quest of it.

In most of the mountains of Galloway and Mayo grows an elegant sort of Heath, bearing large Thyme leaves, a spike of fair purple flowers like

Eyre Square, Galway at the beginning of the twentieth century (Lawrence Collection R776)

some Campanula, and viscous stalks. I know not whether it be any thing related to the *Cisti Ladaniferae*.

In the same places *Pinguicula flore carneo minore* is a common plant, and a sort of *Ros Solis*, which I take to be undescribed.

From *Early Science in Oxford*

Samuel Molyneux

1709

ASTRONOMER AND POLITICIAN Samuel Molyneux (1689–1728) was born in Chester, England, the son of William Molyneux, founder of the Dublin Philosophical Society. He entered Trinity College in 1705 and there received private tutoring from George Berkeley. Molyneux graduated from Trinity in 1708 and the following year undertook a tour of Ireland. His goal was to complete a project of his father's – the writing of a description of Ireland for an atlas. His account of his journey was originally published under his uncle Thomas' name. In 1712, Molyneux left Ireland for England and in 1714 became private secretary to the Prince of Wales, the future King George II. He devoted the rest of his life to the study of astronomy and optics.

I went to vizit old Flaherty, who lives, very old, in a miserable condition at Park, some 3 hours west of Gallway, in Hiar or West-Connaught. I expected to have seen here some old Irish manuscripts, but his ill fortune has stripp'd him of these as well as his other goods, so that he has nothing now left but some few of his own writing, and a few old rummish books of history printed. In my life I never saw so strangely stony and wild a country. I did not see all this way 3 living creatures, not one house or ditch, not one bit of corn, not even, I might say, a bit of land, for stones: in short nothing appeared but stones and sea, nor could I conceive an inhabited country so destitute of all signs of people and art as this is. Yet here, I hear, live multitudes of barbarous uncivilized Irish after their old fashions, who are here one and all in ye defence of any of their own or even other rogues that fly to them, against the laws of Ireland, so that here is the assylum, here are committed the most barbarous murders after shipracks, and all manner of roguerys protected, that the Sheriffs of this county scar[c]e dare appear on ye west side of Gallway bridge, which, tho' Ireland is now generally esteem'd wholly civilized, may well be call'd the end of the English pale, which distinction should still have place as long as the inhabitants live with us in so open a state of nature.

Having got back again safe thro' this barbarous country to Galway, I din'd with some of ye officers who were here quarter'd. After dinner they walk'd me round ye town and citadell: the fortifications are in better order, and seem to have more of present strength, there being a good number of brass and iron ordinance mounted and fitt for use, than any town I saw in Ulster; and indeed, Dublin excepted, this is the best town taken alltogether I have seen in Ireland. The houses are all built of stone, of course kind of marble, all like one another, like castles for their arch'd doors and strong walls, windows, and floors, and seem to have all been built much about the same time, after the modell, as I hear, of some town in Flanders. The inhabitants are most Roman Catholicks, and the trade is wholly in their hands, and indeed in all Connaught, as you go farther from Dublin, you may see the remains of Popery, yet less and less extinct than in ye other parts of Ireland. Here are 2 nunnerys, who, keeping somewhat private, are conniv'd at by the Governour and Mayor. At ye Gates I observ'd ye sentinells have gotten a use of taking 2 turfs from every horse that comes in with turf, allso, I hear, with herrings, (and, I believe, with other things) which is much more than ye toll due to ye Mayor: this greivance the officers told me they think themselves excus'd from redressing till ye civill power thinks itself so injur'd as to complain, which, it seems, they don't yet. They have here 2 mass houses for one church, which is indeed a pretty modell'd one, but with little ornaments; one tomb is in it of very good and well polish'd black marble well streak'd with white, I believe from the Isles of Bofin, where I am told there is a good quarry of such. We saw here ye Town-house, which is built on piazzas, but has nothing remarkable, and is not yet finish'd, ye Barracks, one in ye citadell, the other new built at another end of the town, both for foot: they hold about a regiment. Having view'd the town, I was directed where I might have a map of it, which I bought, and seems pretty exact: 'twas done in Brussells by a fryer who was born and bred in this town, and, they tell you, had been at Brussells 8 years when he made it.

From *Journey to Connaught*

John Wesley

1773

JOHN WESLEY (1703–1791), the founder of Methodism, was a relative of the Duke of Wellington. He was educated at Charterhouse and Oxford University and was ordained an Anglican priest in 1728. While at Oxford, Wesley, with his brother Charles and several others, started a doctrine of living 'according to the methods laid down in the New Testament.' While visiting America in 1735, Wesley came into contact with the Moravian Brethren and departed from the High Church on his return to England. He and his brother began to preach at vast open-air gatherings and Wesley spent the rest of his life travelling and preaching, often covering up to 60 miles on horseback a day.

John Wesley

*M*ay 13. We went on, through a most dreary country, to Galway; where, at the late survey, there were twenty thousand Papists, and five hundred Protestants. But which of them are Christians, have the mind that was in Christ, and walk as he walked? And without

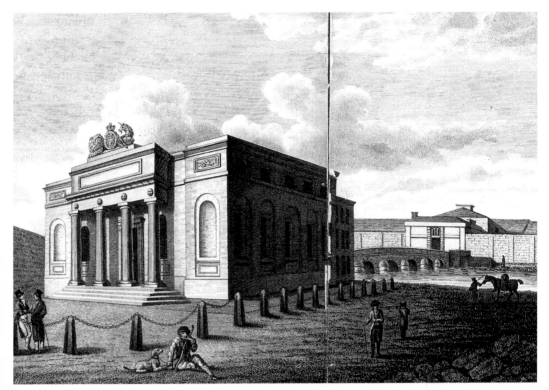

The County Courthouse where John Wesley preached in 1773

this, how little does it avail, whether they are called Protestants or Papists! At six I preached in the Court-House, to a large congregation, who all behaved well.

From *The Journal of John Wesley*

Arthur Young

1776

ARTHUR YOUNG (1741–1820) was born at Whitehall, London. A precocious schoolboy, he spent so much on clothes he had nothing left for his books. To raise money he turned to writing political pamphlets. After his father's death, Young had to leave school and took over a small farm of his mother's. At first he succeeded as a farmer but when he moved to Samford Hall, a larger farm in Essex, he again found himself in dire straits. Young turned to writing and produced a travel book on Southern England. In 1776, he toured Ireland and kept a journal of his trip. Unfortunately, on the return journey his servant stole his trunk containing the journal and all the specimens of soil and minerals he'd collected. He had to recreate his account of his trip from memory and it was finally published in 1780.

$\mathcal{M}$r. Andrew French of Rathone Galway, who I met at Moniva, favoured me with the following particulars. At Galway there is a salmon fishery, which lets at £200 a year; and in the bay of Galway they have a considerable herring fishery. There are belonging to the town 200 to 250 boats, 40 or 50 of which are employed in the spring fishery, for cod, hake, mackarel, &c. &c. These boats are from 4 to 6 tons, some 9 tons. They cost building, £20 a boat, and the nets and tackle, £15; the nets are of hemp, tanned with bark. There are five or six men to a boat; they fish by shares, dividing into sixty: they have had this fishery time immemorial. The plenty of fish has decreased these 15 years. A middling night's take is 5,000 fish; all they get is sold into the country, and the demand is so far from being answered, that many cargoes are brought in from the north. The fish sell at 1s. 4d. to 2s. 2d. a hundred; but the men are far from being industrious in the business: some weeks they do not go out twice.

On the coast of Conna Marra there is, from the 10th of April to the 10th of May, a fishery of sun-fish, which is done by the herring boats. It is not by shares, but the owners of the boats hire the men for the fishery. One fish is reckoned worth £5 and if a boat takes three fish in the month, it is reckoned good luck. There are 40 or 50 boats employed on this. Along the whole bay there is a great quantity of kelp burnt; 3,000 tons are annually exported from Galway: the present price is 40s. to 50s. a ton. The shore is let with the land against it, and is what the people pay their rent by. They use a great quantity of seaweed, drove in by storms, for manuring land. In November they carry it on, the field being ready marked out in beds for potatoes, and leaving it on them; it rots against the planting season, and gives them great crops. They also do this with fern, cutting it in autumn, and, laying it on to the beds, get good crops. The poor people near Galway are very industrious in buying the sullage of the streets of that town; they give 3d. for a horse load of two baskets, and carry it three miles.

September 3d, left Moinva, and took the road to Woodlawn, the seat of Fredrick Trench, Esq; passed many bogs of considerable size, perfectly improveable, and without the uncommon exertions I have just described. None could be more anxious for my information than Mr. Trench.

Woodlawn is a seat improved entirely in the modern English taste, and is as advantageous a copy of it as I have any where seen. The house stands on the brow of a rising ground, which looks over a lawn swelling into gentle inequalities; through these a small stream is converted into a large river, in a manner that does honour to the taste of the owner; it comes from behind a hill, at the foot of which is a pretty cottage hid by plantation, and flows into a large mass of wood in front of the house: the grounds, which form the banks of this water, are pleasing, and are prettily scattered with clumps and single trees, and surrounded by a margin of wood. The house is an excellent one, so well contrived, that the same disposition of apartments would be agreeable upon almost any scale of building.

September 4th, to Kiltartan, the seat of Robert Gregory, Esq. who is engaged in pursuits which, if well imitated, will improve the face of the country not a little. He has built a large house with numerous offices, and taken 5 or 600 acres of land into his own hands, which I found him improving with great spirit. Walling was his first object, of which he has executed many miles in the most perfect manner: his dry ones, 6 feet high, 3 feet and a half thick at bottom, and 20 inches at top, cost 2*s*. 6*d*. the perch, running measure. Piers in mortar, with a gate and irons complete £1 14*s*. Walls in mortar, five feet high, cost 6*s*. a perch. He has fixed two English bailiffs on his farm, one for accounts and overlooking his walling and other business; and another from Norfolk, for introducing the turnep husbandry; he has 12 acres this year; and what particularly pleased me, I saw some Irishmen hoeing them; the Norfolk man had taught them; and I was convinced in a moment, that these people would by practice soon attain a sufficient degree of perfection in it. The soil around is all a dry sound good lime-stone land, and lets from 10*s*. to 12*s*. an acre, some at more. It is in general applied to sheep. Mr. Gregory has a very noble nursery, from which he is making plantations, which will soon be a great ornament to the country.

From *Arthur Young's Tour in Ireland*

Daniel Beaufort

1787

DANIEL BEAUFORT (1739–1821) was born in East Barnet, England, where his father, a Huguenot refugee, was rector. He came to Ireland in 1746 when his father was appointed chaplain to the new Viceroy Lord Harrington. Daniel Beaufort was educated at Trinity College Dublin, and, after his ordination, succeeded his father as rector at Navan. He played a prominent role in the foundation of the Royal Irish Academy, but he is better remembered as a geographer for his *Memoir of a Map of Ireland*, published in 1792. While researching this work Beaufort made several long trips through the country.

Daniel Beaufort

*T*uam September 17th 1787. The town is not so well built as Loughrea, nor can it contain as many people, they say here 3000. Mr. Kirwan at the Grove & Mr. Cheevers opposite the palace, have large well looking houses. The palace is old and old fashioned, ill contrived rooms opening into one another & all with corner chimneys, gloomy & ill furnished. The garden good with a very fine canal [   ] was built by Synge.

The ruins of a parish Church are large & in the midst of the town & of a great burial place – I was also shown the site of Temple Scrine the most antient church here, on which a stable is now built, & the ruins of Trinity Abby – where there is not one stone upon another, no more than of John's Abby.

There are quartered here a troop of lighthorse & 2 Comp. of foot, at the invitance of his Grace, when the white boyism broke out last year.

Mr. Nolan an [   ] Atty. dined with us & gave a very Circumstantial account of an attempt to rob him lately near Kilbeggan, of his being shot in the scuffle, & of the man being taken tried at the last Assizes and hanged all within a week of the fact.

Headford. The Ground is pretty diversified by swells & Hedgerows & Groves about Headford; but the populace have cut down much. – The Church has a steeple & a Chancel and is quite out of the town at one end; – which town is large enough but very poorly built. – It all belongs, with 4900 A. to Capt. St. George. – In his strange old house dwells Mr. Crampton, min of this parish, with 5 sons and as many daughters. – The place has been great, but is now ruinous. From the paved room to the yard there are twelve convex & 3 concave circular Steps, & 10 to the door 25 in all. Stables & offices all tumbling.

The Barrack looks ruinous & has long been unoccupied. In the park, is a fine bath in ruins, a number of large beautiful heiffers of Mr. Reddingtons, & in a paddock 30 prodigious fine Rams.

There is a stream by Donapatrick which runs out of a lough turns a mill, & [   ] There is not at this moment one bishop in all Connaught: – and very seldom more.

Galway. September 20th 1787. Galway is large & very old, pretty well laid out in strait Streets but narrow, & the houses high – a very few of

The Abbey of Clare-Galway

these New – but many in absolute Ruin. – The entrance into all by a Gothick door or stone arch some adorned with pillars & sculpture – this leads thro' a broad entry into a square court, round which are buildings; – On the R. & L. of the entry are stone stairs for one flight – and there the apartments inhabited by Gentlefolks begin. – Some houses contain 2 or 3 families. – No Yards or Gardens & it is said but 3 Cloacinas in town – one of which is at my inn luckily. – Into this inn we enter thro' the kitchen then up stone stairs – from whence the aparts. begin.

Much dirt is thrown out of windows at night, & the streets are perfectly dark. Many people here collect street dirt into the courts of houses, where they make a heap till the season for putting it out, – & they hire the use of [ ] which cleanly & wholesome practice is called renting of Entries.

There is therefore frequent occasion for holding one's Nose in ascending these staircases.

Few or none burn coal here tho' a seaport, & turf sells now at 12d a kish & in winter at 2s 6d, tho' it is all brought by boat from the banks of L. Corrib.

The houses are roofed with large heavy flags near an inch thick, & they are now repairing the Church in the same way – The new infirmary however which is a fine building on an eminence to the E end of the town is covering with [   ] Slates.

There is a charter school here for 40 Boys – in which there are just 23 now; – I saw them at dinner & they looked clean and healthy.

There is a paper mill lately erected here by a Mr. Chambers, & it is said to be the best in Ireland – No other manufacture is attended to.

The herring fishery is built within a few years – tho' a whole quarter of the W. Side of the river is only inhabited by fishermen, who have a law & goverment of their own, & a mayor whom they elect among themselves – They are mostly descendants of Cromwelians & have English names, but are now mere Irish & all papists, riotous & obstinate.

Galway. Oct 4th 1787. At 8 I was summoned to breakfast and after chatting till eleven, set out with young Crampton to see the Abbey of Ross. Nor was I sorry to leave a house which impressed much gloom on my mind. A broad old paved road, now grassy led between high walls to an old decayed mansion surrounded with ruinous office. A number of steps, & an old & mossy iron gate admitted to a great flagged old court, with grass growing between each, from whence another flight led to the house door four steps more from the hall to the parlour, where the venerable looking man, surrounded by 10 children all in mourning appeared still lamenting the untimely death of an amiable mother. – Their primitive Manner, early hour, the cawing of the rooks, & the whistling of the wind through the various walls had too solemn an appearance for my temper to withstand.

The bay is much infested with porpoises & seals & some years ago when the Dogfish made havock among the herrings – the Fishermen made the Priest go out with them in his Vestments & represent pathetically to said Dogfish the injury they were doing. But his eloquence was unsuccessful.

August 2, 1788. Left Galway at 7 and passed through Oranmore. Good large cleared fields (interspersed with some rock) for about one mile. Old church as in Taylor and Skinner. See Tyrone house, large and new but very bleak and too high though some low woods about Claranbridge a very small village with an inn-omitted by Taylor and Skinner. Hereabouts there is much fine corn among the rocks.

Passed Kilcolgan, old castle and church but no village, only 2 or 3 cabins. Just above the bridge the river from Cragwell and Rahassan (about one mile off) rises out of the ground. Here we quit the Gort road and turn to the right and at 1/2 past ten reach Kinvara a small village with a ruined church (not marked in any map). Under this castle we saw (it being low water) 3 or 4 great streams issue from the rocks, much below high water mark on the strand, being the rivers of Gort and which disembogues by a subterranious passage here most curiously. James drew the castle for me.

Kinvara is at the south end of the bay. The church 60 by 27 feet in clear, had only a small spike-hole east window and near the altar a small one on the south side – no other. This village is frequented by boatmen. The inn kept by Mr. and Mrs Sille, where we had a good breakfast and afterwards she took me for a doctor and consulted me but I declined prescribing. The whole village belongs to Mr. Gregory and is distant 14 miles from Galway, 14 miles from Loughrea, 12 from Ciorrofin (computed) and 7 from Gort. Tithes set at 7 and 4 and twenty shillings for 100 sheep, none for hay. Of this parish Mr. Upton had 2 quarters, bishop one and vicar Mr. Ficher 1, and of 8 others united to it and Kilcolgan.

From Daniel Beaufort's journals at Trinity College Dublin

Mary Beaufort

1808

MARY WALLER was born in Allenstown, County Meath, the daughter of William Waller who owned lands in Counties Dublin, Meath, Louth and Cavan. She met and married Daniel Beaufort when he was the rector at Navan. The Beauforts had several children; a daughter, Frances, married Richard Lovell Edgeworth and a son, Francis, invented the Beaufort Scale. In the late 1780s, Mary Beaufort travelled through Ireland with her husband while he was researching his map. She visited Galway again in 1808, while reporting on the Charter School system.

Mary Beaufort

*W*e left Galway about 12 to Mr. St. Georges of Tyrone – at 10 miles of fine, flat road, from Galway for some miles the road runs in full, & very fine view of the Bay interspersed with Gentlemen's Seats – and a small village called Oranmore – with a Castle adjoining, in which has

Tuam Cathedral painted by Daniel Grose

lived, & still does live a Mr. Blake & his Family. At five miles the house
of Mr. St. George appears, it is a High House, standing on high ground
without a Tree, bush, or Offices in sight. Nothing can be more unpromising
than it looks from this road. We soon after approached Two Bridges over
different Rivers, which rise after a subterranean course – Kilcolgan, by
Clairan Bridge – near the first is a well looking House built in the Castle, by
Mr. St Georges Father, who lives there, keeps a Chere Amie - and to please
her is turned Roman Catholic – a Story is told of this dissolute old
Gentleman, which One can Scarcely credit – the first day He went to
Chapel, it happened that the Host was then elevating – at which everyone
kneels. He supposed this obeissance performed in honour of him, and
bowed all around – When Service was over he came forward, and made
a fine harangue returning the Congregation thanks for this Great Civility
to him! It must be an unpleasant circumstance to his son who is a moral
domestic County Gentleman to have his Father living so near him (Not
two miles from his Gate) so despicable a life – the old Gentleman built
the House and an excellent One it is.

From Mary Beaufort's journals at Trinity College Dublin

George Petrie

1821

GEORGE PETRIE (1790–1866) was an artist, antiquarian and musician. Born in Dublin the son of portrait-painter James Petrie, he attended Mr. Whyte's school. He first began touring Ireland as an illustrator of guide books and was so impressed by the ruins of Clonmacnoise that he devoted the rest of his life to antiquarian research. He joined the Ordnance Topographical Survey of Ireland with Eugene O'Curry and John O'Donovan as his assistants. Petrie won a Gold Medal at the Royal Irish Academy with his *Essay on the Round Towers of Ireland. The Petrie Collection of the Ancient Music of Ireland*, a collection of Irish airs, was published in 1857.

*T*he Araners, in short, like the race that inhabit the south-western parts of Ireland, and of which they constitute a part, are remarkable for fine intellect and deep sensibility; but unlike them, they are happily placed in circumstances which more generally call forth *only* the good feelings which that sensibility engenders, while the bad ones, which equally belong to it, are left to slumber.

George Petrie

If the inhabitants of the Aran islands could be considered as a fair specimen of the ancient and present wild Irish – the veriest savages in the globe, as the learned Pinkerton calls them – those whom chance has led to their hospitable shores to admire their simple virtues, would be likely to regret that the blessings of civilization had ever been extended to any portion of the inhabitants of this very wretched country. But, fortunately for them, they cannot thus be designated; much of their superiority must be attributed to their remote, insular situation, which has hitherto precluded an acquaintance with the vices of the distant region, while the wisdom and benevolence of their late proprietor, which from its rarity might be supposed of insular growth also, has not required them, for his selfish gratification, to experience the want and wretchedness that would

On Ard Oilean off Connemara

otherwise reign there. They are still wild Irish, perhaps, and poor certainly – for they have no opportunity, except by smuggling, to become rich – but they are at least well dressed savages, without tails, I believe, and with comfortable houses, and generally enough to eat. These fortunate circumstances of their condition, give them some elevation in the scale of *savage* life, and they are therefore to be considered, not as a fair specimen of the wild Irish of the present day, but rather as a striking example of what that race might generally be, under circumstances equally happy.

To the preceding general observations on the social state of the Aran islanders, I am desirous to add a few traits of individual character that came within my notice.

Society presents but few gradations of rank in these remote, ocean-beaten wilds.

The proprietor of the islands is, of course, an absentee. The aristocracy may be said to consist of two gentlemen, who claim the title more from ancient family rank than from wealth or landed possessions. If to these individuals be added the solitary pastor of the undivided flock, the lightkeeper, and the revenue officers; – a list is formed of the whole aristocracy of the three islands of Aran.

Below this, the only distinctions to be observed are those arising from the entire possession of a fishing vessel, or an advantageous lease of a few acres fit for the purposes of pasturage or agriculture.

We had no opportunity of becoming acquainted with Mr. O'Mally. His brother, a worthy Araner, received us on the shore of our landing, conducted us to the house of Mr. O'Flaherty, to whom we had previously signified, through a friend, our intention of becoming his guests, and in the free spirit of the place, stayed with us for some days to add to our hilarity and comforts. Would that I could convey to the mind of my reader even a faint outline of the character of our never-to-be-forgotten host! But as the most skilful artist finds beauty of form beyond his most laborious efforts to embody, so the beauty of character seems equally difficult for language to describe.

The deviation from symmetry, the irregularities of outline may be accurately traced, and the peculiarities of character may be forcibly depicted, but beauty both of character and form, which is most impressive and delightful, arises altogether from a want of such characteristic features, and is produced by an harmonious concordance of a variety of contrasted parts, and such, though ever so deeply felt, is of all things the most difficult to describe. Mr. O'Flaherty is a native of Aran, and he has never been farther from his native rocks than to the city of Galway and the adjacent coast of Thomond. Even such journeys have never been entirely voluntary; and so deeply does absence from home afflict him with melancholy, that he appears on those occasions a man of quite different character to those who have seen him among the loved scenes of his philosophic musings. He is curious to see Dublin, but he has felt the pains of home-sickness so severely that he cannot trust himself upon a journey that would expose him so much to its severity.

What, then, reader, do you suppose such a man to be? A child, perhaps, or a rustic simpleton. A child he is in innocence and simplicity, but in wisdom and understanding he is most truly a man; nay, more, in manner and conduct a polished gentleman.

Such is the unaffected grace of his politeness, the mild charm of his conversation, and the sincere warmth of his hospitality, that though uninvited strangers, we were but a few minutes in his house when we felt all the full freedom of enjoyment that could belong to our own firesides, with old and congenial friends to share it. From such an abode we could feel no haste to depart; and it is to those circumstances, joined to the capability of our host to give information, and his kindness in procuring it, that the following pages owe their origin, as well as any value they may be found to possess.

From *The Life and Labours in Art and Archaeology of George Petrie*

Patrick O'Flaherty

Martha Louisa Blake

1823

MARTHA LOUISA ATTERSOL was born in Portland Place, London, and lived there until she married Henry Blake of Galway in 1810. The Blakes lived at first near Clew Bay before settling permanently at Renvyle House in 1819. Martha Louisa had six sons and indulged her keen sense of history by giving each one an ancient Anglo-Saxon name. A book of letters by several members of the family was published in London in 1825. It was one of the first books to depict Connemara as a place of beauty rather than a wasteland and it captured the popular imagination.

I ought to have written to you some days ago, but I could not resolve to sacrifice the first moments of fine weather. We are enjoying some of those lovely days, which, in this dripping climate, are given us in compensation for many weeks of driving rain and wind. They come upon us suddenly, and their exhilarating effect is delightful. When I first awoke this morning, scarcely a cloud was to be seen. The rocky valley, the cliffs, the distant mountains, all were smiling in sunshine. Our pretty red and white Durhams were feeding, at their ease, by the side of the lake; and the song of the larks rose, in full chorus, from the meadow. It is impossible to resist the pleasure of this first burst of spring, or to remain within doors, while all nature calls for our sympathy. But we are late this year, very late. The mountain tops are, even now, streaked with snow. The winter has been long and severe; yet not more severe, I fancy, than with you. Our frost and snow, however unseasonable, has but kept pace with yours; and such, indeed, we find to be pretty generally the case. The changes of the weather, here and in England, take place within a day or two at the same time, although the temperature is always more moderate on our side of the channel. We have a much greater proportion of rain, and our situation, on the shores of the broad Atlantic, subjects us, of course, to storms in all their magnificence and in all their horrors. Our highest winds and heaviest rains are from the south-west; yet the western gales are, by the sailors, reckoned the most dangerous, because by them they are exposed to a lee shore. The easterly winds are not so ill received by us as they are by you; we are sheltered by a high mountain range, and, as they generally give us dry weather, we willingly bear the slight extra degree of cold. The winter seldom extends, as it has done this year, into March; the few sunny days of February, which, with you are the fine days of winter, with us are the opening of spring.

On the road between Oughterard and Maam

It was one of these 'angel visits' in early spring that welcomed us into Cunnemarra. We had left the Welch roads a foot deep in snow; we had travelled from Dublin in showery and uncertain weather; and wearied ourselves with repeating, 'if this continues, we cannot cross Mam Turc,' and not to cross Mam Turc, implied a necessity of following the beaten track from Westport, instead of enjoying, in all its wildness, the finest of

A street in Galway City

our mountain passes. But our patience was not put to so severe a test. The sun shone brightly, from the first moment of his rising, and we were delighted to observe the sure presage of a fine day, in the purple mist spread over the rocky valley, and drawn like a fleecy cloud along the sides of the mountain. Our first stage was four miles of level road to the borders of Lough Corrib. There we bid farewell to roads and civilization; our baggage was stowed on board a six-oared boat, and at nine o'clock we embarked. Our sails were of no use, for not a breeze was stirring. It was a sweet tranquil scene; the surface of the lake so perfectly still and smooth, that it seemed difficult to imagine its then unruffled waves could be at times so tempest-tossed, as to render it unsafe for any boat to venture out.

The lake varies much in breadth, and is said to be thirty-seven miles long. It is studded with islands, all varying in form and size, some shewing marks of cultivation, with cabins and potatoe grounds, others affording pasture to a few sheep and cows, who looked picturesque enough, quietly feeding on the very brink of the water; some again so bare and barren as to be given up to the gulls and cormorants; some covered with copse and brushwood; and others, with only a single weather-beaten tree, bending from the western blast. On the north side, is the town of Cong, and the ruins of the abbey where Roderic, king of Connaught, ended his days. To such as do not object to travelling back a few centuries, this Roderic O'Connor would furnish a very good hero of romance. From being one of the provincial kings he was elevated to the imperial purple, and made king of all Ireland. A beautiful princess, carried off by the king of Leinster, and restored by Roderic to her lawful husband, might prove a sufficiently interesting episode, while the main part of the story would be drawn from the circumstances attending the first English invasion, which took place at this time. Here are certainly points of sufficient interest for any historical novel, and, besides, you have a fine variety of scenery, and the contrast of manners between the uncivilized wildness of the Irish chieftains, and the barbarous chivalry of the English knights.

But to leave the ruined abbey of Cong. On the western side of the lake is the town of Oughterard, which stands, as it were, on the very boundary between the primitive mountains of Cunnemarra and the secondary range which forms the lowlands. Along the southern shore are some ruined castles; and in the back ground the waving outline of a chain of hills, melting gradually into the plains, by which the lake is bordered on the eastern side. To the west rise, in abrupt majesty, the mountains of Cunnemarra, their summits at that time completely veiled in clouds. As we slowly advanced towards them, the mist cleared off, and we distinguished the break in the chain through which we were to find our way. Passing first one island and then another, our head boatman pointed out to us places which, during the rebellion of ninety eight, had served as retreats for those whose politics were out of fashion. He had many a long story to tell, for he had been personally engaged at the time, and we found much amusement in tracing the workings of his mind. He had been on the side of government, but it was evident that he was guided by no general principles of loyalty. He had embraced the politics and followed the fortunes of his landlord, a much simpler rule of conduct, and more congenial to the manners and feelings of our peasantry.

One or two little boats were plying among the islands; our good man insisted that our six oars had given the alarm; that we were mistaken for a revenue boat, and that the poor rogues were endeavouring to secure their illicit whiskey. One of them passing rather nearer than the others, we turned our helm a little, as though we meant to cut off their approach to the island, towards which they were making. No small signs of uneasiness were manifested at this manoeuvre; but, whether proceeding from surprise alone, or from some more interested motive, we had no opportunity of ascertaining, as it did not appear worth while, to go out of our own course, with the benevolent design of 'terrifying the poor craturs.' Few situations are more convenient for the manufacture of 'mountain dew' than little islands, embosomed like these in the midst of a lake. The water by which they are surrounded is at once a defence and a means of conveyance. The advance of an enemy can be seen (can be *felt*, as we are allowed to say on this side of the channel) at some distance; and the forbidden treasure can be shipped off from one little island to another, so as to elude almost the possibility of a seizure. How quietly too, in the dead of the night, can the *potsheen* of the mountain districts be distributed among the inhabitants of the plain, whose situation, more immediately under the eye of the law, makes it unsafe for them to distil for their own use. Alas! alas! it is sad that the morals of our peasantry should be assailed by a temptation almost too strong for poor human nature to resist. It seems impossible for the excise officers, argus-eyed as they are, to detect, what the united ingenuity of the most ingenious people in the world is at work to conceal. Not one of our poor boatmen expressed any feeling but compassion for 'the poor craturs,' when we noticed the light blue smoke curling up from some secluded corner of a little valley; and not one would have hesitated to give them warning of their danger, and assist their escape, had our six-oared boat really carried an excise officer on board. That the poor should make it a common cause is by no means wonderful; and, who can say that the rich do not give it something more than indirect countenance and support, while their bread is so often lightened with whiskey-barm, and their table is supplied with potsheen in preference to parliament whiskey? If laws are said to be cobwebs, in which the small flies are entangled, while the more powerful one escapes, what shall we say of them in Ireland? where neither rich nor poor are secured, until now and then the cords are tightened, and then how frightful a scene is presented of outrage on the one side, and retribution on the other. But let us leave this tender point, with the hope that, ere long, the wisdom of the age will rather to remove the temptation of infringing the law, than to increase the terrors of its execution.

The scene changed a little when we quitted the open part of the lake: the mountains closed in upon us, and the expanse of water gradually narrowed till we entered the little river of Bealnabrack. It was a true mountain stream, and its serpentine course along the valley was soon too shallow to admit our boat. We ate our cold dinner on board, and then mounting the ponies, which we found in waiting, pursued our journey.

And now, if you wish to follow us, it must be along a path so wild and rugged, that it seems to have been marked out by the mountain goats, or

Overlooking Lough Inagh

by the red deer, which are said still to haunt these untamed regions. We have quitted the rocky bed of the torrent, which however rough, yet preserved the semblance of a road, and must prepare to climb the mountain's side, following the flight of the eagle, who, at this moment, supplies the only ornament that the nature of the scenery will admit, and, soaring across the valley, from the giddy height, lets fall her quarry, which she has abandoned in terror at our approach.

I was desired to let the reins hang loose round my pony's neck, and I did it with perfect confidence, for he was a thorough-bred mountaineer, perfectly aware of his powers, and of the capabilities of his road. Ignorance upon either of these points would have led him and his rider into no small difficulties. But I had no such fear. My little friend had never been known to refuse a step which he might safely have taken, or to take a step which he was forced to retract; and, leaving to him all the toil and anxiety of the undertaking, I was at leisure to admire the surrounding scene. It was Nature in her wildest garb, and in all the majesty of solitude; for no human being was to be seen, and scarcely the vestige of a human habitation. The cattle, of which there were one or two browsing among the rocks, appeared but as specks at the distance from which we looked down upon them; and the small patches of land, cultivated for potatoes were, at that season, undistinguishable in the valley. Yet it was a scene that might well reward the labours of a poet or a painter; who, in every varying tint, thrown by the last gleams of the western sun, would find something worth preserving in the storehouse of his fancy. The new road, projected by Mr. Nimmo, is marked out along this valley; and, when it is finished, will certainly offer to the traveller scenery more sublime, though perhaps less beautiful, than any which he finds in passing from Shrewsbury to Holyhead: would that I could say as varied, and presenting as rich a contrast of cultivated valleys, wooded hills, well-built cottages, and well-clothed peasantry, with the more majestic features of Nature's landscape.

Cultivated valleys, well-built cottages, and well-clothed peasantry we may hope to see; but who will restore to us our wooded hills? The boasted wisdom of this enlightened age will not, surely, much longer suffer that Ireland should remain a blot on England's crown! a mark for the scorn of her enemies, and the wonder of her friends! The physicians, animated as we may believe them to be by every interested motive, must, sooner or later, discover the seat of the disease, and agree upon the remedies to be applied: meanwhile we beg them to observe the decided improvement that a few short years have rendered visible on some Irish estates; and we entreat them to inquire whether on those estates any thing has been granted beyond justice, even-handed and impartial justice, a discreet encouragement of industry, and a small portion, in some cases a very small portion, of alms-giving.

Now do not tell me that you are not one of the Faculty, and that we have your good wishes, and must look for nothing else. If you are not allowed to write the prescription, you may at least make the case known. All that we ask of our English friends is, not to be forgotten. Let our situation be fully understood, – our wants and our sufferings accurately weighed, and we will then look with confidence to that humanity which has so often penetrated even to the farthest corners of the globe, to seek out the objects of her care; and which regards no obstacle where the happiness of a fellow-creature is at stake. Look upon us with the same benevolent eye that you regard the half frozen Icelander, or the negroes in your West Indian plantations, and we will forgive all past injuries, even to the burning of our forests.

Tradition accuses you of having had a chief hand in their destruction; and do what you will to assist us, centuries must pass before the stately pine and spreading oak can again rear their majestic heads, and bid defiance to the rude blast of the Atlantic. The difficulties we have to contend with are so much the greater, by the number of degrees of west longitude in which we exceed our Welsh rival. We break the force of many a tempest that would else fall roughly on her wooded valleys; and if Mona have not yet recovered the desolation of the Roman conquerors, what hope is there for Cunnemarra!

If the absence of trees can any where be overlooked, it is in the midst of scenery so wild and majestic as ours; yet even here we could wish to set some of our bogs upright again with 'all their leafy honours thick upon them!' How much would the beauty of our view from the height of Mam Turc have been increased, if the valley below had been studded with groups of forest-trees! Where every thing is on so grand a scale, the apparent height and distance of many objects are diminished for want of some points by which the eye may be guided in forming an estimate. But it is useless to think of trees on this side of the mountains; and, to say the truth, I should not perhaps have thought of them, even while I was climbing the side of Mam Turc, had not a stunted oak, bleached by many a winter's storm, stretched out her white arms from the rock, and reminded us of all that had once stood there!

I must digress no more, or we shall never reach the summit. Within a few yards of it we were obliged to dismount, for the slaty rock was laid bare, and presented a surface so smooth and slippery that it was necessary for each one to trust to his own footing. We passed without any accident, and

When we reach'd the mountain's brow,
What a prospect lay below!

The rugged declivity by which we were to descend, the plain, the conical pins of Bennabola, the lake of Rylemore, receiving their dark shadows on her bosom; beyond lay other plains, and other mountains arose, enriched by the crimson tints of evening, and bounded by the Atlantic. If no stranger can behold this scene unmoved, what, think you, were the feelings of one returned from foreign wanderings, whose eye had long, in vain, sought relief from the tameness of French vineyards, and the monotony of their pleasure gardens?

The descent of the mountain's side was more dangerous than the ascent had proved, which we were at full leisure to remark, for our view, upon leaving the summit, was confined to the neighbouring mountains and the plain immediately before us. With us a plain is seldom a picturesque object. The proportion of cultivated land is small, compared with the wide extent of the bogs: we have few trees; and the cabins, although they must give an interest to the scene, yet seldom add to its beauty. This remark is applicable, pretty generally, throughout Ireland. At this moment I recollect but one exception: it is between Carlow and Naas, on the Dublin road. To the right are the Wicklow mountains, and to the left an extensive plain, well cultivated, sufficiently wooded, and watered by a pretty little river. It presents as fine a view as can be expected from any extent of level ground.

The evening was now closing in apace, and we were not sorry to find ourselves once more upon a sound road, and the carriage ready to convey us home. The day was, by one hour, too short for us. The last three miles were completely lost in the darkness of the evening. The murmur of the sea rising on the pebbled shore, heard more and more distinctly, gave notice that we were near the end of our journey, and we heartily rejoiced when we drove into the court-yard, over the heather, which, in the true spirit of a mountain welcome, the children had amused themselves in strewing before us.

From *Letters from the Irish Highlands of Connemara.*

Hermann von Pückler-Muskau

1828

GERMAN PRINCE Hermann von Pückler-Muskau (1785–1871) first visited England in 1815 and was so impressed with the country's gardens that he created an English-style park around his house in Muskau. This proved so expensive an undertaking that he soon ran out of money. Pückler-Muskau then married Lucie Hardenburg, the daughter of the wealthy Prussian Chancellor but her father cut them both off without a penny. However Pückler-Muskau was so taken with Lucie that together they hatched up an insidious plot to secure funds – they would divorce and Pückler-Muskau would travel to England and Ireland to find a rich wife. He sent long letters home to Lucie describing his adventures.

*A*thenrye, Sept. 10. I write to you this morning from the house of one of the sweetest women I ever saw in my life: an African too, – and as she tells me, by birth a Mademoiselle H – . 'Que dites vous de cela?' But more of her hereafter. You must now accompany me to the 'race-course,' and see the running and leaping from the beginning. It is a remarkable sight of its kind, and exactly suited to a half-savage nation. I confess that it far exceeded my expectations, and kept me in a state of intense anxiety; only one must leave pity and humanity at home, as you will see from what follows. The race-course is an elongated circle. On the left side is the starting post; opposite to it, on the right, is the goal. Between them, at the opposite points of the circumference, are built walls of stone without mortar, five feet high and two broad. The course, two English miles in length, is run over once and a half. You see then, from my description,

Ruins of Athenry Friary

that the first wall must be leaped twice, the second only once in each heat. Many horses run, but none is declared winner till he has beaten the others in two heats; so that this is often repeated three, four, or even five times, if a different horse comes in a-head each time. To-day they ran four times; so that the winner, in a space of less than two hours, reckoning the intervals, ran twelve English miles at full speed and leaped the high wall twelve times!—a fatigue which it is difficult to conceive how any horse can stand. Six gentlemen in elegant jockey dresses of coloured silk jackets and caps, leather breeches and top-boots, rode the 'race.' I had an excellent hunter belonging to the son of my host, and could, therefore, by crossing the course, keep up perfectly well, and be present at every leap.

It is impossible not to have a favourite on such occasions. Mine, and indeed that of the public, was an extremely beautiful dark bay, called Gamecock, ridden by a gentleman in yellow, a handsome young man of good family, and a most admirable rider.

After him the horse which pleased me the most was a dark brown mare called Rosina, ridden by a cousin of Captain B-; a bad rider, in sky blue. The third in goodness, in my opinion, Killarney, was a strong, but not very handsome horse, ridden by a young man who showed more power of endurance than perfect horsemanship: his dress was crimson. The fourth gentleman, perhaps the most skilful, though not the strongest of the riders, rode a brown horse, not remarkable in its appearance, and was dressed in brown. The other two deserve no mention, as they were 'hors du jeu' from the beginning: they both fell at the first leap; the one sustained a severe injury on the head, the other came off with a slight contusion, but was disabled from riding again. Gamecock, who darted off with such fury that his rider could hardly hold him in, and flew, rather than leapt, over the walls with incredible bounds, won the first heat with ease. Immediately after him came Rosina without her rider, whom she had thrown, and took the remaining leaps of her own accord with great grace. Gamecock was now so decidedly the favourite that the bets were five to one upon him: but the result was far different from these expectations, and very tragical. After this noble animal had distanced the other two in two successive heats, and had achieved the two first leaps in the most brilliant manner, he set his foot, in the third, on a loose stone which one of the less skilful horses had pushed down as he fell, *and which it was not permitted to remove out of the course.* He fell backward upon his rider with such violence that both lay motionless, when the other riders came up, took not the slightest notice of them, and accomplished the leap. After a few seconds Gamecock got up, but his rider did not recover his senses. A surgeon present soon pronounced his state to be hopeless; both his breast-bone and skull were fractured. His old father, who stood by when the accident happened, fell senseless on the ground, and his sister threw herself with heartrending cries on the yet palpitating though unconscious body. But the general sympathy was very slight. After the poor young man had been repeatedly bled, so that he lay on the turf weltering in his blood, he was taken away, and the race began again at the appointed time as if nothing had happened.

The brown rider had been the first in the preceding heat, and hoped to win the last and decisive one. It was what the English call 'a hard race.' Both horses and men did their part admirably, they ran and leaped almost in rank. Killarney at last won only by a quarter of a head: – it was necessary therefore to run again. This last contest was of course the most interesting, since one of the two running must of necessity win everything. There was a great deal of betting, which at first was even. Twice did the victory appear decided, and yet at last terminated on the contrary side. At the first leap the horses were together; before they reached the second it was evident that the brown was exhausted, and Killarney gained so much upon him that he reached the second wall more than a hundred paces before him. But here, contrary to all expectations, he refused to leap, and the rider had lost all power over him. Before he could be brought to obey, the brown came up, – made his leap well; and now putting out all his strength, was so much a-head that he seemed sure of winning. Bets were now ten to one. But the last wall was yet to cross, and this was fatal to him. The tired animal who had exhausted his last remaining strength in fast running, tried the leap willingly enough indeed, but had no longer power to effect it; and half breaking down the wall, he rolled bleeding over and over, burying his rider under him so that it was impossible for him to rise. Killarney's rider had in the mean time brought his refractory horse into subjection, achieved the two remaining leaps amid the cheers of the multitude, and then rode at a foot pace, perfectly at his ease and without a rival, to the goal. He was so exhausted, however, that he could scarcely speak.

In the intervals between the preceeding heats I was introduced to many ladies and gentlemen, all of whom most hospitably invited me to their houses. I however preferred following my young host, who promised to show me the fairest of the fair, if I would give myself up to his guidance, and not object to riding ten miles in the dark. On the way he told me that this lady was called Mrs –, and was the daughter of the late Dutch governor of –, that she had had a complaint in the lungs, and was now staying in the solitary village of Athenrye, on account of the salubrity of its air.

We did not arrive till ten; and surprised her in her little cottage (for the place is miserable) at tea.

Galway fish market

I wish I could describe this sweet and lovely being to you in such manner as to place her visibly before you; certain that you, like me, would love her at the first glance. But I feel that here all description falls short: – all about her is heart and soul, and that is not to be described; – she was dressed in black, with the greatest simplicity, her dress up to the neck, but fitting closely to her beautiful form. Her person is slender and extremely youthful, full of gentle grace, and yet not without animation and fire in her movements. Her complexion is of a pure and clear brown, and has the soft polish of marble. More beautiful and brilliant black eyes, or teeth of more dazzling whiteness, I never beheld. Her mouth too, with the angelic, childlike character of her smile, is enchanting.

Her refined unaffected good-breeding, the sportive graces of her gay and witty conversation, were of that rare sort which are innate, and must therefore please, whether in Paris or in Pekin, in town or country. The greatest experience of society could not give more ease or address, and no girl of fifteen could blush more sweetly, or jest more joyously. And yet her life had been the most simple and uniform, and her youth was rather the unfading spring of the soul than that of the body; for she was mother of four children, near thirty, and but just recovered from an attack on the lungs which had threatened to prove fatal. But the fire of all her movements, the lightning-flashes of her conversation, had all the freshness and all the power of youth, imparting a resistless charm to the gentleness of her nature. One felt that this was the child of a warmer and kindlier sun, of a more luxuriant soil, than are to be found in our misty climes. And indeed she felt the most melancholy longings after her native land, and a painful expression passed over all her lovely features as she said, she should never more breathe that balmy air charged with sweet odours. I was too much absorbed in looking at her to think of food, had she not, with all the kind activity of a good housewife, made preparations for entertaining us as well as she could in her little cabin. A table was set in the room in which we sat; so that our frugal meal caused no interruption to the conversation, and it was long after midnight ere we separated.

It was not till I was in bed that I learned that, finding it impossible to get us beds in a place consisting of only a few cabins, this kind-hearted and unceremonious woman had quitted her own for me, and gone to sleep with her eldest daughter.

Concerning her family, whose name was necessarily so striking to me, Mrs. – herself could tell me but little. She had married Mr.– , then a captain in the British army, in her twelfth year: immediately afterwards she lost her father, and embarked with her husband for Ireland, which she has never left. She had heard, indeed that she had relations in Germany, but never corresponded with them. Three years ago she received a business letter from a cousin in A-, announcing that her father's brother had died and had left her heir to his whole property. The indifference of this African child of nature went so far, that she had not only up to the present time left this letter unanswered, but, as she told me, had never been able to decypher the whole of it, as it was written in Dutch, and she had almost entirely forgotten the language. 'I don't know the man,' added she innocently, 'and the money affairs I left to my husband.'

This bathing-place, Athenrye, is also one of the curiosities of Ireland. From what I have already said, you will conclude that no Polish village can have a more wretched aspect. The cluster of cabins is on a bare hill rising out of the bog, without tree or bush, without an inn, without any convenience, inhabited only by ragged beggars, and by the few invalids who bring with them everything they want, and must send for even the most trifling article of food to Galway, a distance of twelve miles. Once it was otherwise; and it saddens one to see at the further extremity of this wretched village the proud ruins of better times. Here stood a rich abbey, now overgrown with ivy: the arches which once protected the sanctuary lie in fragments amid the unsheltered altars and tombstones. Further on is a castle, with walls ten feet thick, in which King John held his court of justice when he came over to Ireland.

I visited these ruins with a most numerous company: I do not exaggerate when I say that at least two hundred half-naked beings, two-thirds of whom were children, had collected round my carriage at a very early hour in the morning, doing nothing: they now thronged round me, all begging, and shouting, 'Long life to your honour!' Every individual among them stuck faithfully by me, leaping over stones and brambles. The strangest compliment now and then resounded from the midst of the crowd: at last some called out, 'Long life to the King!' On my return I threw two or three handfuls of copper among them; and in a minute half of them, old and young, lay prostrate in the sand, while the others ran with all speed into a whiskey-shop, fighting furiously all the way.

Such is Ireland! Neglected or oppressed by the government, debased by the stupid intolerance of the English priesthood, and marked by poverty and the poison of whiskey, for the abode of naked beggars! I have already mentioned that even among the educated classes of this province, the ignorance appears, with our notions of education, perfectly unequalled: I will only give you one or two examples. To-day something was said about magnetism, and no one present had ever heard the slightest mention of it. Nay, in B-m, in a company of twenty persons, nobody knew that such places as Carlsbad and Prague existed. The information that they were situated in Bohemia did not mend the matter: Bohemia was not less unknown; and in short, everything out of Great Britain and Paris, was a country in the moon. 'And where do you come from?' asked one. 'From Brobdignag,' said I in jest. 'O! is that on the sea? Have they whiskey there?' asked another. The son of my host, whom I have repeatedly mentioned, asked me one day very seriously as we met some asses, whether there were any such animals in my country? 'Ah ! but too many,' replied I.

From *Tour in England and Ireland*

Maria Edgeworth

1834

NOVELIST MARIA EDGEWORTH (1767–1849) was born in England, but at fifteen moved to Edgeworthstown, County Longford, to an estate her father had inherited. Her father gave her the task of writing moral tales for her younger brothers and sisters which were published as a series starting in 1796 with *The Parent's Assistant*. They were influential in both England and America, but it was her novel, *Castle Rackrent*, that made her famous. Edgeworth went on to write several other novels, among them *Ennui* and *Ormond*. Her works had a considerable influence on Sir Walter Scott, with whom she maintained a correspondence throughout her lifetime.

*W*e did not reach Ballinasloe till it was almost dark. There goes a story, you know that no woman must ever appear at Ballinasloe Fair; that she would be in imminent peril of her life from the mob. The daughters of Lord Cloncarty, it was said, had tried it and scarce were saved by fate. Be this as it may, we were suffered to drive very quietly through the town; and we went quite through it to the outskirts of scattered houses, which are on either side of the spacious Fair green, large as any race ground I have ever seen. We stopped at the door of the Vicarage. And well for us that we had a letter from the Dean of Ardagh to the Rev. Mr. Pounden, else we might have slept in the streets, or have paid guineas

Maria Edgeworth

apiece for our beds, all five of us for three nights. Now 3 by 5 equals 15 which would not have been agreeable even to Sir Culling Smith and Lady Culling Smith, much less to me who had insisted on paying my share of expense. Mr. and Mrs. Pounden were the most hospitable of people, and they were put to a great trial, dinner just over, and that day had arrived unexpectedly one family of relations, and expectedly another, with children without end. And how they did stow them and us, to this hour I cannot conceive; they had, to be sure, one bedroom in a house next door, which luckily, Lord and Lady Somebody had not arrived to occupy. Be it how it might, here we stayed till Monday; and on Sunday there was to be a charity sermon for schools under the patronage of Lord and Lady Cloncarty. Lady Cloncarty no doubt you do remember is Lady Pakenham's sister. And by whom do you think this charity sermon was to be preached? Not by the Archbishop of Tuam, though he was at Garbally (Garbally you know is the name of the Cloncarty's fine place adjoining this fine Fair green). The charity sermon was to be preached by a namesake of yours. Pakenham, Archdeacon Pakenham – whom Admiral

Pakenham used to call 'His Reverence the Count.' In walked he to Mr. Pounden's on Sunday morning just before church, and very much surprised to see me and still more to learn who was with me – or rather with whom I was.

Now this next explanation is difficult, unless you happen to know already that there was a Lady Anne Culling Smith who was sister to Lord Wellesley and married a W. Culling Smith, cousin to this Sir Culling, my present travelling companion. That Lady Anne and her husband had, I think, been unkind to the Duchess of Wellington and from several things Mr. Pakenham said to me I perceived that he had not it rightly in his head who my companions were – they were out walking, and he did not see them this morning – and in short this misunderstanding prevented, I suppose, our being invited by Lord and Lady Cloncarty or in any way being noticed by them during our stay, which I think rather mortified Isabella and Sir Culling. A multitude of contradictory apologies were made by poor Mr. and Mrs. Pounden for their patrons' neglect. Admiral Pakenham himself, in reply to my having asked for a note of introduction for the Smiths, had written me word that he would not give one just at this time because the family at Garbally were all in the deepest affliction, would see nobody on account of the sudden death of a nephew of Lord Cloncarty.

That was all very well till we saw the ladies out in their open carriages as gay as you please, and till we heard from the Archdeacon, who did not know what the Admiral had said, that the house at Garbally was at this moment surprisingly full – eight and twenty sat down to dinner yesterday, every plate and platter called into requisition.

Well, this was to be explained afterwards by Mr. and Mrs. Pounden. All the eight and twenty were Lord and Lady Cloncarty's own relations – no strangers were ever invited on any account during the Ballinasloe fair – an invariable rule – Mrs. Pounden adduced cases in point of the grandest people having being uninvited at the last and every preceding fair.

Well, this was good till somebody came and told us that Lord Somebody who had come to the fair and Mr. Secretary Littleton were invited to dinner this day at Garbally. But Mrs. Pounden was sure it was a mistake – and at last as a great secret she told me the real reason, viz, that Lady Cloncarty, who is the most intellectual lady in the world, would have been delighted to see Miss Edgeworth in particular at Garbally, but that she dared not invite any stranger, because Lord Cloncarty could not bear to see any stranger there – there was no knowing what effect it might have on him – 'he has epileptic fits and the sight of any new face might throw him into one.' I have now written two pages upon this nonsense. What a fool I am! But if it makes you laugh, no waste. We were very much entertained.

The horse fair of Ballinasloe drawn by Jack Yeats

This Sunday after a charity sermon, seeing horses leaping, wicked though it was, and good very good as we all were and railing against the sin all the time. An immense crowd before the windows, filling the Fair green – we went out to see – and fine horses and fine leaping we saw over a loose wall built for the purpose in the middle of the Fair green, and such shouting and such laughing and such hurraing for those who cleared or those who missed. And then came deaf Basset Saunderson, and I was very near being run over before I could make him understand how I came there, while he with his eyebrows up, kept asking me if he might believe his eyes. As to the rest of the cattle fair, I give it up. It is beyond my powers of description, even if I had seen it, which I did not; for we left Monday morning before the thick of it came on.

I forgot to tell you though that on Sunday, between the times of Church and Fair green leapings, arrived Mr. Strickland, and he with maps and road-books and common sense explained to Sir Culling where he should go, and how he was to accomplish his objects, and attempted (but that was a vain attempt) to get into his head that he could not expect to get on in Connemara bogs and wilds with his fine carriage and four horses. It was settled that we were to go this night to Loughrea, not Loughglynn, and to see certain ruins by going a few miles out of our way; and this we accomplished and actually did see, by an uncommonly fine sunset, the beautiful ruins of Clonmacnoise Abbey, where so many bones were left after some famous battle, whose name has escaped me, that the English used to send ships for them for shiploads to manure their ground – believe it who may. And we slept this night at Loughrea, where we had been assured there was a capital inn, and may be it was, but the rats or the mice ran about my room so, and made such a noise in the holes of the floor, that I could not sleep, but was thankful that they did not get on or into my bed.

Next day we went on to Galway, and still it was fine weather, bright for the open carriage. Galway, wet or dry, and it was dry when I saw it, is the dirtiest town I ever saw, and the most desolate and idle-looking. But I am told, and indeed saw, that it has a prodigious fine harbour, and that it might be, and has been one of the most prosperous towns in the world, I am assured. As I had heard from Captain Beaufort and Louisa and others of the curious old Spanish houses in Galway, I was determined not to go through the town without seeing these; so as we got to the inn, I summoned landlord and landlady, and begged to know the names of the principal families in the town. I thought I might light upon somebody who could help us, Sir Culling never having thought of getting a single letter of introduction. In an old history of Galway, which Mr. Strickland

A Salmon Haul

picked up from a stall at Ballinasloe, I found prints of some of the old buildings and names of the old families; and the landlord having presented me with a list as long as an alderman's bill of fare of the names of the gentlemen and ladies of Galway, I pitched upon the name of a physician, a Dr. Veitch, of whom I had found a fine character in my book. He had been very good to the poor during a year of famine and fever. To him I wrote, and just as I had finished reading his panegyric to Lady Smith, in he walked; and he proved to be an old acquaintance. He was formerly a surgeon in the army, and was quartered at Longford at the time of the rebellion; the year before Fanny was born; remembered our all having been driven to take shelter at Longford, and remembered how well we were sheltered there, and how near my father was to being killed by the mob, and how courageously he had behaved. Dr. Veitch had been kindly received by him, and now he seemed anxious, thirty-five years afterwards, to return that kindness to me and my companions. He walked with us all over Galway and showed us all that was worth seeing, from the new quay projecting and the new green marble-cutters workshop to the old Spanish houses with projecting roofs and piazza walks beneath, more like the Rows of Chester than any houses I recollect; and wading through seas of yellow mud thick as stirabout, we went to see arches that had stood centuries, and above all to the old mayoralty house of that Mayor of Galway who hung his own son, and the black marble marrowbones and death's head and inscription, with the date 1493 still on the walls; it has formed the groundwork very lately of a tragedy. The son had – from jealousy as the tragedy had it, from avarice according to the vulgar version – committed a murder, killed a Spanish friend of whom he became jealous; and the father, a modern Brutus, condemns him to death and then goes to comfort him. This is at any rate better than showing him at the window and passing the rope around his son's neck himself. Human nature sickens at such extreme of justice – truly injustice. I really felt it worth while to wade through mud to see these awful old relics of other times and other manners. But coming back again, at every turn it was rather disagreeable to have 'fish' bawled into one's ears, and 'fine flat fish' flapped in one's face. The fish-market was freshly supplied, and Galway is famous for John Dorys. 'A John Dory, ma'am, for eighteen pence – a shilling – sixpence.' A John Dory could not be had for guineas in London. Quin, the famous actor, wished he was all throat when he was eating a John Dory. But still it was not pleasant to have ever so fine raw Dorys flapped in one's face. Sir Culling bought one for sixpence, and it was put into the carriage; and we took leave of Dr. Veitch and left.

From Galway Sir Culling was obliged to take job horses for our Connemara tour, as we were warned that we were entering a country where post horses were not to be found, and were never even heard of. Dr. Veitch bid us not think of entering Connemara this night. 'You will have to send after me soon, if you don't take care. You have no idea of the places you are going into, and that you may have to sleep in.'

The next place we were to go to, and where Dr. Veitch advised us to sleep, was Outerard, a small town or village, where was as he told us an inn or an hotel, as even in these out of the world regions it is now called. It was but fifteen miles, and this with four horses was not two hours drive; and Sir Culling thought it would be sad waste of daylight to sleep at Outerard, for still he measured his expected rate of travelling by his Bath Road standard. Though we left Galway at three, we were not at

Outerard till past seven, with our fine fresh horses; and excellent horses they really were, and well harnessed too, with well-accoutred postillions in jackets of dark blue frieze and good hats and boots, all proper, and an ugly little dog running joyously along with the horses. Outerard as well as we could see it, was a pretty mountain-scattered village with a pond and trees, and a sort of terrace road, with houses and gardens on one side, and a lower road with pond and houses on the other. There is a spa at Outerard to which bettermost sort of people come in the season; but this was not the season, and the place had that kind of desolate look, mixed with pretensions too, which a watering-place out of season always has.

When we came to the hotel, our hearts sank within us. Dusk as it was, there was light enough to guess, at first sight, that it would never do for sleeping – half covered with overgrown ivy, damp, forlorn, windows broken, shattered look in all about it. With difficulty we got at the broken gateway into the small and very dirty courtyard, where the four horses could hardly stand with the carriage. Out came such a master and such a maid! And such fumes of whiskey punch and tobacco. Sir Culling got down from his barouche-seat to look if the house was practicable, but soon returned, shaking his head, and telling us in French that it was quite impossible. So the horses were turned round, which was also nearly impossible; and the master of the inn with half-threats, half-laughter, assured us we should find no other place in Outerard. I inquired for the Priest's house, and when the maid came up to answer, I was on the very point of asking: 'Has the Priest any family?' but luckily I recollected myself in time, and asked whether the Priest's house was large enough to hold us. 'Not an atom of room to spare in it, ma'am.' Then I inquired for the Chief of Police, the Clergyman, or the Magistrate. 'Clergyman not in it, Magistrate neither, none; and the Chief of Police was upon the hill; but you will not get in nor like to get in there.'

We went there however, and up the hill toiled, and to the door of a sort of spruce-looking lanthorn of a house, without tree or shrub near it. But still it might be good to sleep in; and nothing daunted by the maid's prophecies and ominous voice, we determined to try our fate. Sir Culling got down and rubbed his hands; while, after his man's knocking at the door several times, no one came to open it, though through the drawing-room window we saw figures gliding about. At last the door half opened by hands unseen, and Sir Culling pushing it wholly open went in; and we sat in the carriage, waiting as patiently as we could. The figures in black and white came to the window, and each of them had pocket hand-kerchiefs in their hands or at their eyes. Sir Culling reappeared, ordered the horses to be turned about again, and when he had remounted his barouche seat, which he did with all convenient speed, he informed us that a lady had died in the house a few days before of cholera; that she had this day been buried; that in any other circumstances the master and mistress would have been happy to relieve us, but now it was quite impossible for our sake and their own. The damp and window-broken hotel was preferable; so back we went. But as we went along the high road, down in the low road on the other side of the pond, through the duskiness we saw lights in several houses, and in front of one long house that looked whiter than the rest, we stopped at a cross in the road where was a path which led to the valley beneath, and Sir Culling, who proved in our need an active knight, sallied down to adventure another trial, and in a few minutes after immerging into this mud castle, and emerging from it, he waved his arm over his head in sign of triumph and made a sign to the postillions to turn down into the valley, which they did without overturning us; and to our satisfaction we found ourselves housed at Mrs. O'Flaherty's, who did not keep an inn, observe; her admitting us, observe, depended upon our clearly understanding that she did not so demean herself. But she in the season let her house as a boarding house to the quality, who came to Outerard to drink the waters or to bathe. So, to oblige us poor travellers, without disgrace to the blood and high descent of the O'Flaherties, she took us in, as we were quality, and she turned her two sons out of their rooms and their beds for us; and most comfortably were we lodged. And we ate the John Dory we had brought with us, and I thought it not worth all the talking about it I had heard; and for the first time in all my days or nights, I this night tasted a toombler of anti-Parliament whiskey alias potsheen and water; and of all the detestable tastes that ever went into my mouth or smells that ever went under my nose, I think this was the worst – literally fire-spirit and water. But I can tell you that with our knight and the fair Isabella it went down quite natural and with glee. Isabella observed that she had often drunk Inishowen and water with dear Agnes and Joanna Baillie, whose Scotch taste never degenerated by their long residence in England. There's no disputing about tastes; therefore I did not dispute, only set down the tumbler and sip took never more; for I could as soon have drunk the chimney smoking. The doors, just opening with a latch, received us into our bedrooms, with good turf fires on the hearth, coved ceilings and presses, and all like bedrooms in an English farm-house more than an Irish; wonderful comfortable at Outerard after fear of the cholera and the dead woman especially.

Next day, sun shining and a good breakfast, our spirit of travelling adventure up within us, we determined that, before proceeding on our

main adventure into Connemara, we should make a little episode to see a
wonderful cave in the neighbourhood, about which my curiosity had been
excited by the description of it in the story of the lady and the white trout
in Lover's *Legends*, a book which if you have never read, pray order from
Calcutta. You will pay five shillings for it, and it will give you five guineas
worth of amusement, even by the incomparable Irish sketches with which
it is illustrated. Lover is a real name of author and painter, and in my
opinion his pencil is superior in Irish character to Crookshanks or any
drawing I ever saw in comic annual or anywhere. Oh! that those vile cuts
were out of the new edition of Miss E.'s Tales which you will soon see,
and that Lover had drawn his notions of Castle Rackrent and King
Corny. Pray whenever you have seen Lover's book, give me the
satisfaction of knowing how you like them. Don't forget.

It is called the Pigeon-hole; not in the least like a pigeon-hole, but it is
a subterraneous passage, where a stream flows which joins the waters of
Lough Corrib and Lough Mask. Outerard is on the borders of Lough
Corrib, and we devoted this day to boating across Lough Corrib, to see
this famous cavern, which is on the opposite side of the lake, and also to
see a certain ruined monastery. We passed over the lake admiring its
beauty and its many islands – little bits of islands of which the boatmen
tell there are three hundred and sixty-five – be the same more or less, one
for every day in the year at least. We saw the ruins, which are very fine as
well as the lake, but I have not time to say any more about them. We
crossed the churchyard and a field or two, and all was as flat and bare and
stony as can be imagined; and as we were going and going further from
the shore of the lake, I wondered how and when we were to come to this
cavern. The guide called me to stop and I stopped; and well that I did; I
was on the brink of the Pigeon-hole – just like an unfenced entrance to a
deep down well. The guide went down before us and was very welcome!
Down and down and down steps almost perpendicular, and as much as
my little legs could do to reach from one to the other; darker and darker,
and there were forty of them, I am sure, well counted – though certainly
I never counted them – but was right glad when I felt my feet at the
bottom on terra firma again, even in darkness, and was told to look up
and that I had come down sixty feet and more. I looked up and saw
glimmering light at the top, and as my eyes recovered, more and more
light through the large fern leaves which hung over the opening at the
top, and the whole height above looked like the inside of a limekiln,
magnified to gigantic dimension, with lady fern – it must be lady fern
because of the fairies – and lichens, names unknown, hanging from its
sides. The light of the sun now streaming in, I saw plainly, and felt why

the guide held me fast by the arm – I was on the brink of a very narrow dark stream of water, which flowed quite silently from one side of the cavern to the other! To that other side, my eye followed the stream as it flowed, I now looked, and saw that the cavern opened under a high archway in the rock. How high that was or how spacious, I had not yet light to discern. But now there appeared from the steps down which we had descended, an old woman with a light in her hand. Our boy guide hailed her by the name of Madgy Bourke. She scrambled on a high jut of rock in the cavern: she had a bundle of straw under one arm, and a light flickering in the other hand, her grizzled locks streaming, her garments loose and tattered, all which became suddenly visible as she set fire to a great wisp of straw, and another and another, she plucked from her bundle and lighted, and waved the light above and underneath. It was like a scene in a melodrama of Cavern and Witch – the best cavern scene I ever beheld. As she continued to throw down, from the height where she stood, the lighted bundles of straw, they fell on the surface of the dark stream below, and looking like tiny fire-ships, one after another sailing on and disappearing. We could not help watching each as it blazed till it vanished. We looked till we were tired, and then turned about and clambered up the steps we had scrambled down, and found ourselves again in broad daylight, in upper air and on the flat field; and the illusion was over, and there stood, turned into a regular old Irish beggar woman, the Witch of Outerard, and Madgy Bourke stood confessed, and began to higgle with Sir Culling, and began to flatter the quality, the English quality, for a sixpence more, and following us across the churchyard path she told heaps of lies about her high rent and her cruel landlord – all which Sir Culling sifted – for he is a great sifter – and found not a word of truth at the bottom, which surprised him, being an Englishman born and bred, and never could he in the least comprehend how people can tell so many lies about everything. To which they with all their hearts could answer 'Very aisy.' Well, Madgy got her sixpence extraordinary from me at any rate, and I believe from Isabella, but Sir Culling held out and slipped into the boat with the consciousness of being worthy, no doubt, of all Miss Martineau's political economy admiration. And may be, Mr. Pakenham, you don't know who Miss Martineau is – though all London has been ringing many months with her fame and her political economy stories exemplifying the mischief of charity, etc. I have not time to explain. But in time the waft of perfume of her fame will reach Indy and you, no doubt at Amballah, perhaps by the time that there is no whiff of it left in these countries.

Meanwhile I have to cross Lough Corrib; and well for us that we had the prudence to declare that we would not take a sail-boat, for a sail-boat is dangerous in the sudden squalls which rise in these mountain regions and on these lakes, very like the Swiss lakes for that matter, where, for instance on the Lake of Lucerne, I have seen sunshine and glassy surface change in five minutes to storm and cloud so black and thick that Mount Pilate himself could not be discerned through it more than if he never stood there in all his sublimity.

From *Tour in Connemara*

Alexis de Tocqueville

1835

FRENCH-BORN POLITICAL writer Alexis de Tocqueville (1805–1859) came from an aristocratic family and studied law at the Sorbonne. In 1831 he visited the United States to investigate the penal system and wrote *La Démocratie en Amérique* on his return. Writing and politics were to occupy him for the rest of his life. In 1839, de Tocqueville was elected to the Chamber of Deputies of France and served briefly as Foreign Minister after the 1848 Revolution. He was imprisoned for opposing the *coup d'état* of Louis Napoleon. In his books, the best known being *L'Ancien Régime et la Révolution*, de Tocqueville argued for the abolition of aristocracies and for strong central rule.

2 August 1835. The Protestant congregation is in possession of the ancient Catholic cathedral; a handsome Gothic nave which is used by the hundredth part of the population (the 99 others [who] are Catholics obtained permission only sixty years ago to build elsewhere at their own expense a chapel). The church (the cathedral) is badly maintained. The paving stones are disjointed; one would say that they have difficulty in preventing the grass from growing there. The walls are dirty and have the appearance of being half-repaired. In the middle of the transept are a certain number of very clean and comfortable benches ('pews'). In the middle of the choir a large stove. All

Alexis de Tocqueville

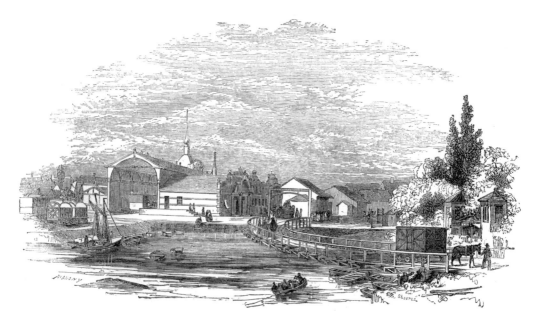

The Galway Railway Station in the eighteen fifties

the rest of the church is deserted. The pews can seat two or three hundred persons. The presence of the court of assizes has almost filled them. All the rest are vacant. The entire congregation seems composed of the rich or at the very most of their servants (as well). An hour before we had seen a vast population crowded on the bare paving stones of a Catholic church that was too small to receive them.

The preacher, who is a man who speaks well, attends to his delivery, has white gloves and a large notebook in his hand, goes into the pulpit. He utters some commonplaces about charity, then turning suddenly to politics, he explains that God indeed had prescribed the principle of alms-giving to the Jews. But he had never made it a *legal* obligation. That the principle of charity is sacred but that its performance, as that of all moral principles, ought to be subject to conscience, (allusion to the poor law against which the Orangemen contend in Ireland). Passing from there to the advantages of charity, he discovers that it forms the greatest bond in society and that he did not know there were any others. There are indeed, it is true, senseless and perverse men who believe that it is possible to make men equal and dispense in consequence with this bond that establishes the kindness and gratitude between the rich and the poor. But such doctrines are manifestly contrary to the will of God, who made men weak and strong, clever and stupid, capable and incapable. Society ought to form a consistent ladder and its happiness depend on the respect each will have for the rank of his neighbor and on the satisfaction with which he will fill his own. Opposite doctrines can be preached only by the enemies of order, by agitators who, after having deprived the people of celestial lights (the Bible), will push them towards actions destructive of civilization.

The preacher ended by assuring his audience that the collection was not intended to relieve the wretchedness of Catholics; without doubt all misery ought to concern Christians, but does not scripture say that it is necessary to relieve your own before thinking of strangers? And is not this moral especially applicable to a small body like that which the Protestants of Galway form, who need to be all united among themselves to endure as a living witness of the true religion, without the support of numbers?

I left thinking that charity, so restricted, will hardly destroy the congregation. For in Galway, almost all the Protestants are rich and all the poor, with very few exceptions, are Catholics.

I saw in Galway a very characteristic trial which throws a strong light on the social and political state of this country.

About sixty years ago a Catholic priest by the name of O'Rock became a Protestant and married.

His son was brought up in the Anglican religion, became a minister, and thanks to the good example given by his father, was provided with the benefice of Mylock, a large parish in the neighborhood of Galway.

Soon afterwards he was appointed justice of the peace and finally the court of *Chancery* charged him with the management of a considerable estate. The parish of Mylock is composed of 10,000 Catholics and about a hundred Protestants. The income of the rector was considerable, his duties few; as minister he demanded the tithe, as justice of the peace he saw to it that it was paid without resistance. To occupy his spare time, he bought or rented land and took over a farm (it is his lawyer who said this) of 1200 acres of land. All prospered for thirty years for Mr. O'Rock. He married three times, had a large family, established his daughters, placed his sons and lived in the hope of a happy old age.

Mr. O'Rock, by the fact of his birth, as may be believed, was particularly abhorred by Catholics, who formed the great mass of the surrounding population. He became far more (hated) still when the question of tithes was raised; he persisted in levying the tithe, while his neighbors agreed not to pursue it, and exacted it with the utmost rigor. As a magistrate he showed himself an inflexible and violent persecutor of the poor. He had, furthermore, the misfortune to attract the animosity of the local Protestants. Twice there were attempts to assassinate him. But he faced the storm and hoped to intimidate his enemies.

In the parish of Mylock lived a Catholic solicitor (Attorney). The latter embraced with ardor the cause of his co-religionists, and with the assistance of legal means began the warfare against the Reverend Mr. O'Rock of which we have seen the last act.

This solicitor, who was called Killkelly, set about watching the conduct of Mr. O'Rock. And every time the latter strayed from the letter of the law, Killikelly took him or had others take him to court. Seven cases thus succeeded each other in a short time. Mr. O'Rock lost them all and was condemned each time to pay his adversaries considerable damages and costs. Killikelly declared that his intention was not to apply any of this money to his own use. He bought a piece of ground opposite the house of Mr. O'Rock, and, with the help of the money extracted from the latter by the decrees of the courts, he began to build under his very eyes a pretty little Catholic chapel.

Mr. O'Rock, it appears, is known in the district for having irregular morals. Two years ago he had in his service the daughter of a Catholic peasant named Molly X. Molly became pregnant. Her father chased her out of the his house; her friends refused to receive her. But a shepherd of Kilikelly was more compassionate, he took her into his hut, kept her for six weeks. And the child having come into the world, Molly took it to the house of a local priest, to whom she declared that Mr. O'Rock had seduced her, that he had taken her honor actually inside the Protestant church of Mylock, and that he was the father of the child. The priest gave the little girl the name of Mary O'Rock and the news was spread through the county. Killikenny, having learned these facts, took the father of the young girl into his service, and he, at the instigation and with the help of his master (so Killikelly declared himself at the hearing), instituted the case of which we have been witnesses.

The jury is what is called a '*special jury*' (the parties agree on 40 names from which are drawn 12 jurors by lot). These jurors are respectable local landlords. The draw yielded 9 Catholics and three Protestants. But unanimity is necessary to reach a verdict. The room is packed. The two populations, the two religions are face to face. The case is followed with the most lively interest. Mr. Kilikelly's counsel speaks. He is a Protestant; he knows, says he, that most of his audience have come with the hope of seeing the Church of England humiliated. But such is not his intention. He believes, himself, that the Church of England ought to expel unworthy members and O'Rock is of that number. In this way, he preserved his personal position and dealt only surer blows to the minister.

The witnesses are heard. Their animosity against the Protestant priest was manifestly apparent. However they are precise and unanimous. The audience is in suspense. The judge (a Protestant and a Tory) sums up in favor of the accused. The jury retires and after an hour, it returns and delivers a verdict of guilty. Everybody understands that such a verdict was a decree of banishment against the Rev. O'Rock and many people think that this motive has influenced the jury more than the proofs of the plaintiff. What is certain is that to us as strangers they did not appear sufficient.

The next day we left Galway to go to Tuam. Some coaches going in the opposite direction stop us. Well! What news? What did the jury decide in the case of Mr. O'Rock? – The verdict has been unfavorable to him – So, he is ruined? – and this time at least, he will be forced to leave the country. – What a blow for the Church of England! And we separate with mutual satisfaction.

From *Alexis de Tocqueville's Journey in Ireland*

Caesar Otway

1838

CAESAR OTWAY (1780–1842) was born in County Tipperary and graduated from Trinity College Dublin in 1801. He spent the next seventeen years as a country curate before becoming assistant chaplain at Leeson Street Magdalen Chapel, Dublin. He became one of their leading preachers and, with Joseph Henderson Singer, started *The Christian Examiner*, the first religious magazine of the Established Church. Deeply interested in antiquarian research, Otway collaborated with George Petrie on the *Dublin Penny Journal*, for which he wrote under the pseudonym Terence O'Toole. Otway made several tours in Ireland and wrote *Sketches in Ireland* and *A Tour in Connaught* about his experiences.

*B*efore I go farther, I may as well tell all I know about this tribe of Joyces, that have given their name to this part of Connaught. They were a troop or band that came over from Wales or the West of England, under the command of Bermingham of Athenry in the reign of Edward I, their name was Joyes or Jorse, and they were said to be descended from ancient British princes. Transplantation improved them in stature, for certainly the Welsh are not a tall race. This people not only settled in these western highlands, so very like those in Wales, but they became important in Galway town, and formed one of the thirteen tribes of that ancient and extraordinary corporation, – the *merry* Joyces!! For all tribes had their *soubriquets*, and perhaps a Blake is positive, and a D'arcy stout, (quere, fire-eating duellists), and a Martin litigious; and so on respecting each characteristic whereby they were formerly designated. Only this I think I have heard say, that however a Martin loved litigation in the good town of Galway, he allows no writs or issues of law to extend beyond his gateway at Oughterard, just twenty miles from his mansion-house.

Of the Joyces many were mayors and bailiffs of the capital of Connaught, and not only the men bustled and battled away against the rough-riding rogues, the O'Maddens and the ferocious O'Flaherties, but even the women were sometimes of big note; amongst others, I may mention, Margaret, the daughter of John Joyce, who one day going down to wash her household clothes in the broad transparent stream that runs out of Lough Corrib, and as she stood in the current, as did the daughters of Grecian kings in the time of Ulysses, who should come by but Don Domingo De Rona, a Biscayan merchant of great wealth and note, who had arrived at Galway with a carrack of Benecarlo wine, which was much in demand for doctoring the claret, the Galway merchants were so famous for concocting.

Now, as fair Margaret beetled away in the stream, and as with ruddy legs and untrammelled toes, (as straight and fair as her fingers, not a corn or bunnion on one of them), she trampled the linen, the Don was captivated, with the maid; he made love as Spaniards do; produced proofs of his pedigree, and his cash, and in due time they were married, and proceeded to Corunna; but not long after he died, (as old cavaliers are apt to do who marry late), and Donna De Rona came home a sparkling and wealthy widow, and by and by her hand was solicited by Oliver Oge Ffrench, one of the heads of that tribe, and in due time they were married, and after the marriage he became mayor and one of the greatest merchants of the city. He traded much to foreign ports, and as it was no shame to smuggle in those days, and as the good town of Galway never was allowed to be lighted by night, in order that smuggling might go on and prosper, so Oliver Oge was often on the sea, showing a good example of enterprise and free trade – exporting wool and importing brandy and wine.

In the meanwhile the Donna was not idle; she was the greatest improver in the west; she had particularly a passion for building bridges. She might have made as good a pontifex as Pope Joan, and heaven's blessing was on her for her good works; for one day as she was superintending her masons, an eagle came soaring from the ocean, and balancing itself with poised wing just over the dame, it dropped at her feet a ring formed of a single stone, so strange and outlandish in its make and form, but yet so beautiful and so precious that, though the most skilful lapidaries admired it, and would have given any price for it, none could say of what kind it was, or of what country or age was the workmanship: it has been kept in the family since.

Derry Island in Lough Derg

I wish I could tell the reader which of the Joyces now owns this precious relic. All I can say is, that it is *not* on the finger of big Jack, or his wife. But indeed the Joyees seem to have been a favoured race; it is a favour that they should be named and known as merry; for he who has 'a merry heart hath a continual feast.' I assume it to be a favour also that they were under the especial patronage of eagles. One of the family in the religious and valorous times, when men went to fight for the love of Christ against the Saracens, a fine, tall stalwart fellow, a fair specimen of a Joyce, had gone to the wars of the Holy Land, and there he was taken prisoner by the Paynim, and there the dark, gazelle eye of an Arab maid fell on him, and she loved *his* blue eye and *merry* countenance, which even captivity could not sadden, and also his large proportions, and she set him free, and followed her Irish cavalier through Egypt, Barbary, and into Spain; and there they were wandering as pilgrims in sordid state and apparel, just favoured with food and lodging, because returning from Palestine, when the guardian eagle of the family, as they were winning their weary way over the Sierra Morena, came fluttering over his head, and gave such signs as led him along a certain path until he reached a spot where a Moorish king had deposited, after a defeat, all his treasures. How the stout Joyce contrived to appropriate and make his own these heaps of gold, history does not inform. All it says is, that he came (I hope not unaccompanied

59

Connemara peddler

by his Arabian true love) to Galway, there lived and died, and showed his gratitude to God, and his love to his country, by building churches and strengthening the town wall.

I must conclude my remarks on the Joyces by observing, that Mr. Hardiman, in his excellent History of Galway, says that he has heard and witnessed many instances of the size and strength of the Joyces. 'I saw,' says he, 'an elderly man of that name of uncommon stature and strength, who, (as I was informed,) when in his youth elevated by *the native*, never was satisfied until he had drove every man out of the fair green; those who knew his humour, and also his strength, generally retired beyond a certain small bridge; when his caprice was satisfied by submission, he permitted them to retire quietly; resistance would not only have been useless but almost certain destruction, for nineteen in twenty were of that name and all related; when I saw him he was the remains of a noble figure, remarkably gentle and kind to every one, and heard, with great regret, the pranks of his youth mentioned.' So much for the Joyces; yet still, I say, that I do not consider that (take them *now* as a tribe or race) they are superior in strength or stature to the well-fed mountaineers, who are *not* pressed on for the means of subsistence, in Connemara, Clare, Tipperary, or Kerry. I have a mountain farm in Tipperary, and I will engage (leaving Jack Joyce and his son out of the question) to produce ten men off that farm as tall and well-proportioned as those of any district of the same extent and population in Joyce's country.

The descent is very rapid from the high grounds on which Jack Joyce's new farm and public-house is situated, to the Killery Bay, and the inn of Leenane. As you descend by a very good road, there are noble mountain views, and the long Killery, stretching its dark and deep cut line through the mountains, was certainly a fine sight, and very unlike any thing I have seen elsewhere in the island – not, perhaps, presenting so grand a prospect as either Bantry Bay or Lough Swilly, but it has features all its own. About either of these fine estuaries there appears something that man has done – man has *some* share in the decoration, or even grandeur of the scene; but here at the Killery man and his works are out of the question; no sail upon the waters; no cultivation along the shore; all as rough nature has left it; even trees seem out of character with the place; and *there* is the deep bay, and *there* are the high mountains all around, the same, we may suppose, as when the first sea-rover turned inwards his prow for shelter or curiosity, and sought, and that in vain, for something that marked the occupation and dominion of man.

Some have said that Killery Bay is like a Norvegian fiord. Never having been in the Scandinavian peninsula I cannot decidedly contradict, but it certainly does not meet *my* idea of a fiord, which supposes pine-crowned precipices hanging and frowning over the deep blue wave; but this is not the case here: perfectly bare of any timber, the mountains, though rising all around, and assuming all manner of outlines, yet shelve gradually down to the shore, and I would say that the character of the place is not *sublime* but *savage*.

We arrived in good time at Leenane, and found the new owner, or rather renter, a civil but inexperienced woman, who had lately taken possession, and who complained bitterly of her landlord, who had promised to put the house in good repair, and make it sufficiently decent to induce travellers to stop with her.

From *A Tour in Connaught*

Claddagh ring

John O'Donovan

1839

TOPOGRAPHER AND CELTIC SCHOLAR John O'Donovan (1809–1861) was born in County Kilkenny and brought to Dublin as a child after his father died. He was appointed to a post in the historical department of the Ordnance Topographical Survey of Ireland, working with George Petrie and Eugene O'Curry, whose sister he married. He travelled throughout the country and his findings were published as essays on topography and history in *The Dublin Penny Journal*. His books include *A Grammar of the Irish Language*, but his greatest achievement is his translation of *The Annals of the Four Masters*.

*W*e set sail from Galway on the 11th of July for Aran in the *Mountain Maid*, one of the best boats in the Claddagh, the property of Conneely alias Connolly to whom I paid 18 shillings for transporting us to Aran. We set out from the old quay of Galway at 3 o'clock, the wind being very scant, and from the south east. When we had sailed three miles into the Bay of Galway there came a dead calm, and the boatman began to feel certain that we could not reach Aran till the following day. They therefore wished to lie at Blackhead till the break of day from fear of fogs which often lie brooding on the sea between Blackhead and the Isles of Aran. I would not consent to their doing so, not wishing to sit shivering in the boat, nor to loose the next day; so I desired them to sail away, and tack away whatever time they might reach the island. I saw the sun set in the Atlantic, a glorious sight, but so often described that I wont say one word about his meteor eyes, but the Aran light house shed such a stream of light as astonished me. It is a revolving light, and the reflectors are so good that while it remains in view (it takes 3 1/2 minutes to revolve) it looks like a meteor. It sheds such a flood of radiant light upon the welkin, the sea, and the eyes of the spectators, as apparently to put out the nocturnal lamps blazing in the firmament (as a tasteless poet would say).

We neared the little harbour of Kilronan exactly at two minutes after three, when the day began to shew the first symptoms of its birth in the east, by streaking the north, east, with its capuscle glimmer, and filling the canvass with a colder and fresher breeze.

We climbed up the big stones of which the little quay of Kilronan is built, and finding ourselves on the solid rocks of Aran we proceeded by the guidance of two Claddaghmen, and one native Aranite, to the head Inn of Aranmore, in which being now chilly and fatigued, we were very anxious to get our heads in, and to lay down our heads to sleep for a few

The Church of Kilcannanagh drawn by William Wakeman

hours. I was astonished as I trod upon the smooth and level lime stone pavement of the village, and many wild associations of ideas flitted across my brain, about creation, earth-quakes, and other incomprehensibilities before we reached the head Inn. On arriving at the house, our sailors rapped at the door several times, but no answer was made, which made me believe that they brought us to the wrong house, at which the youngest of them pushed in the door!

On the following day we proceeded to Kilmurvy and thence to St. Breccan's church in the townland of Onaght, and on our way back examined several churches lying between Port Murvy and Monaster. On the next day we examined the most ancient and most curious fortress on Aranmore, ie Dubh-Chathair with the antique aspect of which I was much gratified.

On the next day I was determined, if possible, to sail back to Galway, or get myself landed somewhere on the north shore leaving Mr. Wakeman to go over the three islands again to make careful sketches of all the remains which we had identified with their ancient names. The priest procured the best boat on the island for me for the moderate charge as the owner averred, of 12/6. Up to near 12 o'clock the sea presented too angry an aspect to venture on it at all, but about 12 exactly the storm abated a little, and Paidin O'Flaherty, the proprietor of the boat, said that he would venture out, his boat being so very good. I embarked at the little quay of Kilronan and the men hoisting the sail with great courage and cheerfulness we soon found ourselves riding on the swollen billows. A pháidín a mhic na caillíghe

Lynch's Castle

nach breág an fhairge í! the wind blowing directly from the south-east point. We sailed very well for about two hours nearly in the direction of Caslah Bay, when suddenly the breeze grew brisker, the clouds assumed a louring aspect, and the waves dashed over the boat from stem to stern, which wet us to the skin.

The sailors wishing to land me on the north shore, asked me if I wished it (thinking that I was a good deal terrified) but I told them that there was no danger, which they knew very well themselves. When they came near Caslah bay they tacked and steered in the direction of Black head, which looked very far off. At the hour of seven o'clock we came after countless tackings very close to Black head, when a violent storm arose which alarmed the men very much. They took down the two sails during this squall, and we were tossed sailless about for about 1/2 an hour.

I got into the forecastle of the boat to avoid the dashing of the waves which annoyed me not being able to bear much wet, but there I got quickly sick from the smoak and water dashing down through the scuttle hole which served for a chimney.

When the storm had subsided a little, the sailors reefed and hoisted the sails again and finding to their great satisfaction that during the squall the wind had veered about a little to the S.W., at seeing which the stiurasmann cried out in Irish: 'All is right now, thank God, we shall get to Galway now in a few half hours.'

In this, however, he was disappointed for we did not reach Galway till 10 o'clock.

From *Aran Islands of Legend*

Anthony Trollope

1841

ANTHONY TROLLOPE (1815–1882) was the son of a famous novelist, Fanny Trollope. In 1834 he went to work at the General Post Office in London as a clerk and five years later was sent to Ireland as deputy postal surveyor. Trollope began to write while in Ireland and in 1859 returned to London and settled at Waltham Abbey. He became one of the most popular novelists of the Victorian Age with novels such as *Barchester Towers* and *Phineas Finn*. He visited Connemara in June of 1882 researching another novel with an Irish setting but died before it was written.

I had not been a fortnight in Ireland before I was sent down to a little town in the far west of county Galway, to balance a defaulting postmaster's accounts, find out how much he owed, and report upon his capacity to pay. In these days such accounts are very simple. They adjust themselves from day to day, and a Post Office surveyor has nothing to do with them. At that time, though the sums dealt with were small, the forms of dealing with them were very intricate. I went to work, however, and made that defaulting postmaster teach me the use of those forms. I then succeeded in balancing the account, and had no difficulty whatever in reporting that he was altogether unable to pay his debt.

From *Autobiography of Anthony Trollope*

William Makepeace Thackeray

1842

BORN IN CALCUTTA, William Makepeace Thackeray (1811–1863) was taken to England after his father died. He was educated at Cambridge University and studied art but the prospect of a large fortune induced idleness in him. After squandering his fortune, and having failed to sell any paintings, Thackeray turned to journalism. He attracted attention with his articles in *Punch* and his first book, *The Paris Sketch Book*, was published in 1842. That same year he visited Ireland under contract to write *The Irish Sketch Book*, for which he also drew illustrations. His best known novels are *Vanity Fair*, *Barry Lyndon*, *Henry Esmond* and *The Virginians*.

The Clifden car, which carries the Dublin letters into the heart of Connemara, conducts the passenger over one of the most wild and beautiful districts that it is ever the fortune of a traveller to examine; and I

William Makepeace Thackeray

could not help thinking, as we passed through it, at how much pains and expense honest English cockneys are, to go and look after natural beauties far inferior, in countries which, though more distant, are not a whit more strange than this one. No doubt, ere long, when people know how easy the task is, the rush of London tourism will come this way: and I shall be very happy if these pages shall be able to awaken in one bosom, beating in Tooley Street or the Temple, the desire to travel towards Ireland next year.

After leaving the quaint old town behind us and ascending one or two small eminences to the north-westward, the traveller, from the car, gets a view of the wide street of Lough Corrib shining in the sun, as we saw it, with its low dark banks stretching round it. If the view is gloomy, at least it is characteristic: nor are we delayed by it very long; for though the lake stretches northwards into the very midst of the Joyce country (and is there in the close neighbourhood of another huge lake, Lough Mask, which again is near to another sheet of water), yet from this road henceforth, after keeping company with it for some five miles, we only get occasional views of it, passing over hills and through trees, by many rivers and smaller lakes, which are dependent upon that of Corrib. Gentlemen's seats, on the road from Galway to Moycullen, are scattered in great profusion – perhaps there is grass growing on the gravel walk, and the iron gates of the tumble-down old lodges are rather rickety; but for all that, the places look comfortable, hospitable, and spacious, and as for the shabbiness and want of finish here and there, the English eye grows quite accustomed to it in a month; and I find the bad condition of the Galway houses by no means so painful as that of the places near Dublin. At some of the lodges, as we pass, the mailcarman, with a warning shout, flings a bag of letters. I saw a little party looking at one which lay there in the road crying, Come, take me! but nobody cares to steal a bag of letters in this country, I suppose, and the carman drove on without any alarm. Two days afterwards, a gentleman with whom I was in company left on a rock his book of fishing-flies; and I can assure you there was a very different feeling expressed about the safety of that.

In the first part of the journey, the neighbourhood of the road seemed to be as populous as in other parts of the country; troops of red-petticoated peasantry peering from their stone-cabins; yelling children following the car, and crying, 'Lash, lash!' It was Sunday, and you would see many a white chapel among the green bare plains to the right of the road, the courtyard blackened with a swarm of cloaks. The service seems to continue (on the part of the people) all day. Troops of people, issuing from the chapel, met us at Moycullen, and ten miles further on, at Oughterard, their devotions did not yet seem to be concluded.

A more beautiful village can scarcely be seen than this. It stands upon Lough Corrib, the banks of which are here, for once at least, picturesque and romantic: and a pretty river, the Feogh, comes rushing over racks and by woods until it passes the town and meets the lake. Some pretty buildings in the village stand on each bank of this stream, a Roman Catholic chapel with a curate's neat lodge; a little church on one side of it, a fine courthouse of grey stone on the other. And here it is that we get into the famous district of Connemara, so celebrated in Irish stories, so mysterious to the London tourist. 'It presents itself,' says the Guide-book, 'under every possible combination of heathy moor, bog, lake, and mountain. Extensive mossy plains and wild pastoral valleys lie embosomed among the mountains, and support numerous herds of cattle and horses, for which the district has been long celebrated. These wild solitudes, which occupy by far the greater part of the centre of the country, are held by a hardy and ancient race of grazing farmers, who live in a very primitive state, and, generally speaking, till little beyond what supplies their immediate wants. For the first ten miles the country is comparatively open; and the mountains on the left, which are not of great elevation, can be distinctly traced as they rise along the edge of the heathy plain.

'Our road continues along the Feogh river, which expands itself into several considerable lakes, and at five miles from Oughterard we reach Lough Bofin, which the road also skirts. Passing in succession Lough-a-preaghan, the lakes of Anderran and Shindella, at ten miles from Oughterard we reach Slyme and Lynn's Inn, or Half-way House, which is near the shore of Loughonard. Now, as we advance towards the group of Binabola, or the Twelve Pins, the most gigantic scenery is displayed.'

But the best guide-book that ever was written cannot set the view before the mind's eye of the reader, and I won't attempt to pile up big words in place of these wild mountains, over which the clouds as they passed, or the sunshine as it went and came, cast every variety of tint, light, and shadow; nor can it be expected that long, level sentences, however smooth and shining, can be made to pass as representations of those calm lakes by which we took our way. All one can do is to lay down the pen and ruminate, and cry, 'beautiful!' once more; and to the reader say, 'Come and see!'

Wild and wide as the prospect around us is, it has somehow a kindly, friendly look; differing in this from the fierce loneliness of some similar scenes in Wales that I have viewed. Ragged women and children come out of rude stone-huts to see the car as it passes. But it is impossible for the pencil to give due raggedness to the rags, or to convey a certain picturesque mellowness of colour that the garments assume. The sexes with regard to raiment, do not seem to be particular. There were many boys on the road in the national red petticoat, having no other covering for their lean brown legs; as for shoes, the women eschew them almost entirely; and I saw a peasant trudging from mass in a handsome scarlet cloak, a fine blue cloth gown, turned up to show a new lining of the same color, and a petticoat quite white and neat – in a dress of which the cost must have been at least 10/-; and her husband walked in front carrying her shoes and stockings.

The road had conducted us for miles through the vast property of the gentleman to whose house I was bound, Mr. Martin, the member for the county; and the last and prettiest part of the journey was round the Lake of Ballynahinch, with tall mountains rising immediately above us on the right, pleasant woody hills on the opposite side of the lake, with the roofs of the houses rising above the trees; and in an island in the midst of the water a ruined old castle that cast a long white, reflection into the blue waters where it lay. A land-pirate used to live in that castle, one of the peasants told me, in the time of 'Oliver Cromwell.' And a fine fastness it was for a robber, truly; for there was no road through these wild countries in his time – nay, only thirty years since, this lake was at three days' distance of Galway. Then comes the question, What, in a country where there were no roads and no travellers, and where the inhabitants have been wretchedly poor from time immemorial – what was there for the land pirate to rob? But let us not be too curious about times so early as those of Oliver Cromwell. I have heard the name many times from the Irish peasant, who still has an awe of the grim, resolute Protector.

The builder of Ballinahinch House has placed it to command a view of a pretty, melancholy river that runs by it, through many green flats and picturesque rocky grounds; but from the lake it is scarcely visible. And so, in like manner, I fear it must remain invisible to the reader too, with all its kind inmates, and frank, cordial hospitality; unless he may take a fancy to visit Galway himself, when, as I can vouch a very small pretext will make him enjoy both.

It will, however, be only a small breach of confidence to say that the major-domo of the establishment (who has adopted accurately the voice

Ballynahinch

and manner of his master, with a severe dignity of his own which is quite original) ordered me on going to bed 'not to move in the morning till he called me,' at the same time expressing a hearty hope that I should 'want nothing more that evening.' Who would dare, after such peremptory orders, not to fall asleep immediately, and in this way disturb the repose of Mr. J—n M—ll—y?

There may be many comparisons drawn between English and Irish gentlemen's houses; but perhaps the most striking point of difference between the two is the immense following of the Irish house, such as would make an English housekeeper crazy almost. Three comfortable, well-clothed, good humored fellows walked down with me from the car, persisting in carrying one, a bag, another a sketching-stool, and so on; walking about the premises in the morning; sundry others were visible in the court-yard and near the kitchen-door; i the grounds a gentleman, by name Mr. Marcus C—rr, began discoursing to me regarding the place, the planting, the fish, the grouse, and the Master, being himself, doubtless, one of the irregulars of the house. As for maids there were half a score of them skurrying about the house; and I am not ashamed to confess that some of them were exceedingly good-looking. And if I might venture to say a word more, it would be respecting Connemara breakfasts; but this would be an entire and flagrant breach of confidence, and, to be sure, the dinners were just as good.

One of the days of my three days' visit was to be devoted to the lakes; and as a party had been arranged for the second day after my arrival, I was glad to take advantage of the society of a gentleman staying in the house, and ride with him to the neighbouring town of Clifden.

The ride thither from Ballinahinch is surprisingly beautiful; and as you ascend the high ground from the two or three rude stone huts which face the entrance-gates of the house, there are views of the lake and the surrounding country which the best parts of Killarney do not surpass, I think, although the Connemara lakes do not possess the advantage of wood, which belongs to the famous Kerry landscape.

But the cultivation of the country is only in its infancy as yet, and it is easy to see how vast its resources are, and what capital and cultivation may do for it. In the green patches among the rocks, and the mountain-sides, wherever crops were grown, they flourished; plenty of natural wood is springing up in various places; and there is no end to what the planter may do, and to what time and care may effect. The carriage-road to Clifden is but ten years old: as it has brought the means of communication into the country, the commerce will doubtless follow it; and in fact, in going through the whole kingdom, one can't but be struck with the idea that not one hundredth part of its capabilities are yet brought into action, or even known perhaps, and that, by the easy and certain progress of time, Ireland will be poor Ireland no longer.

For instance, we rode by a vast green plain, skirting a lake and river, which is now useless almost for pasture, and which a little draining will convert into thousands of acres of rich productive land. Streams and falls of water dash by everywhere: – they have only to utilize this water-power for mills and factories – and hard by are some of the finest bays in the world, where ships can deliver and receive foreign and home produce. At Roundstone especially, where a little town has been erected, the bay is said to be unexampled for size, depth, and shelter; and the Government is now, through the rocks and hills on their wild shore, cutting a coast-road to Bunown, the most westerly part of Connemara, whence there is another good road to Clifden. Among the charges which the Repealers bring against the Union, they should include at least this – they would never have had these roads but for the Union, roads which are as much at the charge of the London tax-payer as of the most ill-used Milesian in Connaught.

A string of small lakes follow the road to Clifden, with mountains on the right of the traveller for the chief part of the way. A few figures work in the boglands – a red petticoat passing here and there – a goat or two browsing among the stones – or a troop of ragged whity-brown children who came out to gaze at the car, form the chief society on the road – the first house at the entrance to Clifden is a gigantic poor house – tall, large, ugly, comfortable; it commands the town and looks almost as big as every one of the houses therin. The town itself is but of a few years' date, and seems to thrive in its small way. Clifden Castle is a fine chateau in the neighbourhood, and belongs to another owner of immense lands in Galway – Mr. D'Arcy.

Here a drive was proposed along the coast to Bunown, and I was glad to see some more of the country, and its character. Nothing can be wilder – we passed little lake after lake, lying a few furloughs inwards from the shore. There were rocks everywhere, some patches of cultivated land here and there, nor was there any want of inhabitants along this savage coast. There were numerous cottages, if cottages they may be called, and women, and above all, children in plenty. Here is one of the former – her attitude as she stood gazing at the car. To depict the multiplicity of her rags would require a month's study.

At length we came in sight of a half-built edifice, which is approached by a rocky, dismal, grey road, guarded by two or three broken gates, against which rocks and stones were piled, which were removed to give an entrance to our car. The gates were closed so laboriously, I presume, to prevent the egress of a single black consumptive pig, far gone in the family-way – a teeming skeleton – that was cropping the thin dry grass that grew upon a round hill which rises behind this most dismal castle of Bunown.

If the traveller only seeks for strange sights, this place will repay his curiosity. Such a dismal house is not to be seen in all England; or, perhaps, such a dismal situation. The sea lies before and behind; and on each side, likewise, are rocks and copper-coloured meadows, by which a few trees have made an attempt to grow. The owner of the house had, however, begun to add to it, and there, unfinished, is a whole apparatus of turrets, and staring raw stone and mortar, and fresh ruinous carpenters' work; – and then the courtyard! – tumbled-down out-houses, staring empty pointed windows, and new-smeared plaster cracking from the walls – a black heap of turf, a mouldy pump, a wretched old coal-scuttle, emptily sunning itself in the midst of this cheerful scene! There was an old Gorgon, who kept the place, and who was in perfect unison with it – Venus herself would become bearded, blear-eyed, and haggard – if left to be the housekeeper of this dreary place.

In the house was a comfortable parlour, inhabited by the Priest, who has the painful charge of the district. Here were his books and his

The Royal Mail in the eighteen eighties

breviaries, his reading-desk with the cross engraved upon it, and his portrait of Daniel O'Connell the Liberator to grace the walls of his lonely cell. There was a dead crane hanging at the door on a gaff; his red fish-like eyes were staring open, and his eager grinning bill – a rifle-ball had passed through his body. And this was doubtless the only game about the place; for we saw the sportsman who had killed the bird hunting vainly up the round hill for other food for powder. This gentleman had had good sport, he said, shooting seals upon a neighbouring island, four of which animals he had slain.

Mounting up the round hill, we had a view of the Sline lights – the most westerly point in Ireland.

Here too was a ruined sort of summer-house, dedicated DEO HIBERNIAE LIBERATORI. When these lights were put up I am told the proprietor of Bunown was recommended to apply for compensation to Parliament, inasmuch as there would be no more wrecks on the coast; from which branch of commerce the inhabitants of the district used formerly to derive a considerable profit. Between these Sline lights and America nothing lies but the Atlantic. It was beautifully blue and bright on this day, and the sky almost cloudless; but I think the brightness only made the scene more dismal, it being of that order of beauties which cannot bear the full light, but require a cloud or a curtain to set them off to advantage. A pretty story was told me by the gentleman who had killed the seals. The place where he had been staying for sport was almost as lonely as this Bunown, and inhabited by a priest too – a young, lively, well-educated man. 'When I came here first,' the priest said, '*I cried for two days*;' but afterwards he grew to like the place exceedingly, his whole heart being directed towards it, his chapel, and his cure. Who would not honour such missionaries – the virtues they silently practise, and the doctrines they preach? After hearing that story, I think Bunown looked not quite so dismal, as it is inhabited, they say, by such another character. What a pity it is that John Tuam, in the next county of Mayo, could not find such another hermitage to learn modesty in, and forget his Graceship, his Lordship, and the sham titles by which he sets such store.

A moon as round and bright as any moon that ever shone, and riding in a sky perfectly cloudless, gave us a good promise of a fine day for the morrow, which was to be devoted to the lakes in the neighbourhood of Ballinahinch: one of which, Lough Ina, is said to be of exceeding beauty. But no man can speculate upon Irish weather. I have seen a day beginning with torrents of rain, that looked as if a deluge was at hand, clear up in a few minutes, without any reason, and against the prognostications of the glass and all other weather-prophets – so in like manner, after the astonishingly fine night, there came a villanous day which, however, did not set in fairly for rain, until we were an hour on our journey, with a couple of stout boatmen rowing us over Ballinahinch Lake. Being, however, thus fairly started, the water began to come down, not in torrents certainly, but in that steady, creeping, insinuating mist, of which we scarce know the luxury in England; and which, I am bound to say, will wet a man's jacket as satisfactorily as a cataract would do.

It was just such another day as that of the famous stag-hunt at Killarney, in a word; and as, in the first instance, we went to see the deer killed, and saw nothing thereof, so, in the second case, we went to see the landscape with precisely the same good fortune. The mountains covered their modest beauties in impenetrable veils of clouds; and the only consolation to the boat's crew was that it was a remarkably good day for trout-fishing – which amusement some people are said to prefer to the examination of landscapes, however beautiful.

O you who laboriously throw flies in English rivers, and catch, at the expiration of a hard day's walking, casting, and wading, two or three feeble little brown trouts of two or three ounces in weight, how would you rejoice to have but an hour's sport in Derryclear or Ballinahinch, where you have but to cast, and lo! a big trout springs at your fly, and, after making a vain struggling, splashing, and plunging for a while, is infallibly landed in the net and thence into the boat. The single rod in the boat caught enough fish in an hour to feast the crew, consisting of five persons, and the family of a herd of Mr. Martin's, who has a pretty cottage on Derryclear lake, inhabited by a cow and its calf, a score of fowls, and I don't know how many sons and daughters.

Having caught enough trout to satisfy any moderate appetite, like true sportsmen the gentlemen on board our boat became eager to hook a salmon. Had they hooked a few salmons, no doubt they would have trolled for whales, or for a mermaid; one of which finny beauties the waterman swore he had seen on the shore of Derryclear – he with Jim Mullen being above on a rock, the mermaid on the shore directly beneath them, visible to the middle, and as usual 'racking her hair.' It was fair hair, the boatman said; and he appeared as convinced of the existence of the mermaid, as he was of the trout just landed in the boat.

In regard of mermaids, there is a gentleman living near Killala Bay, whose name was mentioned to me, and who declared solemnly that one day, shooting on the sands there, he saw a mermaid, and determined to try her with a shot. So he drew the small charge from his gun and loaded it with ball, that he always had by him for seal shooting, fired, and hit the mermaid through the breast. The screams and moans of the creature, whose person he describes most accurately – were the most horrible, heart-rending noises that he ever, he said, heard; and not only were they heard by him, but by the fishermen along the coast, who were furiously angry against Mr. A—n, because, they said, the injury done to the mermaid would cause her to drive all the fish away from the bay for years to come.

But we did not, to my disappointment, catch a single glimpse of one of these interesting beings, nor of the great sea-horse which is said to inhabit these waters, nor of any fairies (of whom the stroke-oar, Mr. Marcus, told us not to speak, for they didn't like bein' spoken of): nor even of a salmon, though the fishermen produced the most tempting flies. The only animal of any size that was visible we saw while lying by a swift black river that comes jumping with innumerable little waves into Derryclear, and where the salmon are especially suffered to 'stand'; this animal was an eagle – a real wild eagle, with grey wings and a white head and belly: it swept round us, within gunshot reach, once or twice, through the leaden sky, and then settled on a grey rock and began to scream its shrill, ghastly aquiline note.

The attempts on the salmon having failed, the rain continuing to fall steadily, the herd's cottage before named was resorted to: when Marcus, the boatman, commenced forthwith to gut the fish, and taking down some charred turf-ashes from the blazing fire, on which about an hundredweight of potatoes were boiling, he – Marcus – proceeded to grill on the floor some

Lake of Ballynahinch

of the trout, which we afterwards ate with immeasurable satisfaction. They were such trouts as, when once tasted, remain for ever in the recollection of a commonly grateful mind – rich, flaky, creamy, full of flavor – a Parisian *gourmand* would have paid ten francs for the smallest *cooleen* among them; and, when transported to his capital, how different in flavor would they have been – how inferior to what they were as we devoured them, fresh from the fresh waters of the lakes, and jerked as it were from the water to the gridiron! The world had not had time to spoil those innocent beings before they were gobbled up with pepper and salt, and missed, no doubt, by their friends. I should like to know more of their 'set.' But enough of this: my feelings overpower me: suffice it to say, they were red or salmon trouts – none of your white-fleshed brown-skinned river fellows.

When the gentlemen had finished their repast, the boatmen and the family set to work upon the ton of potatoes, a number of the remaining fish, and a store of other good things; then we all sat round the turf-fire in the dark cottage, the rain coming down steadily outside, and veiling everything except the shrubs and verdure immediately about the cottage. The herd, the herd's wife, and a nondescript female friend, two healthy young herdsmen in corduroy rags, the herdsman's daughter paddling about with bare feet, a stout black-eyed wench with her gown over head

Overlooking Leenane

and a red petticoat not quite so good as new, the two boatmen, a badger just killed and turned inside out, the gentlemen, some hens cackling and flapping about among the rafters, a calf in the corner cropping green meat and occasionally visited by the cow her mamma formed the society of the place. It was rather a strange picture; but as for about two hours we sat there, and maintained an almost unbroken silence, and as there was no other amusement but to look at the rain, I began, after the enthusiasm of the first half-hour, to think that after all London was a bearable place, and that for want of a turf-fire and a bench in Connemara, one *might* put up with a sofa and a newspaper in Pall Mall.

From *The Irish Sketch Book*

Asenath Nicholson

1845

ASENATH HATCH (1795–1855) was born in Vermont and moved to New York City when she married Norman Nicholson in 1833. She got to know the Irish while working among the poor in New York. After her husband died, Nicholson went to Ireland to investigate conditions there. Wearing a polka-dot coat and carrying a suitcase full of Bibles, she walked the countryside. Her account of the destitution she encountered was published in America in 1847 as *Ireland's Welcome to a Stranger*. By then the Famine had struck and Nicholson stayed on, providing relief from her own funds. After spending some time in Cork with her friend Father Matthew, the Apostle of Temperance, she returned to America in 1852.

*S*abbath. Paid threepence for my lodging, and took the car for Gort, reaching it at ten o'clock.

Here I went from street to street, and almost from door to door, to find a roll of bread and a cup of cocoa. There seemed to be nothing to eat, and twice when I asked for bread, the answer was 'the people of Gort don't eat, ma'am; we have no bread.' At last I found a few small loaves, took a penny's-worth, and left the town to walk to Oranmore, a distance of fourteen miles.

On my way a woman called out, 'Good-morrow, ma'am; ye look wairy, come in and rest ye a bit.' I found her ignorance was painful; she seemed to know nothing beyond her own cabin. Seeing that she wanted a pin, I gave her a couple of rows; the paper was red, and she admired it with great wonder. A son of twenty came in, and she immediately presented the paper to him. They both held it up, and endeavoured to look through it, and seemed delighted at the novel sight.

The next day I attempted to walk to Galway, as I had sent on my carpet-bag, and felt a little uneasy. The distance was but four and a half miles, but my feet soon became so painful, that it seemed quite impossible to proceed. An old woman saluted me, 'An' ye'll be kilt with walkin,' an' wouldn't ye ride for sixpence? I know a poor man who keeps a little ass, that would gladly take ye for that.' She took me to a hovel, and called out, 'Here, John, wouldn't ye take a lady to Galway for sixpence?' 'An' that I would.' said John, jumping out of bed. It was eight o'clock; the children were preparing for school, and though ragged they were not dirty. The man had but one arm, and no means of support but by his cart and ass. I insisted that he should eat his potato first, though I saw none preparing. I found afterwards he had none, and no prospect of any till the sixpence should be earned. It was a touching case of uncomplaining want. When we were going away, the woman said, 'Maybe the lady hasn't got the change now.' Taking the hint that she wanted the sixpence, I said, 'Yes.' But the poor man's sensitiveness was awakened, and he hurried me away with, 'Never mind – never mind.'

I gave him a few pennies more than the sixpence, and this so affected him, that I was glad when he bade 'God speeed' and hastened to buy his potatoes.

At Galway I hastened to the car office to make arrangements for Clifden, and there found my carpet-bag upon the floor broken open, and the contents lying in fragments. I inquired the cause of the agent, who insolently answered, 'Your things are all there. An officer's wife said she had examined them, and found the value was not much, and she left them as she found them, but I must have an additional shilling for my trouble, or the luggage shall not leave the office.' I asked him whether as a stranger I had merited such treatment. He cared nothing, he said, for strangers, nor anything for Americans. Offering him a sovereign to change, 'he should change it when he knew the weight, but should not trust to my honesty.' The sovereign was weighed, and proved to be more than weight. He took the shilling, and asked my name to enter on the book. I declined, and told him that I should have no more to do with Bianconi's cars, since this was not the first time I had been treated rudely and unkindly by his agents.

I passed out, found the one-armed man, and agreed with him to take me fourteen miles for two shillings. His price was a shilling a day, and he could perform this journey in a day. Early in the morning I was prepared for the ride, but no man appeared. I took my parasol, leaving my luggage, and went on, hoping the old man might soon follow. The wife of a poor curate soon joined me, who deplored greatly the delusions of Romanism, but the divisions among Protestants, she thought, were more to be regretted than all. Her husband, she said, was an indefatigable labourer in the cause of Christ, and had lost a promised promotion from the bishop, because he had sought to obey a higher Master than an earthly one.

My place of stopping was Outerard. I turned into a house where were huddled a group of boys and girls. When I entered, the 'master skilled to rule' was standing, one foot upon a chair, his elbow resting upon his knee, spectacles across his nose, a pen in his hand, which he was mending, ever and anon flourishing it, as he vehemently expatiated on some clause in the lesson he was explaining. He bowed long and low to me, and then spoke in Latin to a boy who answered in the same language. Then turning to a bevy in a dark corner, who were urging their rights by

Clifden Waterfall

hunches and threats, he told them that the wandering Arab in the great desert of Sahara, or the Siberian at the frozen regions of the north, could as well understand the meaning of civility as they; and should he enjoin taciturnity (though that was too refined a word for such boors as he had before him), they would as readily obey him.

'I have done much, honoured lady, for these lads before you, and to say the truth they are the first fellows in the kingdom. Come here; let's hear you conjugate this verb.' Before the boy had half run through, 'There, lady, what do you think of my manner of teaching?' 'It cannot be disputed, sir.' 'I ought to be promoted for what I have done. Go on, honey, and tell the whys and the wherefores. And so you see, lady, no stone's unturned.' I assured him I had seen nothing like it in all Ireland. 'Hear, hear, my good fellows! Here's a lady of the first order speaking, and mark what she says. I knew when she entered, by her looks and language, she was a lady of the highest order. Now mark!'

Full well they laughed, and counterfeited glee.

Hear, hear! I made a speech somewhat in keeping with the place and persons, and had I never before felt my own greatness, now was the favourable moment. A long and low bow, ended by two or three short ones and a hearty good-bye on my part, finished the morning comedy.

My journey lay through a wild mountainous country, and the red petticoats scattered here and there upon hill and lake-side gave a romantic touch to the strange scenery for many a mile. An old man and his daughter joined me on the way; each had a heavy burden, which they tried to lighten at every cabin upon the mountains. They were dealers in dry goods. The father, after a 'God save ye kindly, we're all travellers together,' said 'I rair'd the little gal yonder, and a blackguard of a fellow kept his eye on her for a twelvemonth, till by her consent and mine he married her, stopped with her one month, took the few pounds she had gained by dailin', and went away, the villain, and set up the business, and has never put the two eyes on her sence.'

We were all fatigued, our feet blistered, and we sat down upon a bank of one of the beautiful lakes which are dotting this wild mountain scenery for many a mile. Having my Testament in my hand, 'Ye have a nice little book,' said the old man. 'Shall I read a little?' I asked. 'Plaise God, ye will,' was the answer. I opened at the 14th of John, and read. 'Where,' said the daughter, 'did you get that beautiful book?' 'It sounds,' said the father, 'like our Catholic raidin', and what the priest has told us from the altar.' They had heard portions of the Scripture, but did not know that this was the Word of God till I told them. The daughter took it in her hand, turned over the leaves, read a few portions intelligibly, and asked, 'Where could I get one? Would you sell me this?' I promised one from my basket, should it reach Clifden while she was there. The old man clasped his hands, raised his eyes, blessed the good God that he had met such a lady, and such blessed words which 'melt the heart.' We needed no cushioned desk or fringed drapery, to adorn our pulpit. We wanted no lighted gas to enable us to read our prayers from gilt-edged books, for the chandelier of day was hanging in heaven's high dome. Our temple was a lofty one, and as we sat together within its broad portals, we read the sweet and condescending words, 'Let not your heart be troubled. In my Father's house are many mansions.' 'Yes,' ejaculated the old man, 'blessed be His Holy name, there are many mansions.' I then felt that God was truly a Spirit, and could be worshipped on the mountain-top or lowly valley, and needed no temple made with hands.

They stopped as the sun was setting, at a miserable-looking lodging-house for the night, leaving a three miles' walk for me alone. Darkness soon came over me, and no smoke of a cabin cheered my eye. I heard a footstep, and as it approached, inquired if my lodging-house on the mountain was near. 'A perch or two under yer fut, and ye are in it.' I went on; as I reached the door I heard laughing, music, and dancing. It was a barrack; and a piper, with more whisky than good sense in his brain, was blowing with all his might for the barefooted girls and merry lads, who were in the highest glee. 'Is this a lodging-house?' I inquired. 'Go back, and you will find it.' I stumbled to the back of the barracks, and opened a door. A clean bed was provided; two others, well filled, were in the room; but never was rest more refreshing. The next day was rainy, and I employed my time reading, writing, and listening to the music of two fiddlers, who told me they were employed by gentlemen to amuse them at their houses. So fond are the Irish of music, that, in some form or other, they must and will have it. A piper entered on a wooden leg, and called for a glass of whisky, which was given him, and feeling a little jealous lest the fiddlers might be thought more than rivals, he gave such proofs of dexterity as put all to silence. 'We live so remote,' said he, 'that these little droppings now and then on a rainy day make the time pass very pleasantly. In fact, I don't know how we should get along without them. It's nature, you see,' holding a grand-daughter of the host, eight months' old, upon the floor to see her dance. 'you see, ma'am, they'll dance before they can walk.'

When I had gone about a mile on my road, the wind increased almost to a tornado, and the rain was pouring in torrents. I was now in a woeful plight – my parasol, which had withstood many a buffeting, soon turned inside out, and became a wreck.

I turned my back, and strove to ascend a hill in that way. In despair I stood; when looking to my left I saw at a distance a cabin, and a little girl standing in the door. She was gazing at me, as I supposed, from idle curiosity, and as the last alternative, I heasitatingly turned towards the dreary abode. 'Welcome, welcome, stranger, from the stawrm; ye're destroyed. I told the little gal to open the door and stand in it, that ye mightn't think we was shuttin' ye out in the stawrm; we've got a good fire and plenty of turf; and though the cabin is small, and not fittin' for sich a lady as ye, I'll make it better than the mad stawrm without; and I'll soon heave over a pot of potatoes, and get ye a sup of milk, and I wish my wife were here. I'm but a stranger; but here sence Monday.' All this passed before I had time to tell my country, pedigree, or business to Ireland. A huge pile of blazing turf soon dried my clothes, and I was sitting 'high and dry' against the heels of a stage-horse, who was taking his lunch from a pile of straw at the foot of a bed. In an hour the potatoes were ready, and the kind little girl brought me a broken soup-plate with two eggs on it, and a 'sup of milk.' The eggs I gave to a coachman who had dropped in to exchange horses, and took some salt and my teaspoon, which I carried in my pocket; and upon a stool by the side of the pot, on which a basket was placed containing the lumpers, I ate my supper with the family and coachman, not only with a cheerful, but a grateful heart.

Night came; the horse, to my great delight, was removed by the coachman, leaving two good bundles of clean straw untouched, which

The Square, Tuam (Lawrence Collection R6759)

were more inviting than the only bed. The father went out; a little son fell asleep, and I persuaded him to go to bed, the girl saying, 'He mustn't lie there; father told us that we are to sit by the fire, and ye are to lie in the bed.' I refused, telling her I should not do it; but when the father came in, he told the son in anger, 'he'd break every bone in his body if he didn't go out of that.' I at last prevailed on the father to allow him to remain, and told him I had an excellent bed in my eye. 'An' sure it isn't the bundle of straw; not a ha'p'orth of yer wet and wairy bones shall lie there to-night.' I insisted that I greatly preferred it as a luxury, and finally took one bundle, removed the band, made a little opening, and placed it before the fire, put a second one at the bottom of the door, as the breach was large and the wind piercing; and then with some loose handfuls stopped the crevices above and around, till all was quite snug. Then wrapping my coat closely about me, I lay down in as comfortable a nest, and slept as sweetly, as I ever had in America or Ireland.

The fire died upon the hearth, and the cold awakened me. The day was the Sabbath; the storm had not in the least abated. I had my Testament, and spent the morning reading the crucifixion and resurrection of the Saviour to the family. The father assured me that he 'had never heard a ha'p'orth of it read before; we are as ignorant, good lady, as the goats upon the mountain. God help us!' A woman entered with a red petticoat turned over her head, and the man told her in Irish who I was, and that I had come to see the poor. She reached her hand, and said in Irish, 'Then she is my sister.' The little girl explained, 'She is a very religious body, and means you are her sister if you are religious.' She was a mountain Connemara girl, but not a facsimile of the one I met in Oranmore. She gave a hearty shake of the hand as she went out, telling the man she must come and see me again. The man said, 'If ye could spake in Irish, ye could do good to these craturs, for they are as stupid as the marble stone.' One told me that they wore red petticoats to keep off the fairies; 'and this,' he added, 'they fully believe.' While he was deploring their ignorance, his little son told him he had dreamed a bad dream. 'Bless yourself, then, nine times, in the name of the Father, Son, and Holy Ghost, when ye are goin' to sleep, and ye won't drame at all.' 'Do you believe this?' I asked. 'I do, ma'am; the priest told me so, and the priest must know.' 'The priest, sir, insulted you if he told you so; it is all nonsense, and you should not listen to it.' He shook his head at my incredulity, but said no more.

The rain ceased, and I must go to the next lodging-house, about two miles. Asking the man if he could change half-a-crown. 'For what?' As I hesitated, 'not a ha'p'orth shall the childer take, for that blackguard bed ye laid yer wairy bones upon. If I had a half-crown, I would give it to let ye ride to Clifden.' This was true Connemara hospitality, and I went out without paying a farthing.

From *The Bible in Ireland*

Thomas Carlyle

1849

THOMAS CARLYLE (1795–1881) was born in Scotland, the son of a stonemason. He entered Edinburgh University at 15 intending to become a clergyman, but religious doubts put an end to this ambition. He worked as a schoolteacher and a private tutor before turning to writing. Carlyle's interest in German literature resulted in his *Life of Schiller*, and his translation of Goethe's *Wilhelm Meister* was praised by the author. In 1826, he married Jane Welsh and moved to Chelsea, London. He had almost completed his most famous work, *The History of the French Revolution* when disaster struck. He had given it to his friend John Stuart Mill to read but the manuscript was accidentally burned at Mill's home.

Galway from the south west

Some green fields, even parks and trees, tho' rather roughish, and with barren hills beyond, this lasts for a mile or two: then fifteen miles of the stoniest barest barrenness I have ever yet seen. Pretty youth mounts beside, polite enough in his air and ways, not without some wild sense; 'Connaught young gentleman,' he too is something: on the box sits a fat Irish tourist in oilskin, beyond my own age; eager to talk, has squireen tendencies; no sense or too little; don't. Connaught rangers 88th, memorable to me for repute of blackguardism in Dumfries: natives proud of them for prowess here. Big simple driver, d. d. guard: I think we had no further company, and in the inside there was none. Stone cottages, stone hamlets, not nearly so ugly as you might have looked for in such a country, – stony, bare, and desolate beyond expression. Almost interesting as the breezy sunshine lay on it: wide stony expanse, in some places almost like a continuous flagged floor of grey – white stone; pick the stone up, build it into innumerable little fences, or otherwise shove it aside, the soil, when free, or freed of water, seems sharp and good. Parks here and there; where wood has thriven: greenest islets in the sea of stone. Martin of Galway's representative, in one; Browne or Black (Blake); plenteous names these. English-Irish air in all *our* company, Redlington's (secretary) draining, trenching goes on here; our stage, and I see that my writing case is inside,

84

beneath a big corn-bag. Galway bay, and promontory, where Galway city is. Stones, stones, – with greenest islets here and there. Oh for men, pickmen, spademen, and masters to guide them! 'Oranmore,' with grey masses of old monastic architecture (Clanricarde's *Castle* this!). Silent as a tomb otherwise: not a hammer stirring in it, or a bootfall heard, stagnant at the head of its sleeping tide-water: how on earth do the people live? Barest of roads towards Galway: dusty, lonely, flanked by ill-built dry stone walls, poor bare fields beyond. Pauper figures, and only a few, the women all with some red petticoat or something very red, plodding languidly here and there under the bright noon; tatterdemalion phantasm, 'piece of *real* Connaught,' with some ragged walletkins on him, at a turn under some trees. Parkl*ets*, as if of Galway merchants; very green indeed, and wood growing bravely when once tried. Galway suburbs; long row of huts mostly or all thatched, – true Irish houses, 'Erasmus Smith's school'; young gentleman knows of it; to the right; a big gaping house; – in vacation just now. Road always mounting, has now mounted, got into *streets*; gets into a kind of central square; – Duffy visible; Hotel (all full of assize people); and here are letters for me, a Galway editor for guide, with car ready for yoking, – and we must be in Tuam *this* evening.

Letters read, we mount our car: straight steep streets, remarkable old city; how in such a stony country it exists! Port wine and Spanish and French articles inwards, cattle outwards, and scantlings of corn; no *other* port for so many miles of country; *enough* of stony country, even that will make a kind of feast. Inlet of river from Lough Corrib the Connemara country: extensive government works here too. 'Godless College,' turreted grey edifice, just becoming ready; editor warmly approves of it, – Maynooth pupil this editor, a burly thick-necked, sharp-eyed man; – couldn't *be* a priest; in secret counterworks M'Hale, as I can see, and despises and dislikes his courses and him. 'Give them light': no more a *Protestant* act than that 'Maynooth grant.'

If the devil were passing through my country and he applied to me for instruction on any truth or fact of this universe, I should wish to give it him. He is *less* a devil, knowing that 3 and 3 are 6, than if he didn't know it; a light-spark tho' of the faintest is in this fact; if he knew *facts enough*, continuous light would dawn on him, he would (to his amazement) understand what this universe *is*, on what principles it conducts itself, and would *cease* to be a devil! – Workhouse, well enough for *it*, – 'human swinery'; can't be bothered looking much at any more of them. Model-farm or husbandry school; can't find time for it, – sorry. 'Piscatory school,' means only school *for* fishermen's children: in the Claddagh, – whither now, past old sloop lying rotting in the river, along granite quays, government works, (hives *without* bees); and enter the school at last, and there abide mostly.

Queen's College

Good school really, as any I saw, all catholics, – can't speak English at first, 'Dean Burke' not there, over in England; substitute, with undermaster and d. mistress, handy Irish people, man and wife if I rememebr; geography &c, finally singing: and substitute goes out with us, 'show you the Claddagh.' Complexity of silent narrow lanes, quite at the corner of the town, and clear of it, being over the river too; kind of wild Irish community; or savage poor republic trying still to subsist on fishing here. Dark, deep-sunk people, but not naturally bad. We look into many huts; priestly schoolmaster, a brisk frank clever kind of man, knows Irish, seems to be free of them all. Petticoats, as usual, high-dyed, however dirty; lilac, azure, especially red. Old woman at a live coal of languid turf; likes 'tay'; net-weaving (tho' not entirely) is going on too: husbands all out at the fishing. The herrings are still here? 'Yes, your riverence.' – Hope they *stay* till you get *ready* to catch them! He answered. Claddagh as like Madagascar as England. A kind of charm in that poor savage freedom; had lately a revd. senior they called their 'admiral' (a kind of real *king* among them), and priests and reverence for priests abound. – Home to our editor's lodgings now, (inn uninhabitable for assize tumult): one 'Councillor Walker' has been inquiring twice for me (editr. has told me); I cannot yet recollect him for *Petrie's*, and A. Sterling's 'Chambers Walker' near Sligo, nor try much to make him out at all.

Hospitable luncheon from this good editor, Duffy's *sub*-editor now, I think; – in great tumult, about 3 1/2 p.m. in blazing dusty sun, we do get seated in the 'Tuam car,' quite full and, – Walker recognizing me, inviting warmly both Duffy and me to his house at Sligo, and mounting up beside me, also for Tuam this night, – roll prosperously away, Duffy had almost rubbed shoulders with Attorney General Monahan; a rather sinister polite gentleman in very clean linen, who strove hard to have got him hanged lately, but couldn't, such was the *bottomless* condition of the thing called 'Law' in Ireland. Long suburb again, mostly thatched, kind of resemblance to 'the Trench' near Dumfries. Bad seat mine, quite *under* driver's, won't admit my *hat*, or hardly even my head; Walker politely insists on exchanging when the horses change. Talk, talk from Wr. Very polite, conciliatory, rational too, not very deep. Bare country; not quite so stony as the morning's, not quite so barren either. Romantic anecdote (murder,? Ghost,? or what) of a family that lived in some bare mansion visible to the left, – totally forgotten now. Country flattens, gets still more featureless; 'John of Chume's' Cathedral tower; 'little influence John of Chume'; anecdotes of some Roman-Irish Bishop and him; – Tuam itself, happily, and dismount, about 7 p.m.; reverence of landlady to Duffy; tea, Walker joining us; walk out, McHale's big not beautiful Cathedral (towers like *pots* with many *ladles*); back of McHale premises, 'College' or whatever he calls it, outer staircase wants parapet; ruinous enough, – this *is* St Jaralath's, then? If we go into the street the protestant bishop's house stands right opposite too. Across then to protestant cathedral; old, very good, – don't go in. Ancient Cross, half of it, is *here*, other half (root or basis of it) is at McHale's standing on the open circuit there. 'Judgement of Solomon has not answered for these two mothers!' On emerging a crowd has gathered for Duffy's sake; audible murmur of old women there, 'Yer hanar's wilcome to Chume!' Brass band threatening to get up, simmering crowd in the street; a letter or so written; get off to bed,–high up mine, and not one of the *best* in nature!

From *Reminiscences of my Irish Journey of 1849*

Harriet Martineau

1852

POLITICAL ECONOMIST Harriet Martineau (1802–1876) was born in Norwich, the daughter of a manufacturer of bombazine. A sickly child, she was educated at home and started writing at an early age. When forced to earn a living, she turned out social, economic and historical articles until her *Illustrations of Political Economy*, of which she wrote twenty-five volumes, made her a celebrity. In 1834, Martineau toured America and was lionized by both North and South, until she declared her anti-slavery beliefs at a Boston abolitionists' meeting. She caused a sensation when, after a long illness, she declared herself cured by mesmerism and wrote *Letters on Mesmerism* about her experience.

*A*ugust 31, 1852. *Whatever* we may find that is strange in the wild parts of Ireland, we shall hardly find anything stranger than this town of Galway. If we should encounter a wilder barbarism in remote places, it will, at least, not be jumbled together with an advanced civilization. See here what has struck us already.

We approached the place through a series of limestone bottoms which ought to afford the finest pasturage. Nothing can be fresher, sweeter, or more delicate than the grass that grows there, though there is no great weight of it. The people destroy these slopes and levels as pasture, breaking it up to grow potatoes, of which they lose this year 80 per cent. As, owing to natural advantages, nothing can altogether stop the grazing, butter of the finest quality is sold in Galway (none being exported) at *1s.* a lb. throughout the year; the pound consisting of 28 oz. Yet there is no manure whatever saved or made from any kind of stock or land-growth. The people will have seaweed, and no other manure whatever. Now, see what a story belongs to this seaweed. It is the red weed, which is thrown up in vast quantities, in every bay and on every promontory, from the north coast of Mayo to the extreme south-west of Ireland. After all is taken for manure that the people will use, two-thirds are left to rot and be lost. A professor of chemistry examined this weed, and saw reason to be confident that, if properly burned, it might be made an article of profitable production. He is certain that the extinguished kelp fires might be profitably relighted all along the coasts, not for the sake of the soda, which was the product formerly sought by kelp-burning, but which can now be had more cheaply from common salt, but for the sake of the iodine and potash salts, which this particular weed yields in abundance, when burned in a certain manner. He went over to the island of Arran,

The Claddagh

and there arranged his plans. He purchased seven stacks of the weed, at £1 per stack, and he promised £3 more for the burning. This burning would take one man three weeks, or three men one week. One need not say that this pay is much higher than could be obtained by selling the weed for manure, even if there had not been abundance for both purposes. All was agreed upon; and the professor paid half the money into the hands of the priest, in the presence of the men, promising the remainder when, the work should be finished. In the morning, as he was proceeding to the spot with the rake he had brought over for the men's use, they met him, and, under various pretences, threw up their bargain.

There is a fish abounding in these bays, and near the land (for the Claddagh fishermen will not go far to sea) called the basking shark. To what extent it abounds may be judged by the fact that eighty were taken last season, under all disadvantages. Each fish yields six barrels of oil; and the liver of a single fish fills one of the Claddagh boats. The oil is almost inestimable as a commercial resource, if its value was understood; but the people do not understand or believe it; and they sell it all, as train-oil, to a purchaser from Dublin, who comes and buys it up. This oil burns with a light as brilliant as sperm; and the professor of chemistry here vouches that its value for medicinal purposes is nearly or quite equal to that of cod-liver oil. Yet, there is no inducing the Claddagh men to use any harpoon in pursuing the basking shark, but the antique one, which allows many more fish to escape than it secures. We were, the other day, in a boat with.a man who last season struck seven fish which escaped, and which he might have secured with a proper harpoon: and he sticks by the old one yet. To appreciate the mournfulness and vexatiousness of this perverseness one must walk through Claddagh, looking into the houses as one goes.

It is a spectacle never to be forgotten by an Englishman. Claddagh is a suburb of Galway – a village of fishermen's cabins. The cottages are in rows; and there are therefore streets or alleys, where grass springs between the stones, or moss tufts them, and where a stunted elder-bush, or other tree, affords a strange little patch of verdure in the dreary place. The rest of the verdure is on the roofs. Nettles, docks, and grass grow to the height of two feet, and the thistle, and ragwort shed their seeds into the thatch. Where the thatch has tumbled in, the holes are covered with matting, kept down by large stones, which make new holes in the rotten mass. The once white walls are mossy and mouldy. The sordidness is indescribable. But infinitely worse is the inside. Some have no windows at all. Voices were heard from the interior of one where there was no window, and where the door was shut. In several, men were mending their nets by the light from the door; in one we saw, through the darkness a woman on her knees on the mud floor, netting, at a net which was suspended from the roof; and again we saw, kneeling at a bench, a mother and daughter, whose faces haunt us. The mother's eyes were bleared, and her hair starting like a patient's in Bedlam. Elsewhere we saw a litter of pigs wallowing in the mud close by the head of the bed. Many mothers in the street, and even in the fish-market, were performing that operation on their daughters' heads or on their own persons, which is apt [to] turn English stomachs in Naples or Lisbon. But enough. This mere fragment of description will show something of how the Claddagh people live, while the basking shark abounds on the coast, and dozens of Claddagh boats are laid up in the harbour. On inquiring whom this village belonged to, we were informed that it has lately been purchased by a Mr. Grattan, and that he is hoping to induce the people to use a modern harpoon which he is sending them. But, till this is achieved, what is to be done about those cabins? How can any man endure to call them his?

There is a clergyman on the island of Arran who has set up a trawling-boat, with a crew of two men, said to be Scotch. The success of this little fishery is what might be expected on such a coast, and what might attend any other well-served trawling-boats. It is necessary to be cautious in receiving details in this part of the world; but the profits of that fishery are said to have been, in the past season, from £12 to £16 per week. The Claddagh men attacked the boat, and threatened, in all seriousness, the life of the clergyman. He applied to Government for protection, and a steamer has been sent in consequence. Some Claddagh men were asked, in our presence, the other day, whether it would not be better for them to try for a share in so profitable a fishery; and why they did not club together to get trawling boats, and prosper like the clergyman. They replied that they had their own boats in the harbour; that they were poor men; that they did not want any new ways; that they had always been used to their own boats; and so forth. The answer to all proffers of advantage to the people here is, that they don't want any improvements.

'Here is the barbarism,' you will say; 'but where is the civilization?' You have had news of the railroad. Here is a new canal – a massive and admirable work, to all appearance, opening the great lakes to the bay. A short canal connects Lough Mask with Lough Corrib; and this new line, very short also, with some improvement of the navigation of the river Corrib, and some deepening of parts of the lake, establishes an admirable waterway for the conveyance of produce from the interior. Of the interior and its produce we may say more when we have seen them. As to the aspect of Galway, the place seems to have been furnished with a vast apparatus for various social action, for which there is no scope. Here is the railroad, with, as yet, very little traffic. Here is this canal, with, as yet, no trade. Here is a nobly situated port, with, at present, no article of export. Here is a great hotel, built apparently in some prophetic anticipation of custom in future years. Here is the very handsome Queen's College, with its staff of twenty professors, and its forty-two scholarships, while its halls echo to the tread of seventy-five students. The number on the books is about one hundred and twenty; and the attendance is seventy-five. The grey marble edifice stands up strangely amidst bare plots of ground and desolate fields, heaped up or strewed over with stones, and inlets of water, which glitter in the sun on every side. The sea runs in wherever it can find an opening; and there is the river Corrib, and the canal; and a cut through the rocks for the water power which turns the great wheel at Franklin's marble-cutting establishment. The amount of water-power would make a great manufacturing centre of the place at once, if Galway were in America; here it seems to add to the desolation of the scene. Well, there is, besides, the new workhouse, also of grey stone; and the model schools under the National Board – the most hopeful feature, perhaps, of the singular scene. Across one arm of the bay there are woods; and, when your boat approaches the beach there, you see gay gardens, productive orchards, rows of stacked corn and hay; and, across another inlet, more stacks, another orchard, verdant pastures, a pretty farm-house, some splendid stock; and you believe you have found one piece of sound prosperity on the shores of Galway Bay. You find that the tenant of the farm is the agent of the whole estate, under whose management it has reached this prosperity; but he is going away. His stock is to be sold off; the pastures he has retrieved to their natural use will be broken up into potato-grounds. He is the Professor of Agriculture in the college. He has only five pupils there but his example on this farm might have done more than his instructions in the college. Why is he leaving his farm? Because the noble owner of the property which has been so much benefited by his science and skill died of cholera last year, and the widow will not (possibly cannot) grant the tenant a lease which will justify his remaining on his farm.

So much for the agriculture. We have seen how it is with the fisheries and the seaweed. There are marble quarries at hand, – the fine black marble of Galway, and the green marbles of Connemara, so well known by name, but of which so little use is made. With all these resources, and many more, Galway has no trade; and people who desire improvement look for it from the place being made an American packet station. For passengers, and mails, and latest news by the electric telegraph, it may serve; but surely not for goods traffic: the trans-shipment for the passage of the Irish Channel must be a fatal objection. However this may be, we would fain see the Galway people using now their great advantages, while awaiting what the future may bring. The difficulty seems to lie in the absence of a middle class of society. The people are, in this, like the buildings. There are imposing edifices – hotel, college, schools – and there are the thatched cottages of the old town, and the Claddagh cabins. If, after looking round for middle-class abodes, you think you have discovered a row or group, you find they are convents, and you are shown the cross upon the roof. In the same way, you find two kinds of aristocracy in the place – the proud old families, either rolling in their gay carriages through the narrow old streets (and past, among other houses, the weedy grey mansion of the Warden of Galway), or secluding themselves within their own gates, because they are too poverty-stricken to come abroad; and the implanted society of the college professors and their families, and other officials. Between these and the poor you find scarcely anybody – the poor, of whom not one in forty can read, and whose ignorance is of a worse kind than an absence of all notion of books. There are a few shops, languid and old-fashioned; and there must be industrial people of sufficient intelligence to carry on the business of life: but there is no substantial, abounding middle class, from whom the rise of a place of such capabilities might be confidently expected.

Of the religion of the region we will say little till we know more. Taking all the Irish colleges together, there was a decided increase of Catholic students after the Synod of Thurles. This is a cheering fact. In

The Church of St Nicholas

the Galway College and Model Schools the proportion of Catholics and Protestants accords very fairly with that of society generally. The Vice-president of the College is a Catholic; but he has lost caste among his own order who are vehemently opposed to the institution; he has been absent for six months past – gone to Rome, to represent the mistakes that the Pope has been led into about these colleges. We shall see whether any good results from his voluntary mission. Meantime, we have seen something. We yesterday turned, after leaving the college and schools, into the parish chapel, – a dim, large, sordid-looking building, with a shadow of an old woman on the steps, selling rosaries; and four blind, crippled, and decrepit persons within; two telling their beads on their knees, and two asking charity. All this we should have expected; and the dressed altar, and the confessionals. But there was more, which we could not have anticipated. Panelled in the wall, there was a barbarous image of Christ, for the most part hung with cobwebs, but with one leg and foot black and shining – no doubt with the kisses of worshippers; and worse – there was another panelled image, a bas-relief, of God the Father, as a hideous, bearded, mitred old man; and God the Son, as a lamb with a human face, equally hideous. We turned away, and, when in the open street again, felt as if we had passed, with one step, from the recesses of a pagan temple into the vestibule of our own home.

From *Letters from Ireland*

Thomas Colville Scott

1853

THOMAS COLVILLE SCOTT was born in England. When the Martin estate was put up for auction after the Famine, Scott was sent to Ireland to survey it for a prospective buyer. He arrived in Dublin in February 1853 with a 'full hand of stereotypes of Irishness.' Over the next six months he travelled throughout Connemara surveying the estate which covered nearly 200,000 acres. His experiences in Ireland caused him to rethink many of his attitudes towards the Irish. The journal he kept of his trip was finally published in 1995.

*L*eft Galway, at 10 a.m., by Bianconi's car, for Ballynahinch, a distance of 44 miles. In the immediate neighbourhood of Galway there are numerous clusters of Cottages of the poorest description, and whenever 10 square yards of soil can be found between the rocks, it is scraped up with exemplary industry into 'lazy beds' for potatoes. These patches, although appearing to be only a light sharp loam, incumbent on decomposing Granite and other rocks, must be of a very fertile nature, for they are invariably planted with potatoes, year after year, and continue productive, though no manure is raised and applied them. These small patches continue for ten or fifteen miles along the road, and if ever the painstaking squatters, now upon them, are superceded by larger Farm Tenants, they must all be laid down to grass, as it would be impossible to till them with the plough as they are, and it is equally impossible to clear them of stones and lay them together. Being on the margin of a limestone formation, the herbage would soon become good and sweet.

Many Farms could be thus formed between Galway and Oughterard, suitable for Dairy Farmers wishing to keep from 10 to 30 Cows; but this would involve a *present outlay* and likewise *a great sacrifice of annual rent* to the existing owners of the land. The prescribed national system of allotments seems then to have a natural origin here, and be best calculated to afford fair rent on an average of years and to sustain and supply the population. The Bogs between Oughterard and Ballynahinch are immense in extent, and apparently all drainable, and worth improving.

Approaching Roundstone (Lawrence Collection R954)

There are gravelly subsoils everywhere in conjunction with these Bogs, which if spread on the surface would, of itself, produce herbage of a useful description. The water from all these Bogs, is *pure*, showing the Bog soil to be of a different character, from that of the English and Scotch Bogs, exuding their black and poisonous waters.

The Limestone in this district is very frequently blended with decomposing Granite, but here and there it is found pure, and burned with peat turf for lime.

Suitable and economical buildings could be put up for new Tenants along this line of country, and the shootings and Fishings preserved and let to advantage, – at present this is all neglected, and there is stock on the lands.

Reached Ballynahinch at 4 p.m., having walked from the Oughterard and Clifden road to the 'Castle,' a distance of about a mile. Met Mr. John Robertson and his wife on the road. Mr. R. is a Dumbarton man and came here about twenty years ago to fish the Salmon rivers and the Oyster beds in the Bays of 'Kilkerran,' 'Burtenbuy.' He has a lease of these fishings, and also of some land, and seems to have managed all his business well, both for himself and the poor people in the district whom he extensively employs. When the Martin Estate came into the hands of the 'Law Life Insurance Company,' in 1848, Mr. R. was appointed their Agent, being the only person resident in the district who had sufficient knowledge of the people and energy to manage them. He has a salary of £500 a year and £100 for expenses and now resides in the 'Castle of Ballynahinch,' having an office near at hand, where two Clerks are constantly in attendance to receive rents from the numerous O's on the Estate.

Two nephews attend to his interests in the fishings, namely Mr. Wm. Robertson, – son-in-law of Mr. James Pendlebury of the Dukes Dock, Liverpool, – who manages the Oyster beds, – and Mr. James Crawford, who attends to the Salmon and river fishing. Mr. R. Senr. has built what he calls a 'Hotel' at the Salmon Weirs about a mile from the Castle and he thus avoids the expensive luxury of Irish hospitality in which 'the Martins' used so freely to indulge.

He has built some Cottages for his men, and preserving houses for the Salmon and the Oysters, which are boiled in Canisters, hermetically sealed & then sent to Dublin, London, and other markets.

Sunday, February 6th. Drove from Ballynahinch House to Roundstone Episcopal Church, 6 miles. The Rev. Mr. Ashe, the incumbent, read the service, and Mr. Brook from London, preached. The subject was 'Transubstantiation' which he handled with considerable 'cunning of fence' but not in a way likely to enlighten the understandings or improve the feelings of the congregation consisting principally of those patted children who are now so ardently pounced upon in the West as the fittest subjects for proselytism. There appears to be 'open war' waging at present between the Protestant and Roman Catholic Clergy, headed by the Rev. Mr. Dallas of London, who are lately here, and is establishing Schools in almost every parish, & even in isolated spots amongst *rocks* and *lakes*, which appear almost inaccessible. These Schools are drawing in many deserted or orphaned Roman Catholic children & the converts are opprobriously designated 'Jumpers,'–This work of conversion is done with rather too much chuckling triumph over the Roman Catholics to obtain the support of others than the interested casuists.

The village of Roundstone is nearly all under a principal Lease to the late Mr. Nimmo, – who came from Scotland about 30 years ago, and made the principal roads in the district,–and who subleases to others. The Herring trade once flourished here; but is now gone and many of the houses are forsaken and decaying.

The land round the village is good, but the quantity available for tillage, very small. There is a monastery here, which I attempted to look into, but was thwarted by the dingy screens suspended on the windows.

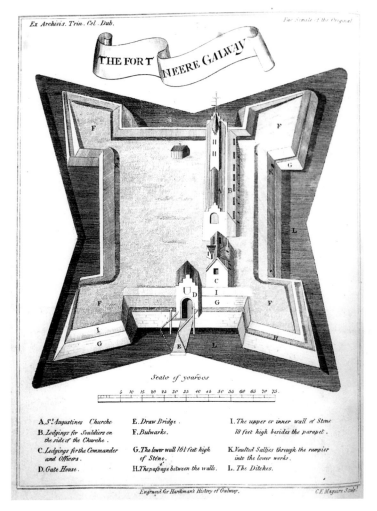

A fort near Galway

The monks appear to have felt the pinch of the late famine & are evidently in no plight at present to join in the jolly chorus of the Friars of old.

In going and returning from Roundstone, I looked at many of the rude graves in the Bogs, Quarry holes and even on the ditches, into which the unfortunate people were flung in the time of the famine of '47. The very dogs which had lost their masters or were driven by want from their homes, became roving denizens of this district & lived on the unburied or partially buried corpses of their late owners and others, and there was no possible help fot it, as all were prostrate alike, the territory so extensive, and the people so secluded and unknown. The luxuriant tufts of grass and heath shew the spots where they lie.

From *Connemara after the Famine*

Samuel Ferguson

1853

SAMUEL FERGUSON (1810–1886) was born in Belfast and educated at Trinity College Dublin. He founded the Protestant Repeal Association but soon turned his attention to antiquities. He was called to the Irish Bar in 1838, but retired from practice in 1867 when he was appointed the first Deputy Keeper of Public Records of Ireland. Ferguson wrote many essays on antiquities for the Royal Irish Academy and served as its President in 1882. His most famous antiquarian work is his *Ogham Inscriptions in Ireland, Scotland & Wales*. He also wrote long narrative poems based on Gaelic legends as well as humorous verses.

Samuel Ferguson

A row of two hours, against an unfavourable wind and through a rough sea, brought us to a little creek on the south side of Inishere. Here the canoe was drawn up, inverted, and carried on the backs of two of the crew, to one of the country dry-docks for the reception of craft of this kind, which might, without much impropriety, be called a corragh-haggard. Half a dozen other corraghs were already laid up within the little enclosure, resting with their gunnels on stone props, so as to clear their curved prows of the ground; and ours being deposited on a vacant stand, we proceeded to the village. Our path lay across a vast sheet of grey limestone rock which separates a capacious pool that nature seems to have designed for a floating dock, from the external waters. On the opposite side of this lake, the ridge of limestone rises with a mural front all along the ascent to the higher part of the island. This natural wall is quite smooth, save where it is diversified by patches of ivy, and in some places is about twenty feet high. A natural stair, wonderfully resembling the architectural approach to the platform of an Assyrian palace, leads up this escarpment to the upper division of the island. A section of the rock, of some thirty feet in length, and about a yard thick, had detached itself from the face of the wall behind, and stands forward just at a sufficient distance to admit two people between; and the debris accompanying its disruption has so fallen in this interval, as to form two stairs of stone, leading symmetrically from either side to the top, and there meeting at the centre. It would make a pretty picture, with the faces of some of the handsome young Arran people peeping over the rock parapet to gaze at the unusual sight of a stranger – for this South Island is still very rarely visited.

Following the pathway, which is defined only by the polish of the rock-surface, over a further succession of limestone ridges, we reached the principal village, consisting of about a dozen cabins, in the midst of irregular stone enclosures, sheltered on the north and west by a craggy knoll, exhibiting the first patches of verdure that had so far caught my observation. The cabins are of a better character than on the mainland. That of the respectable Widow O'Flaherty, to whom I am indebted for the rites of hospitality, contains a cheerful, though unceiled and earthen-floored sitting-room, with a little bed-room attached, not to be despised by one accustomed to sea-side lodgings. As elsewhere along the western coast, the thatch is tied down by a net-work of ropes fastened by pegs projecting from the wall. To admit of the insertion of these pegs, the top part of the wall immediately under the eaves, is sometimes built of mud; but the masonry of the walls is generally of the most massive kind. There are many cabins in the hamlets of Inishere which would be called Cyclopean, if they were of ancient date. Indeed it is scarce possible to avoid the employment of very large stones in building here, the ground, or rather the rock-surface, being everywhere strewed with masses of limestone ready squared and cut by the hand of nature; for the natural cleavage of the rocks detaches it in blocks and slabs disposed in the most convenient way to the hand of the builder. Masses which would not disgrace the foundations of the Temple at Jerusalem, may be seen in the lower courses of many of these cabin-walls; and, I have no doubt, if a block of the dimensions of Cleopatra's Needle were required, such a one might be found without going beyond the ready-cleft segments of the surface. The patches of vegetable soil which occur here and there over this rugged tract are carefully enclosed, and generally planted with potatoes. The soil is light and sandy, but owing to the absorption of heat by the rock, peculiarly warm and kindly; and the islanders here have had the singular good fortune never to have been visited by the potato blight; never to have had a death from destitution; and never to have sent a pauper to the poorhouse. They are a handsome, courteous, and amiable people. Whatever may be said of the advantages of a mixture of races, I cannot discern anything save what makes in favour of these people of the pure ancient stock, when I compare them with the mixed populations of districts on the mainland. The most refined gentleman might live among them in familiar intercourse, and never be offended by a gross or sordid sentiment. This delicacy of feeling is reflected in their figures, the hands and feet being small in proportion to the stature, and the gesture erect and graceful. The population consists principally of the three families or tribes of O'Flaherty, Joyce, and Conneely. Martin Joyce, an obliging young fisherman, conducted me to the objects of interest, and beguiled the way, which, for the most part, is the roughest imaginable, with conversation full of intelligence and good-nature.

On the northern side of the rocky knoll I have described, a sandy beach, terminating in a strip of verdure, runs up between it and the central eminence of the island. The sands occupy a considerable extent of beach, and have risen round the picturesque ruin of the church of St. Cavan (brother of him of Glendalough), which stands at the opening of the little valley, till the surface is nearly on a level with the top of the side wall next the sea. But the doorway in the inland wall has so guided the draught of the wind, as to keep a passage on that side clear, the sand sloping down to the threshold, as in the upper half of an hour-glass. The aspect of these graceful ruins, with their airy chancel-arch, and ivied gables, surrounded by a surface so pure and untrodden, is singularly impressive. On the sea-side all the hillock is covered with tombs and headstones. A rugged pillar-stone, higher than the rest, marks the site of *Leaba coemhain*, or St. Cavan's bed – a grave held in great veneration, which the blowing sands have risen around till it now forms a pit of about five feet in depth. An engraved cross, of very ancient design, decorates the flagstone at the bottom, but there is no inscription. The clear, fine sand alternating with patches of verdure, and backed by the blue, incorruptible ocean, gives an air of purity to the scene very congenial to the idea of a last resting place for people of a simple and virtuous life. 'Our island is clean – there are no worms here,' were the repeated expressions of my companion; and when, on passing a little farther on, we came to where the wind had stripped the sand from a skeleton, I could see that the cleansing, calcerous envelope had brought the bones to the whiteness of chalk. I thought of Archytas, *prope, littus Matinum,* and bestowed the rites of ancient piety – *ossibus et capiti inhumato.* Old as this interesting ruin is – I judge it to be of the twelfth century – it is the most modern of all the ecclesiastical remains on the Isles of Arran. It is, at the same time, the most picturesque and, perhaps, the best calculated to awake, while it tranquilises the soul.

From *The Dublin University Magazine*

Martin Haverty

1857

MARTIN HAVERTY was serving as secretary of the Ethnological Section of the British Association when they made their excursion to the Aran Islands on September 6th, 1857. The group was a distinguished one, including all the luminaries of Irish antiquarian research of the day – George Petrie, William Wilde and John O'Donovan as well as the Provost of Trinity College Dublin and the French Consul. Seventy persons in all left Galway on the *City of Tribes* and the *Vestal* and dropped anchor in Cill Éinne Bay. In addition to his report of the Aran excursion, Haverty wrote *The History of Ireland Ancient & Modern*.

From Dun Onaght the party crossed the island to the great cliffs on the ocean side, at one of which an exciting exhibition was prepared, which few of the party can ever expect to witness again. We had all heard how the inhabitants of Aran, and the Hebrides, and some other places, descend the dizzy ocean cliffs by means of ropes, in search of sea-fowls' eggs, and of the birds themselves for the sake of the feathers: and here our ethnologists were to be treated to a view of the appalling feat performed in the most perfect manner. Fifteen or twenty of the hardy islanders had brought their ropes, and when we had assembled at a point which might be called the horn of a crescent-shaped cliff, the rope was fastened around the middle of an old man, upwards of sixty years on the island, who boldly let himself over, whilst a dozen of his comrades payed out the rope from above. When he got down some few yards, this active and fearless old man, striking the rock with his foot, holding the rope with one hand, and preserving his balance with the other, flew, as it were, outwards and downwards, his feet constantly moving like paddles in the air and as the oscillations of the rope, which grew longer and longer as he descended, brought him towards the cliff, in imminent danger of being dashed to pieces, he struck out again with a bold and graceful movement, until at last, becoming smaller to our eyes as he descended, he reached the bottom. He took off the rope, which was then hauled up, when another and younger man, and after him a third who was a mere lad, performed the same perilous feat in a manner precisely similar. The old man then assumed the rope again, and was swung outwards by his companions below, and during the first long vibration of the living pendulum ascended about fifty feet. The process of striking the cliff was repeated each time he approached it on the ascent, until arriving within thirty feet of the brow of the precipice, he literally commenced to run up the face of it, his body projecting horizontally, supported and raised by the men above; and thus he reached the summit again. Within a few minutes the other men were also brought up in safety, amid the applause of all who beheld the exciting and novel exhibition. It should be added that, with the experienced men who performed those feats, there was really no danger to be apprehended.

Dun Aengus. The name of this fort is pronounced Dun Eanees in Irish; but the tradition of the name has been almost lost on the island, where it is usually called the Great Dun. It is built on the brow of an overhanging precipice, the loftiest in the three islands, being 302 feet above the surges at its caverned base. These great precipices are composed of four enormous strata of limestone, each about seventy feet thick, and piled one above the other like the stones of some fabulous cyclopean building, one of the upper strata projecting fearfully over the black abyss beneath it. It is necessary to retire to some of the lower cliffs on either side in order to see this great precipice in all its terrific grandeur; and but few heads are steady enough to venture on a peep down the yawning gulf itself. The walls of Dun Aengus are built in a horse-shoe form on the summit of the cliff, at which they terminated on either side. There are three enclosures or semicircles, one outside the other, the innermost wall being by much the thickest; and outside the second wall is a *chevaux-de-frise*, composed of erect slender stones, securely fastened in the rock, and so close to each other that it is impossible to make one's way through them without much time and caution. These must have presented a formidable obstacle to a foe when the walls within were well manned by desperate defenders. None of the Aran forts seem to have suffered so much from dilapidation as Dun Aengus; and it is difficult even now, in many parts, to ascertain its dimensions. The innermost enclosure or keep measures 150 feet from north to south, and 140 feet along the edge of the cliff from east to west. The wall which enclosed this space was, as in the other duns, composed of three distinct coatings, the aggregate thickness of which, as far as can be ascertained in their present ruinous state, was 12 feet 9 inches. The doorway which led into this keep measures only about five feet in height, and rather less than 3 feet 6 inches in width.

This was our culminating point of interest – the chief end and object of our pilgrimage. To have seen this would have amply repaid any of the party for the whole fatigue and trouble of the expedition. This was the Dun Aengus whose name is always associated with that of Aran, which it has immortalized in the mind of the archaeologist more than all the other remains of antiquity with which the island abounds. This was the Acropolis of Aran, – the Palace-fortress of the days of Queen Maeve, –

Dun Aengus

the venerable ruin which Dr. Petrie, in his evidence before a Government Commission in 1843, described as 'the most magnificent barbaric monument now extant in Europe.' We can here only describe its dimensions, its remote antiquity, its site on the beetling brow of the precipice, its walls, now reduced to little more than crumbling piles of loose stones; but the indescribable feelings of sadness, and awe, and enthusiasm, which the place itself inspired, cannot be conveyed to the reader by any words of ours. . . .

Dinner-hour having arrived, and all our company being assembled within the great Firbolgic fort of Dun Aengus, which was most judiciously selected by Mr. Wilde as our banquetting-hall on the occasion, and order being, with some difficulty, restored in the ranks of the hungry savans, it was proposed, to the great joy of all, that the repast should commence without further delay. The stewards commenced their duties; the hampers were unpacked; and the company were arranged in a spacious circle on the grass in the centre of the fort, separated from the overhanging brow of the terrific precipice by a wide, low ledge of limestone, which formed a sort of table, upon which a part of the viands were laid: the waves of the great Atlantic breaking all the while on the rocks below, yet, at such a distance beneath us that their roaring only sounded like the gentlest murmurs.

It was a glorious day, the sun being almost too warm, notwithstanding the ocean breeze which fanned us, and groups of the islanders looked on from the crumbling ruins around. With such scenery and such associations, cold would have been the bosom which did not feel a spark of enthusiasm within it. An abundant dinner, in serving which both the stewards and some of the *Vestal's* crew exerted themselves in a most praiseworthy manner, and which was washed down with some excellent sherry, left nothing wanting to give effect to the impressions of the scene. The repast being disposed of, the party assembled on the grass near the platform of level rock which has been already mentioned, and, on the motion of Mr. Wilde, the Provost of Trinity College was called on to preside, and took his seat on the rock.

From *The Aran Isles*

William Wilde

1860

PIONEERING SURGEON William Wilde (1815–1876) was born in County Roscommon and studied in London, Berlin and Vienna before returning to Dublin to become the city's leading eye and ear specialist. In 1851 he married Jane Francesca and they had a son, Oscar. A man of great generosity, he used the first £1000 he earned to found St. Mark's Opthalmic Hospital. He invented the opthalmoscope and a now common procedure for mastoiditis and also served as Medical Commissioner of the Irish Census, for which he was awarded a knighthood. Wilde wrote several travel books – including *The Beauties of the Boyne & the Blackwater*, and *Lough Corrib & Lough Mask*.

*L*och Coirib, which is the second largest sheet of inland fresh water in Ireland, is about thirty-five miles in length from Gaillimh to Mám; and varies in breadth from eight miles, as between Uachtar Ard and Cunga, to one quarter of a mile, as from the Wood of Dún to Corrán Point, where it narrows between the Joyce Country and Iar-Connacht hills. Its general direction is from west-north-west, in a curvature, to south-south-east. In depth it varies considerably, being in many parts full of rocky shoals, left dry in summer; and, even in the navigation course, having but six or seven feet of water in some places; and in other parts descending to 152 feet, as between the island of Inis mhic a' trír and Cunga, and between Dubhros Island and Fornocht Point, which portions are styled by the fishermen 'The Old Loch.' The accompanying map,

St. Macdara's church

reduced to a scale of half an inch to the statute mile, taken from the Admiralty Chart made in 1846, and the Ordnance Survey Maps, shows the principal islands, the navigation course, the rivers, and the chief objects of interest along its shores, referred to in this work.

At the commencement of its tortuous course among the Western mountains, it has the county of Galway on both sides, along the baronies of Ross and Magh Cuillin. At the north-east, it divides the counties of Mayo and Galway, along the south margin of the barony of Kilmaine in the former, from the river of Cunga to the Black-river of Srúil, about a mile to the north of the ruins of Eanach Caoin Castle, on the east shore. From thence southwards, during the remainder of its course, it has the county of Galway on both sides–the barony of Clare on the east, and that of Magh Cuillin on the west; but the river between the south end of the lake and the sea passes through the Barony, formerly styled 'the county of the town' of Galway.

The old Irish name of this sheet of water was Lough Oirbsein or Orib, now corrupted into Coirib, and derived from the ancient Danann navigator, Orbsen Mac Alloid, commonly called Mannanán Mac Lir, 'The Son of the Sea,' from whom the Isle of Man is designated. He was slain in conflict by Uillin, grandson of Nuada of the Silver Hand, the Danann King of Ireland, in a great battle on the western margin of the lake; and from that circumstance this district is called Magh-Uillin, or Magh Cuillinn, the plain or field of Uillin; and O'Flaherty says that in his day a great stone thereon, six miles from Galway, marked the scene; it still exists. See Parish of Magh Cuillinn.

The ancient territories along it were Iar or West Connacht, comprising Gnó Mor and Gnó Baeg – names derived from ancient chieftains – with Conmaicne – mara, now Connamara, on the west, and Uí Briúin Seóla on the east border, and towards the north-west Duthaigh Seoigheach, between it and Lough Measga; and more to the north-east, Conmaicne Cuile-Tolad, or the plain on which the first great battle of Moytura was fought.

Lough Coirib covers a space of 44,000 acres, and its watershed in the counties of Mayo and Galway comprises an area of 780,000 acres. The summer level of the lake is fourteen feet above the medium data of the sea in Galway Bay, and thirty-seven feet below the surface of Lough Measga. This sheet of water formerly extended over a much larger space; but by the drainage operations, carried on from 1846 to 1850 it was lowered, much valuable land relieved from flooding, and large tracts rendered capable of cultivation; and I myself remember passing in a boat over places now in good pasturage, and fishing in places at present occupied by flourishing plantations. Its chief western supply is from the great catchment basin of the valley of Mám, stretcing westwards towards the salt water fiord of the Killeries, and affording the vast supply of water from the sea clouds caught on the Joyce Country and Connamara Mountains, and pouring it down through the river Bealnabreac, the head or 'mouth of the [ford of the] trout' – generally interpreted as the river of 'the trout's mouth' – (the largest stream in Ireland for its length), and its tributary the Faill Mór, into the lake at Bun Bonáin, near Mám, where they coalesce.

On the north-west the principal supply is from the Dumha Éaga, which collects the watershed between the west and south-west sides of Binn Shléibhe and the south shoulder of the hills that run from Loch na Fúthaí and Lough Measga to Lough Coirib, and which delivers its waters near Cor na Móna-'the rough field of the bog.' The great water source is, however from Lough Measga, that has, with its tributaries, and the Partraighe range of mountains a catchment basin of 225,000 statute acres, and which, filtering subterraneously through the cavernous limestone neck that divides the two lakes between Ross Hill and Cong, rises in an imrnense body of water at the latter place, and forms the great river of Cong, into which the *Eglinton* steamer enters, and conducts us to the termination of our first day's tour; besides which, the waters of Lough

Measga pour into the Corrib lake in numerous places from Cong to Cross, where there is a small stream feeding it with the various springs and turlochs of that end of the barony of Kilmaine, and also from the well of St. Fraochan, in the immediate vicinity of the village of Cross.

Still farther to the south-east the rivers of Srúill, Cloch an Uabhair, Coill Rua, Creaga, and Clár na Gaillimhe, pour in their tributes; the latter, in particular, which is now partially converted into a canal, and has drained several of the principal turloughs on the eastern border of the lake from Tuaim westwards, is, next to the Lough Measga supply, one of the chief water sources of Loch Coirib, and also affords a ready transit and good spawning ground for salmon for many miles inland.

On the west and south sides are a number of small streams, carrying down the surplus waters of the range of hills that stretch from the village of Magh Cuilinn by Carn Suí Finn till they culminate in Leac Aimhréi, which shadows the upper lake opposite the romantic basin in which rest the Island and Castle of Caisléan na Circe. On this side also underground passages and now a canal carry in the waters of Ros and Baile Uí Cuire Lakes; but the chief stream is the Fúthai, or Abhainn Roibhe, which collecting all the waters from the chain of lakes that margin the great road into Connamara, and especially those of Loughs Bó Finne and Gleann Gabhla, to the east of the summit level, enters the lake at Uachtar Árd. The Acha 'n Iúbhair river also affords a full stream. From all this it will be seen that the chief supply to Loch Coirib is independent of springs, and hence the water is remarkably soft.

From *Lough Corrib, its Shores and Islands*

Wilfred Scawen Blunt

1888

POLITICAL ACTIVIST, diplomat and author Wilfred Scawen Blunt (1840–1922) was born in Sussex and educated at Stonyhurst. He entered the diplomatic service in 1858 and served in the major European capitals until 1872 when he inherited valuable properties. He travelled throughout North Africa, Asia and India, which made him a strong opponent of imperialism. Blunt supported the Irish Parliamentary Party and was imprisoned for two months in 1887 for advocating the Plan of Campaign. A prolific writer, Blunt was the author of three volumes of poetry. His diaries, with a foreword by Lady Gregory, were published in two volumes in 1919.

Wilfred Scawen Blunt

In the early months of 1888 I served a sentence under the Crimes Act in Ireland, of two months in Galway and Kilmainham gaols. My treatment was that of an ordinary prisoner with hard labour, though hard labour was not named in the sentence – that is to say, I was made to wear prison dress, sleep on a plank bed, pick oakum and perform the other duties assigned to hard labour prisoners. I was forbidden to receive visits or write letters, or to have any books to read but a Bible and a Prayer Book, except during the last week of my confinement, which was strictly silent and separate during the whole two months. With the exception of the plank bed, which prevented sleep for more than a very short portion of the long winter nights passed in darkness, I found little to complain of in the way of physical hardship. The cells were clean and fairly well aired, the food sufficient, and the exercise, a dull round of the prison yard, more than I needed. The oakum picking was so little a trouble to me that I came to be glad to secrete a piece of the tarred rope on Saturday nights so as to have it to pick on Sundays. It gave an occupation to the hands and slightly to the brain of the kind that knitting gives. It was pleasant to the sense of smell and to the eye. The life under these physical heads was hardly worse than one has to put up with on a sea voyage and may pass without special comment. The suffering inflicted on prisoners under the present system I found to be of a different kind, moral, not physical. But this was severe.

The silent and separate system in the treatment of prisoners was, I believe, introduced as a humanitarian reform with the idea of preventing the less depraved among these from contamination with those companions wholly vicious. Some reform of this sort no doubt was needed. But I doubt if those who devised it either understood its full effects or intended that it should be pushed as far as has been the case. Carried out as we see it under the present regulations it is a punishment in addition to the loss of liberty which I do not think society has any right to inflict for less than the most serious crimes, while its effect on the sufferers is wholly evil. Judges who pass long sentences on comparatively innocent breakers of the law, and visiting

Mount Bellew

justices who go the rounds of cells periodically and find all neat and clean, do not understand the severity of the suffering inflicted by leaving the minds of prisoners for long periods of months and years deprived of any spiritual sustenance whatever. It is starvation of a kind quite as real as the cutting off of meat and drink and more enduringly pernicious.

Perhaps I am the better qualified to speak on this head because my experience in the two gaols, Galway and Kilmainham, is diverse in regard to it. Galway gaol was an old-fashioned, rambling place, with cells of various sizes, and the one I was given was well-lighted, showing a good patch of sky and the windows of a building opposite, so that there was some pleasure to be got from watching the sea-gulls as they hovered overhead, and the jackdaws and sparrows, to which it was even possible to throw bread crumbs. The discipline was lax and the warders, most of them Nationalists, were entirely friendly. I was allowed to do many small things contrary to strict regulation, such as to sit on my blanket on the floor, instead of perched on a stool, to have a Bible with good print instead of the hardly readable regulation Bible, and even to scribble verses on its fly leaves. These small infractions of the prison code were connived at, if not permitted, and they mitigated the rigour of the cast-iron laws which rule gaol life, and to make it tolerable. The warders always stopped on their rounds for a few minutes to chat with me; they were polite and kind; the Governor of the gaol paid me a daily visit of a quarter of an hour; the chaplain brought me little packets of snuff besides his spiritual consolation. I was not unhappy. In the first fortnight I read the whole of the historical books of the Old Testament, which for a political prisoner and for one who, as in my case, was acquainted with the East are most consolatory reading from their description of free life in the desert and the trust they inspire in a final justice for the oppressed and the promises they hold out of vengeance on the wicked. 'Thou shalt not bring my soul out of trouble, and in Thy mercy Thou shalt destroy my enemies.' Thus Galway gaol was for me a house of penance rather than of punishment, and my time in it, for the first fortnight, a kind of spiritual retreat. I still look back on it with affection as a softening influence in my life.

A change, however, came with the visit of the Official Inspector of Prisons from Dublin. He happened to be a connection of my own, Charlie Bourke, a brother of the late Lord Mayo, and being a violent Unionist, he made it his business to put a stop to the irregularities he detected in the treatment accorded me. My quatro Bible was taken from me and a regulation one with small print, which hurt my eyes, was substituted. The friendly warders were reprimanded and eventually dismissed, not nominally on my account but later on, as occasion offered, on charges of drunkenness (all prison warders in Ireland at that time were addicted to drink, and so easily dismissable) and the small amenities of my life were stopped. Nevertheless, as long as I remained in Galway, things went fairly well. It was only on my removal to Kilmainham that I was subjected to the full rigours of prison discipline and came to understand the extent of its demoralizing influence and the hatred it excites against society and what is called the 'law and order' which maintains it.

From *My Diaries*

Edith Somerville

1890

BORN ON THE ISLAND OF CORFU, Edith Somerville (1858–1949) was educated at home in County Cork and at art schools in London and on the Continent. In 1886, she met her cousin Violet Martin for the first time and the writing team of Somerville and Ross was born. Their first book, *An Irish Cousin*, was published in 1889 followed by *Naboth's Vineyard* two years later. Between 1890 and 1893 the cousins travelled in Connemara, Denmark and France. In 1899, *Some Experiences of an Irish RM* was published and made them the most famous writing team of the day.

*H*owever, everything, even the waits between the stations between Limerick and Athenry, comes to an end if you can live it out, and at about nine o'clock at night we were in Galway. Scarcely by our own volition, we found ourselves in an hotel 'bus, and we were too tired to do more than notice the familiar Galway smell of turf smoke as we bucketted through Eyre Square to our hostelry. It may be as well at this point to seriously assure English readers that the word 'peat' is not used in Ireland in reference to fuel by anyone except possibly the Saxon tourist. Let it therefore be accepted that when we say 'turf' we mean peat, and when, if ever, we say Pete, we mean the diminutive of Peter, no matter what the spelling.

We breakfasted leisurely and late next morning, serenaded by the screams of pigs, for it was fair day, and the market square was blocked by carts tightly packed with pigs, or bearing tall obelisks of sods of turf, built with Egyptian precision. We cast our eye abroad upon a drove of Connemara ponies, driven in for sale like so many sheep, and my second cousin immediately formed the romantic project of hiring one of these and a small trap for our Connemara expedition.

'They are such hardy little things,' she said, enthusiastically, 'we had two of them once, and they always lived on grass. Of course they never did any work really, and I remember they used to bite anyone who tried to catch them – but still I think one of them would be just the thing.'

'I beg your pardon, Miss,' said the waiter, who was taking away our breakfast things, 'but thim ponies is very arch for the likes of you to drive. One o' thim'd be apt to lie down in the road with yerself and the thrap, and maybe it'd be dark night before he'd rise up for ye. Faith, there was one o' them was near atin' the face off a cousin o' me own that was enticin' him to stand up out o' the way o' the mail-car.'

My second cousin looked furtively at me, and rose from her seat in some confusion.

'Oh, I think we should be able to manage a pony,' she said, with a sudden resumption of the dignity that I had noticed she had laid aside since her arrival in Galway. 'Is there – er – any two-wheeled – er – trap to be had?'

'Sure there is, Miss, and a nate little yoke it'd be for the two of ye, though the last time it was out one of the shafts – .'

'Is it in the yard?' interrupted my second cousin, severely.

'It is, Miss, but the step took the ground – '

My cousin here left the room, and I followed her. A few moments later the trap was wheeled into the yard for our inspection. It was apparently a segment of an antediluvian brougham, with a slight flavour about it of a hansom turned the wrong way, though its great-grandfather had probably been a highly-connected sedan-chair. The door was at the back, as in an omnibus, the floor was about six inches above the ground, and the two people whom it with difficulty contained had to sit with their backs to the horse, rocking and swinging between the two immense wheels, of which they had a dizzy prospect through the little side windows.

'There it is for ye, now!' said the waiter, triumphantly. He had followed us downstairs and was negligently polishing a tablespoon with his napkin. 'And Jimmy,' indicating the ostler, ''ll know of the very horse that'll be fit to put under it.'

'No,' we said faintly, 'that would never do; we want to drive ourselves.'

The ostler fell into an attitude of dramatic meditation.

'Would you be agin dhrivin' a side-car?'

We said 'No.'

Equally dramatic ecastasy on the part of both ostler and waiter. The former, strange to say, had a friend who was the one person in Galway who had the very thing we wanted. 'Letyees be gettin' ready now,' said Jimmy, 'for I'll go fetch it this minute.'

About half an hour later we were standing at the hotel doorsteps, prepared for our trial trip. On the pavement were clustered about us the beggerwomen of Galway – an awesome crew, from whose mouths proceeded an uninterrupted flow of blessings and cursings, the former levelled at us, the latter at each other and the children who hung about their skirts. We pushed our way through them, and getting up on the car announced that we were ready to start, but some delay in obtaining a piece of cord to tie up the breeching gave the beggars a precious opportunity. My second cousin was recognised and greeted by name with every endearment.

'Aha! didn't I tell ye 'twas her?' 'Arrah, shut yer mouth, Nellie Morris. I knew the fine full eyes of her since she was a baby.' 'Don't mind them, darlin',' said a deep voice on a level with the step of the car; 'sure ye'll give to yer own little Judy from Menlo?'

This was my cousin's own little Judy from Menla, and at her invocation we both snatched from our purses the necessary blackmail and dispensed it with furious haste. Most people would pay largely to escape from the appalling presence of this seventy-year-old nightmare of two foot nothing, and she is well aware of its compelling power.

The car started with a jerk, the driver boy running by the horses's side till he had goaded it into a trot, and then jumping on the driving-seat he

Edith Somerville's trap

lashed it into a gallop, and we swung out of Eyre Square followed by the admiring screams of the beggars. The pace was kept up, and we were well out of Galway before a slightly perceptible hill suddenly changed it to a funeral crawl – the animal's head disappearing between its forelegs.

'Give me the reins,' said my second cousin. 'These country boys never know how to drive.' she added in an undertone as she took them from the boy. The horse, a pale yellow creature, with a rusty black mane and tail, turned his head, and fixing a penetrating eye upon her, slightly slackened his pace. My cousin administered a professional flick of the whip, whereon he shrank to the other side of the road, jamming the step of the car against a telegraph post and compelling me to hurriedly whirl my legs up on to the seat. We slurred over the incident, however, and proceeded at the same pace to the top of the hill. A judicious kick from the boy urged the horse into an amble, and things were going on beautifully when we drew near a pool of water by the roadside.

'You see he goes very well when he is properly driven,' my second cousin began, leaning nonchalantly across the car towards me. As she spoke, the car gave a lurch and came to a standstill at the edge of the pool.

Apparently the yellow horse was thirsty. He was with difficulty dragged into the middle of the road again, but beyond the pool he refused to go. The boy got down with the air of one used to these things.

'If ye bate him any more he'll lie down,' he said to my cousin. 'I'll go to the house beyond and gether a couple o' the neighbours.'

The neighbours – that is to say, the whole of the inhabitants of the house – turned out with enthusiasm, and, having put stones behind the wheels, addressed themselves to the yellow horse with strange oaths and with many varieties of sticks.

''Tis little he cares for yer bating,' screamed the mother after several minutes of struggle. 'Let him dhrink his fill o' the pool and he'll go to America for ye.'

We thought that on the whole we should prefer to return to Galway, and though assured by the boy of ultimate victory, we turned and made for the town on foot.

'I scarcely think that horse will do,' said my second cousin, after we had walked about half a mile, turning on me a face still purple from her exertions with the whip. 'We want a freer animal than that.'

She had scarcely finished when there was a thundering on the road behind us, a sound of furious galloping and shouting, and the car appeared in sight, packed with men, and swinging from side to side as the yellow horse came along with a racing stride.

'Ye can sit up on the car now!' called out the boy as they neared us, 'he'll go aisy from this out.'

The car pulled up, and the volunteers got off it with loud and even devotional assurances of the yellow horse's perfections.

But we walked back to Galway.

From *Through Connemara in a Governess Cart*

Arthur Symons

1896

SYMBOLIST POET and critic Arthur Symons (1865–1945) was born in Wales and is best known for translating Baudelaire and for writing *The Symbolist Movement in Literature* which introduced English-speaking readers to this French literary school. In 1896, Symons travelled to the West of Ireland to stay with Edward Martyn at Tulyira Castle and to visit the Aran islands with a group that included W.B. Yeats. Symons also wrote *The Romantic Movement in English Poetry*. In 1905 he suffered a mental collapse and never recovered.

*F*or two hours and a half the fishing-boat had been running before the wind, as a greyhound runs, in long leaps; and when I set foot on shore at Ballyvaughan, and found myself in the little, neat hotel, and waited for tea in the room with the worn piano, the album of manuscript verses, and the many photographs of the young girl who had written them, first as she stands holding a violin, and then, after she has taken vows, in the white habit of the Dominican order, I seemed to have stepped out of some strange, half-magical, almost real dream, through which I had been consciously moving on the other side of that grey, disturbed sea, upon

Arthur Symons

those grey and peaceful islands in the Atlantic. And all that evening, as we drove for hours along the Clare coast and inland into Galway, under a sunset of gold fire and white spray until we reached the battlemented towers of Tillyra Castle, I had the same curious sensation of having been dreaming; and I could but vaguely remember the dream, in which I was still, however, absorbed. We passed, I believe, a fine slope of grey mountains, a ruined abbey, many castle ruins; we talked of Parnell, of the county families, of mysticism, the analogy of that old Biblical distinction of body, soul, and spirit with the symbolical realities of the lamp, the wick, and the flame; and all the time I was obsessed by the vague, persistent remembrance of those vanishing islands, which wavered somewhere in the depths of my consciousness. When I awoke next morning the dream had resolved itself into definite shape I remembered every detail of those last three days, during which I had been so far from civilisation, so much further out of the world than I had ever been before.

It was on the morning of Wednesday, August 5, 1896, that a party of four, of whom I alone was not an Irishman, got into Tom Joyce's hooker at Cashla Bay, on the coast of Galway, and set sail for the largest of the three islands of Aran, Inishmore by name, that is, Large Island. The hooker, a half-decked, cutter-rigged fishing-boat of seventeen tons, had come over for us from Aran, and we set out with a light breeze, which presently dropped and left us almost becalmed under a very hot sun for nearly an hour, where we were passed by a white butterfly that was making straight for the open sea. We were nearly four hours in crossing, and we had time to read all that needed reading of *Grania*, Miss Emily Lawless's novel, which is supposed to be the classic of the islands, and to study our maps and to catch one mackerel. But I found most to my mind this passage from Roderic O'Flaherty's *Chorographical Description of West or H-Iar Connaught*, which in its quaint, minute seventeenth-century prose told me more about what I was going to see than everything else that I read then or after on the subject of these islands. 'The soile,' he tells us, 'is almost paved over with stones, soe as, in some places, nothing is to be seen but large stones with wide openings between them, where cattle break their legs. Scarce any other stones there but limestones, and marble fit for tombstones, chymney mantle trees, and high crosses. Among these stones is very sweet pasture, so that beefe, veal, mutton are better and earlyer in season here than elsewhere; and of late there is plenty of cheese, and tillage mucking, and corn is the same with the seaside tract. In some places the plow goes. On the shores grows samphire in plenty, ring-root or sea-holy, and sea-cabbage. Here are Cornish choughs, with red legs and bills. Here are ayries of hawkes, and birds which never fly but over the sea, and, therefore, are used to be eaten on fasting days: to catch which people goe down, with ropes tyed about them, into the caves of cliffs by night, and with a candle light kill abundance of them. Here are severall wells and pooles, yet in extraordinary dry weather, people must turn their cattell out of the islands, and the corn failes. They have noe fuell but cow-dung dryed with the sun, unless they bring turf in from the western continent. They have *Cloghans*, a kind of building of stones layd one upon another which are brought to a roof without any manner of mortar to cement them, some of which cabins will hold forty men on their floor; so antient that nobody knows how long ago any of them was made. Scarcity of wood and store of fit stones, without peradventure found out the first invention.' Reading of such things as these, and of how St. Albeus, Bishop of *Imly*, had said, 'Great is that island, and it is the land of saints; for no man knows how many saints are buried there, but God alone'; and of an old saying: 'Athenry was, Galway is, Aran shall be the best of the three,' we grew, after a while, impatient of delay. A good breeze sprang up at last, and as I stood in the bow, leaning against the mast, I felt the one quite perfectly satisfying sensation of movement: to race through steady water before a stiff sail, on which the reefing cords are tapping in rhythm to those nine notes of the sailors' chorus in *Tristan*, which always ring in my ears when I am on the sea, for they have in them all the exultation of all life that moves upon the waters.

Salthill Promenade at the beginning of the twentieth century (Lawrence Collection R6560)

The butterfly, I hope, had reached land before us; but only a few sea-birds came out to welcome us as we drew near Inishmore, the Large Island, which is nine miles long and a mile and a half broad. I gazed at the long line of the Island, growing more distinct every moment; first, a grey outline, flat at the sea's edge, and rising up beyond in irregular, rocky hills, terrace above terrace; then, against this grey outline, white houses began to detach themselves, the sharp line of the pier cutting into the curve of the harbour; and then, at last, the figures of men and women moving across the land. Nothing is more mysterious, more disquieting, than one's first glimpse of an island, and all I had heard of these islands, of their peace in the heart of the storm, was not a little mysterious and disquieting. I knew that they contained the oldest ruins and that their life of the present was the most primitive life of any part of Ireland; I knew that they were rarely visited by the tourist, almost never by any but the local tourist; that they were difficult to reach, sometimes more difficult to leave, for the uncertainty of weather in that uncertain region of the Atlantic had been known to detain some of the rare travellers there for days, was it not for weeks? Here one was absolutely at the mercy of the elements, which might at any moment become unfriendly, which, indeed, one seemed to have but apprehended in a pause of their eternal enmity. And we seemed also to be venturing among an unknown people, who, even if they spoke our own language, were further away from us, more foreign than people who spoke an unknown language and lived beyond other seas.

As we walked along the pier towards the three whitewashed cottages which form the Atlantic Hotel, at which we were to stay, a strange being sprang towards us, with a curiously beast-like stealthiness and animation; it was a crazy man, bare-footed and blear-eyed, who held out his hand and sang out at us in a high, chanting voice, and in what sounded rather a tone of command than of entreaty, 'Give me a penny, sir! Give me a penny, sir!' We dropped something into his hat, and he went away over the rocks, laughing loudly to himself, and repeating some words that he had heard us say. We passed a few fishermen and some bare-footed children, who looked at us curiously, but without moving, and were met at the door of the middle cottage by a little, fat old woman with a round body and a round face, wearing a white cap tied over her ears. The Atlantic Hotel is a very primitive hotel; it had last been slept in by some priests from the mainland, who had come on their holiday with bicycles; and before that by a German philologist who was learning Irish. The kitchen, which is also the old landlady's bedroom, presents a medley of pots and pans and petticoats as you pass its open door and climb the little staircase, diverging oddly on either side after the first five or six steps, and leading on the right to a large dining-room, where the table lounges on an inadequate number of legs and the chairs bow over when you lean back on them. I have slept more luxuriously, but not more soundly, than in the little musty bedroom on the other side of the stairs, with its half-made bed, its bare and unswept floor, its tiny window, of which only the lower half could be opened, and this, when opened, had to be supported by a wooden catch from outside. Going to sleep in that little, uncomfortable room was a delight in itself; for the starry water outside, which one could see through that narrow slit of window, seemed to flow softly about one in waves of delicate sleep.

When we had had a hasty meal and had got a little used to our hotel, and had realised as well as we could where we were, at the lower end of the village of Kilronan, which stretches up the hill to the north-west on either side of the main road, we set out in the opposite direction, finding many guides by the way, who increased in number as we went on through the smaller village of Kileaney up to the south-eastern hill, on which are a holy well, its thorn-tree hung with votive ribbons, and the ruins of several churches, among them the church of St. Enda, the patron saint of the island. At first we were able to walk along a very tolerable road, then we branched off upon a little strip of grey sand, piled in mounds as high as if it had been drifted snow, and from that, turning a little inland, we

*An Aran-island
horseman*

came upon the road again, which began to get stonier as we neared the
village. Our principal guide, an elderly man with long thick curls of flaxen
hair and a seaman's beard, shaved away from the chin, talked fairly good
English, with a strong accent, and he told us of the poverty of the people,
the heavy rents they have to pay for soil on which no grass grows, and the
difficult living they make out of their fishing, and their little tillage, and
the cattle which they take over in boats to the fairs at Galway, throwing
them into the sea when they get near land, and leaving them to swim
ashore. He was dressed, as are almost all the peasants of Aran, in clothes
woven and made on the island – loose, rough, woollen things, of drab, or
dark blue, or grey, sometimes charming in colour; he had a flannel shirt,
a kind of waistcoat with sleeves, very loose and shapeless trousers worn
without braces, an old and discoloured slouch hat on his head, and on his
feet the usual pampooties, slippers of undressed hide, drawn together and
stitched into shape, with pointed toes, and a cord across the instep. The
village to which we had come was a cluster of white-washed cabins, a

little better built than those I had seen in Galway, with the brown thatch fastened down with ropes drawn cross-wise over the roof and tied to wooden pegs driven into the wall for protection against the storm blowing in from the Atlantic. They had the usual two doors, facing each other at front and back, the windier of the two being kept closed in rough weather, and the doors were divided in half by the usual hatch. As we passed, a dark head would appear at the upper half of the door, and a dull glow of red would rise out of the shadow. The women of Aran almost all dress in red, the petticoat very heavily woven, the crossed shawl or bodice of a thinner texture of wool. Those whom we met on the roads wore thicker shawls over their heads, and they would sometimes draw the shawls closer about them, as women in the East draw their veils closer about their faces. As they came out to their doors to see us pass, I noticed in their manner a certain mingling of curiosity and shyness, an interest which was never quite eager. Some of the men came out and quietly followed us as we were led along a twisting way between the cabins; and the children, boys and girls, in a varying band of from twenty to thirty, ran about our heels, stopping whenever we stopped, and staring at us with calm wonder. They were very inquisitive, but, unlike English villagers in remote places, perfectly polite, and neither resented our coming among them nor jeered at us for being foreign to their fashions.

The people of Aran (they are about 3000 in all), as I then saw them for the first time, and as I saw them during the few days of my visit, seemed to me a simple, dignified, self-sufficient, sturdily primitive people, to whom Browning's phrase of 'gentle islanders' might well be applied. They could be fierce on occasion, as I knew; for I remembered the story of their refusal to pay the county cess, and how, when the cess-collector had come over to take his dues by force, they had assembled on the seashore with sticks and stones, and would not allow him even to land. But they had, for the most part, mild faces, of the long Irish type, often regular in feature, but with loose and drooping mouths and discoloured teeth. Most had blue eyes, the men, oftener than the women, having fair hair. They held themselves erect, and walked nimbly, with a peculiar step due to the rocky ways they have generally to walk on; few of them, I noticed, had large hands or feet, and all, without exception, were thin, as indeed the Irish peasant almost invariably is. The women too, for the most part, were thin, and had the same long faces, often regular, with straight eyebrows and steady eyes, not readily changing expression; they hold themselves well, a little like men, whom, indeed, they somewhat resemble in figure. As I saw them, leaning motionless against their doors, walking with their deliberateness of step along the roads, with eyes in which there was no wonder, none of the fever of the senses, placid animals on whom emotion has never worked in any vivid or passionate way, I seemed to see all the pathetic contentment of those narrow lives, in which day follows day with the monotony of wave lapping on wave. I observed one young girl of twelve or thirteen who had something of the ardency of beauty, and a few shy, impressive faces, their hair drawn back smoothly from the middle parting, appearing suddenly behind doors or over walls; almost all, even the very old women, had nobility of gesture and attitude, but in the more personal expression of faces there was for the most part but a certain quietude, seeming to reflect the grey hush, the bleak greyness of this land of endless stone and endless sea.

When we had got through the village and begun to climb the hill, we were still followed, and we were followed for all the rest of the way by about fifteen youngsters, all, except one, barefooted, and two, though boys, wearing petticoats, as the Irish peasant children not unfrequently do, for economy, when they are young enough not to resent it. Our guide, the elderly man with the flaxen curls, led us first to the fort set up by the soldiers of Cromwell, who, coming over to keep down the Catholic rebels, ended by turning Catholic and marrying and settling among the native people; then to Teglach Enda, a ruined church of very early masonry, made of large blocks set together with but little cement – the church of St. Enda, who came to Aran in about the year 480, and fifty-eight years later laid his bones in the cemetery which was to hold the graves of not less than a hundred and twenty saints. On our way inland to Teampull Benen, the remains of an early oratory, surrounded by cloghans or stone dwellings made of heaped stones which, centuries ago, had been the cells of monks, we came upon the large puffing-hole, a great gap in the earth, going down by steps of rock to the sea, which in stormy weather dashes foam to the height of its sixty feet, reminding me of the sounding hollows on the coast of Cornwall. The road here, as on almost the whole of the island, was through stone-walled fields of stone. Grass, or any soil, was but a rare interval between a broken and distracted outstretch of grey rock, lying in large flat slabs, in boulders of every size and shape, and in innumerable stones, wedged in the ground or lying loose upon it, round, pointed, rough, and polished; an unending greyness, cut into squares by the walls of carefully-heaped stones, which we climbed with great insecurity, for the stones were kept in place by no more than the more or less skilful accident of their adjustment, and would turn under our feet or over in our hands as we climbed them. Occasionally a little space of pasture had been cleared or a little artificial soil laid down, and a cow browsed on the short grass. Ferns, and occasionally maidenhair, grew in

Spinners on the Aran Island photographed by John M. Synge

the fissures splintered between the rocks; and I saw mallow, stone-crop, the pale blue wind-flower, the white campian, many nettles, ivy, and a few bushes. In this part of the island there were no trees, which were to be found chiefly on the north-western side, in a few small clusters about some of the better houses, and almost wholly of alder and willow. As we came to the sheer edge of the sea and saw the Atlantic, and knew that there was nothing but the Atlantic between this last shivering remnant of Europe and the far-off continent of America, it was with no feeling of surprise that we heard from the old man who led us that no later than two years ago an old woman of those parts had seen, somewhere on this side of the horizon, the blessed island of Tir-nan-Ogue, the island of immortal youth, which is held by the Irish peasants to lie somewhere in that mysterious region of the sea.

We loitered on the cliffs for some time, leaning over them, and looking into the magic mirror that glittered there like a crystal, and with all the soft depth of a crystal in it, hesitating on the veiled threshold of visions. Since I have seen Aran and Sligo, I have never wondered that the Irish peasant still sees fairies about his path, and that the boundaries of what we call the real, and of what is for us the unseen, are vague to him. The sea on those coasts is not like the sea as I know it on any other coast; it has in it more of the twilight. And the sky seems to come down more softly, with more stealthy step, more illusive wings, and the land to come forward with a more hesitating and gradual approach; and land and sea and sky to mingle more absolutely than on any other coast. I have never realised less the slipping of sand through the hour-glass; I have never seemed to see with so remote an impartiality, as in the presence of brief and yet eternal things, the troubling and insignificant accidents of life. I have never believed less in the reality of the visible world, in the importance of all we are most serious about. One seems to wash off the dust of cities, the dust of beliefs, the dust of incredulities.

It was nearly seven o'clock when we got back to Kilronan, and after dinner we sat for a while talking and looking out through the little windows at the night. But I could not stay indoors in this new, marvellous place; and, persuading one of my friends to come with me, I walked up through Kilronan, which I found to be a far more solid and populous village than the one we had seen; and coming out on the high ground beyond the houses, we saw the end of a pale green sunset. Getting back to our hotel, we found the others still talking; but I could not stay indoors, and after a while went out by myself to the end of the pier in the darkness, and lay there looking into the water and into the fishing-boats lying close up against the land, where there were red lights moving, and the shadows of men, and the sound of deep-throated Irish.

From *Cities and Seacoasts and Islands*

William Butler Yeats

1896

WILLIAM BUTLER YEATS (1865–1939) was born in Dublin, the son of artist John Butler Yeats. He lived in London until the age of 16, when he returned to Dublin to study art. In 1889, Yeats met Maud Gonne and maintained an intense involvement with her for the next 30 years. In 1893, he published *The Celtic Twilight* and started to emerge as the voice of the Celtic Revival. His friendship with Edward Martyn brought him to Galway, where he met Lady Gregory. He became a regular visitor to Coole Park. In 1919, Yeats bought and restored Ballylee Tower near Coole and used it as a summer home.

W.B. Yeats

A couple of weeks after my vision, Lady Gregory, whom I had met once in London for a few minutes, drove over to Tullyra, and after Symons's return to London I stayed at her house. When I saw her great woods on the edge of a lake, I remember the saying about avoiding woods and living near the water. Had this new friend come because of my invocation, or had the saying been but prevision and my invocation no act of will, but prevision also? Were those unintelligible words – 'avoid woods because they concentrate the solar ray' – but a dream confusion, an attempt to explain symbolically an actual juxtaposition of wood and water? I could not say nor can I now. I was in poor health, the strain of youth had been greater than it commonly is, even with imaginative men, who must always, I think, find youth bitter, and I had lost myself besides as I had done periodically for years, upon *Hodos Chameliontos*. The first time was in my eighteenth or nineteenth years, when I tried to create a more multitudinous dramatic form, and now I had got there through a novel that I could neither write nor cease to write which had *Hodos Chameliontos* for its theme. My chief person was to see all the modern visionary sects pass before his bewildered eyes, as Flaubert's St. Anthony saw the Christian sects, and I was as helpless to create artistic, as my chief person to create philosophic order. It was not that I do not love order, or that I lack capacity for it, but that – and not in the arts and in thought only – I outrun my strength. It is not so much that I choose too many elements, as that the possible unities themselves seem without number, like those angels, that in Henry More's paraphrase of the Schoolman's problem, dance spurred and booted upon the point of a needle. Perhaps fifty years ago I had been in less trouble, but what can one do when the age itself has come to *Hodos Chameliontos*.

Lady Gregory seeing that I was ill brought me from cottage to cottage to gather folk-belief, tales of the fairies, and the like, and wrote down herself what we had gathered, considering that this work, in which one let others talk, and walked about the fields so much, would lie, to use a

Yeats' Ballylee Tower drawn by Robert Gregory

country phrase, 'Very light upon the mind.' She asked me to return there the next year, and for years to come I was to spend my summers at her house. When I was in good health again, I found myself indolent, partly perhaps because I was affrighted by that impossible novel, and asked her to send me to my work every day at eleven, and at some other hour to my letters, rating me with idleness if need be, and I doubt if I should have done much with my life but for her firmness and her care. After a time, though not very quickly, I recovered tolerable industry, though it has only been of late years that I have found it possible to face an hour's verse without a preliminary struggle and much putting off.

Certain woods at Sligo, the woods above Dooney Rock and those above the waterfall at Ben Bulben, though I shall never perhaps walk there again, are so deep in my affections that I dream about them at night; and yet the woods at Coole, though they do not come into my dream are so much more knitted to my thought, that when I am dead they will have, I am persuaded, my longest visit. When we are dead, according to my belief, we live our lives backward for a certain number of years, treading the paths that we have trodden, growing young again, even childish again, till some attain an innocence that is no longer a mere accident of nature, but the human intellect's crowning achievement. It was at Coole that the first few simple thoughts that now, grown complex through their contact with other thoughts explain the world, came to me from beyond my own mind.

From *Autobiographies*

Maud Gonne MacBride

1899

MAUD GONNE (1865–1953) was born in England and came to Ireland when her father, an army officer, was transferred to the Curragh after the Fenian uprising. Gonne went to France at the age of ten and was educated privately there. In France she met politician and journalist Lucien Millevoye. They had a daughter, Iseult, who married the novelist Francis Stuart. In the 1890s, Gonne became involved in Nationalist activities and travelled the world addressing meetings. In 1903 she married John MacBride in Paris but the marriage did not last. After he was executed for his part in the 1916 Easter Rising, Gonne returned to Ireland and the following year she was imprisoned for six months in Holloway Prison.

There were many constabulary in the village of Woodford as I got off the mail car a day later and also in the hotel.

The landlord's wife ushered me into a little private room for lunch.

'What are the police here for?'

'To stop the proclaimed meeting.'

I enquired for Mr. Tully.

'He's still in Dublin and lucky he is, for they are looking for him,' she answered.

A tall countryman in a freize coat came in. 'It was good of you coming, Miss Gonne,' he said, 'but it isn't fair to ask you to speak at a proclaimed meeting.'

'I am here by chance,' I said, 'but I'll speak at the meeting if you want me to.'

'I thought Mr. Tully had sent you.'

'No, I came to see Mr. Tully but I hear he is away.'

I arranged to meet my new friend and a car at a crossroads outside the village. As we drove he told me the meeting was called to protest against some land-grabbing and call a boycott on the grabbers; the police held

Woodford, so word had been sent out to meet elsewhere. Dagda in great spirits trotted beside the car. Near a little wood we found a couple of hundred men gathered and great cheers were raised when they recognized me.

The chairman was speaking and when he got down I climbed on his car and spoke, first on the National question, that the people would only get their rights when Ireland's freedom was won and then of the immediate duty for them all to stand together and to boycott any land-grabbers. I had not got far before I saw a body of some hundred Royal Irish Constabulary marching along the road towards the meeting. I bent down and asked the chairman, who looked nervous, if we were to go on.

'Just do as you think best, my lady.'

I continued speaking. The constabulary formed up in ranks on three sides of the meeting. The crowd gathered closer round the car. 'Go on, Miss,' they shouted to me and, being excited, I repeated myself; it didn't matter, for everyone was too excited to notice what I said. The officer in charge of the Constabulary and a superintendent of police pushed their way towards the platform. The superintendent said:

'Miss Gonne, if you continue, I shall arrest you.'

'That's your affair and much good it will do you,' I laughed and continued my speech.

'If you go on I shall give the order to fire,' said the officer.

'Go on, go on,' cheered the crowd.

I heard an order given. I saw the constabulary get their rifles at the ready and heard the click of the triggers. Most of the men now had their backs to the platform and were facing the police; they had nothing but ash plants in their hands but were ready to fight; some still shouted to me to go on.

'No,' I said. 'Men, you know your duty; the proclaimed meeting is now over,' and I got off the car.

There was disappointment; one man said: 'You should have gone on.' I heard another man say: 'You couldn't expect a woman to fight.' I said: 'If you had guns I would have gone on; the rifles were pointed at you, not at me; I couldn't see unarmed men shot down.'

Again a wave of depression overwhelmed me. I thought of France; some day help might come from that quarter if the British alliance could be prevented. Perhaps I had been wrong in not letting the Woodford evicted tenants fight and be shot down. Dead men might have aroused the country as living men could not and at least made the evicted tenants a live issue. I had not dared take the responsibility; I had refused leadership and the situation was not of my making.

From *A Servant of the Queen*

George Moore

1900

BORN INTO A Catholic land-owning family in County Mayo, George Augustus Moore (1852–1933) went to Paris at eighteen to study art. He soon abandoned art for literature and moved to London, where his first novel, *A Modern Lover*, was published in 1883. His second novel, *A Mummer's Wife*, shocked Victorian London but made his reputation as a novelist. In the early years of the twentieth century Moore was drawn into the Celtic Literary Movement by Edward Martyn of Tulyira Castle, County Galway, and moved to Dublin. In 1900 he went to Coole to write a play with William Butler Yeats based on the legend of Diarmuid and Grania.

George Moore

*A*s I write, the wind whistles and yells in the street; the waves must be mountains high in the Channel, I said, but the Irish Sea has always been propitious to me – all my crossings have been accomplished amid sparkling waves and dipping gulls, and the crossing that I am trying to remember when I went to Coole to write *Diarmuid and Grania* was doubtless as fine as those that had gone before. I can recall myself waiting eagerly for the beautiful shape of Howth to appear above the sea-line, my head filled with its legends. Or, maybe, my memory fails me, and it may well have been that I crossed under the moon and stars, for I remember catching the morning mail from the Broadstone and journeying, pale for want of sleep and tired, through the beautiful county of Dublin, alongside of the canal, here and there slipping into swamp, with an abandoned boat in the rushes. But when we leave County Dublin the country begins to drop away into bogland, the hovel appears (there is a good deal of the West of Ireland all through Ireland), but as soon as the middle of Ireland has been crossed the green country begins again; and, seeing many woods, I fell to thinking how Ireland once had been known as the Island of Many Woods, cultivated in patches, and overrun by tribes always at war with the other. So it must have been in the fourth century when Grania fled from Tara with Diarmuid – her adventure; and mine – to write Ireland's greatest love-story in conjunction with Yeats.

Athlone came into sight and I looked upon the Shannon with a strange and new tenderness, thinking that it might have been in a certain bed of rushes that Grania lifted her kirtle, the sweetness of her legs blighting in Diarmuid all memory of his oath of fealty to Finn, and compelling him to take her in his arms, and in the words of the old Irish story-teller to make a woman of her. And without doubt it would be a great thing to shape this primitive story into a play, if we could do it without losing any of the grandeur and significance of the legend. I thought of the beauty of Diarmuid, his doom, and how he should court it at the end of the second act when the great fame of Finn captures Grania's imagination. The third act would be the pursuit of the boar through the forest, followed by Finn's great hounds – Bran, Sgeolan, Lomairly.

In happy meditation mile after mile went by. Lady Gregory's station is Gort. Coole was beginning to be known to the general public at the time I went there to write *Diarmuid and Grania* with Yeats. Hyde had been to Coole, and had been inspired to write several short plays in Irish; one of them, *The Twisting of the Rope*, we hoped we would be able to induce Mr. Benson to allow us to produce after *Diarmuid and Grania*. If Yeats had not begun *The Shadowy Waters at Coole* he had at least written several versions of it under Lady Gregory's roof-tree; and so Coole will be historic; later still, it will become a legend, a sort of Minstrelburg, the home of the Bell Branch Singers, I said, trying to keep my bicycle from skidding, for I had told the coachman to look after my luggage and bring it with him on the car, hoping in this way to reach Coole in time for breakfast.

The sun was shining, but the road was dangerously greasy, and I had much difficulty in saving myself from falling. A lovely morning, I said, pleasantly ventilated by light breezes from the Burran Mountains. We shall all become folklore in time to come, Finns and Diarmuids and Usheens, every one of us, and Lady Gregory a new Niamh who – At that moment my bicycle nearly succeeeded in throwing me into the mud, but by lifting it on to the footpath, and by giving all my attention to it, I managed to reach the lodge-gates without a fall. A horn, I said, should hang on the gatepost, and the gate should not open till the visitor has blown forth a motif; but Yeats would be kept a long time waiting, for he is not musical, and thinking of the various funny noises he would produce on the horn, I admired the hawthorns that AE painted last year; and at the end of a long drive a portico appeared in red and blue glass, partly hidden by masses of reddening creeper.

Sir William's marbles detained me on the staircase, and whilst I compared present with past appreciations Lady Gregory came to meet me with news of Yeats. He was still composing; we should have to wait breakfast for him; and we waited till Lady Gregory, taking pity upon me, rang the bell. But the meal we sat down to was disturbed not a little by thoughts of Yeats, who still tarried. The whisper went round the table that he must have been overtaken by some inspiration, and Lady Gregory, fluttered with care, was about to send the servant to inquire if Mr. Yeats would like to have his breakfast in his room. At that moment the poet appeared, smiling and delightful, saying that just as the clocks were striking ten the metre had begun to beat, and abandoning himself to the emotion of the tune, he had allowed his pen to run till it had completed nearly eight and a half lines, and the conversation turned on the embarrassment his prose caused him, forcing him to reconstruct his scenario. He would have written his play in half the time if he had begun writing it in verse.

As soon as we rose from the table Lady Gregory told us we should be undisturbed in the drawing-room till tea-time, and thanking her, we moved into the room. The moment had come, and feeling like a swordsman that meets for the first time a redoubtable rival, I reminded Yeats that in his last letter he had said we must decide in what language the play should be written – not whether it should be written in English or in Irish (neither of us knew Irish), but in what style.

Yes, we must arrive at some agreement as to the style. Of what good will your dialogue be to me if it is written, let us say, in the language of *Esther Waters*?

Nor would it be of any use to you if I were to write it in Irish dialect?

Yeats was not sure on that point; a peasant Grania appealed to him, and I regretted that my words should have suggested to him so hazardous an experiment as a peasant Grania.

We're writing an heroic play. And a long time was spent over the question whether the Galway dialect was possible in the mouths of heroes, I contending that it would render the characters farcical, for it is not until the language has been strained through many minds that tragedy can be written in it. Balzac wrote *Les Contes Drolatiques* in Old French because Old French lends itself well to droll stories. Our play had better be written in the language of the Bible. Avoiding all turns of speech, said Yeats, which immediately recall the Bible. You will not write Angus and his son Diarmuid which is in heaven, I hope. We don't want to recall the Lord's Prayer. And, for the same reason, you will not use any archaic words. You will avoid words that recall any particular epoch.

I'm not sure that I understand.

The words honour and ideal suggest the Middle Ages, and should not be used. The word glory is charged with modern idea – the glory of God and the glory that shall cover Lord Kitchener when he returns from Africa. You will not use it. The word soldier represents to us a man who wears a red tunic; an equivalent must be found, swordsman or fighting man. Hill is a better word than mountain; I can't give you a reason, but that is my feeling, and the word ocean was not known to the early Irish, only the sea.

We shall have to begin by writing a dictionary of the words that may not be used, and all the ideas that may not be introduced. Last week you wrote begging me not to waste time writing descriptions of Nature. Primitive man, you said, did not look at trees for the beauty of the branches and the agreeable shade they cast, but for the fruits they bore and the wood they furnished for making spear-shafts and canoes. A most ingenious theory, Yeats, and it may be that you are right: but I think it is safer to assume that primitive man thought and felt much as we do. Life in its essentials changes very little, and are we not writing about essentials, or trying to?

Yeats said that the ancient writer wrote about things, and that the softness, the weakness, the effeminacy of modern literature could be attributed to ideas. There are no ideas in ancient literature, only things, and, in support of this theory, reference was made to the sagas, to the Iliad, to the Odyssey, and I listened to him, forgetful of the subject which we had met to discuss. It is through the dialect, he continued, that one escapes from abstract words, back to the sensation inspired directly by the thing itself.

But, Yeats, a play cannot be written in dialect; nor do I think it can be written by turning common phrases which rise up in the mind into uncommon phrases.

That is what one is always doing.

If, for the sake of one's literature, one had the courage to don a tramp's weed – you object to the word don? And still more to weed. Well, if one had the courage to put on a tramp's jacket and wander through the country, sleeping in hovels, eating American bacon, and lying five in a bed, one might be able to write the dialect naturally; but I don't think that one can acquire the dialect by going out to walk with Lady Gregory. She goes into the cottage and listens to the story, takes it down while you wait outside, sitting on a bit of wall, Yeats, like an old jackdaw, and then filching her manuscript to put style upon it, just as you want to put style on me.

Yeats laughed vaguely; his laugh is one of the most melancholy things in the world, and it seemed to me that I had come to Coole on a fruitless errand – that we should never be able to write *Diarmuid and Grania* in collaboration.

From *Hail and Farewell*

John M. Synge

1900

JOHN M. SYNGE (1871–1909) was born at Rathfarnham, Dublin, and educated at Trinity College Dublin. He was living in Paris when he met Yeats, who persuaded him that the Irish peasantry were a good subject of drama. Synge returned to the West of Ireland to gather material. His first play *Shadow of the Glen* was performed at the Abbey Theatre in 1903, followed in 1904 by *Riders to the Sea* which caused riots in Dublin. *The Playboy of the Western World*, produced in 1907, confirmed Synge's reputation as a playwright.

Some of the worst portions of the Irish congested districts – of which so much that is contradictory has been spoken and written – lie along the further north coast of Galway Bay, and about the whole seaboard from Spiddal to Clifden. Some distance inland there is a line of railway, and in the bay itself a steamer passes in and out to the Aran Islands; but this particular district can only be visited thoroughly by driving or riding over some thirty or forty miles of desolate roadway. If one takes this route from Galway one has to go a little way only to reach places and people that are fully typical of Connemara. On each side of the road one sees small square fields of oats, or potatoes, or pasture, divided by loose stone walls that are built up without mortar. Wherever there are a few cottages near

J.M. Synge

the road one sees bare-footed women hurrying backwards and forwards, with hampers of turf or grass slung over their backs, and generally a few children running after them, and if it is a market-day, as was the case on the day of which I am going to write, one overtakes long strings of country people driving home from Galway in low carts drawn by an ass or pony. As a rule one or two men sit in front of the cart driving and smoking, with a couple of women behind them stretched out at their ease among sacks of flour or young pigs, and nearly always talking continuously in Gaelic. These men are all dressed in homespuns of the grey natural wool, and the women in deep madder-dyed petticoats and bodices, with brown shawls over their heads. One's first feeling as one comes back among these people and takes a place, so to speak, in this noisy procession of fishermen, farmers, and women, where nearly everyone is interesting and attractive, is a dread of any reform that would tend to lessen their individuality rather than any very real hope of improving their well-being. One feels then, perhaps a little later that it is a part of the misfortune of Ireland that nearly all the characteristics which give colour and attractiveness to Irish life are bound up with a social condition that is near to penury, while in countries like Brittany the best external features of the local life – the rich embroidered dresses, for instance, or the carved furniture – are connected with a decent and comfortable social condition.

About twelve miles from Galway one reaches Spiddal, a village which lies on the borderland between the fairly prosperous districts near Galway and the barren country further to the west. Like most places of its kind, it has a double row of houses – some of them with two storeys – several public-houses with a large police barrack among them, and a little to one side a coastguard station, ending up at either side of the village with a chapel and a church. It was evening when we drove into Spiddal, and a little after sunset we walked on to a rather exposed quay, where a few weather-beaten hookers were moored with many ropes. As we came down none of the crews were to be seen, but threads of turf-smoke rising from the open manhole of the forecastle showed that the men were probably on board. While we were looking down on them from the pier – the tide was far out – an old grey-haired man, with the inflamed eyes that are so common here from the continual itching of the turf-smoke, peered up through the manhole and watched us with vague curiosity. A few moments later a young man came down from a field of black earth, where he had been digging a drain, and asked the old man, in Gaelic, to throw him a spark for his pipe. The latter disappeared for a moment, then came up again with a smouldering end of a turf sod in his hand, and threw it up on the pier, where the young man caught it with a quick downward grab without burning himself, blew it into a blaze, lit his pipe with it, and went back to his work. These people are so poor that many of them do not spend any money on matches. The spark of lighting turf is kept alive day and night on the hearth, and when a man goes out fishing or to work in the fields he usually carries a lighted sod with him, and keeps it all day buried in ashes or any dry rubbish, so that he can use it when he needs it. On our way back to the village an old woman begged from us, speaking in English, as most of the people do to anyone who is not a native. We gave her a few halfpence, and as she was moving away with an ordinary 'God save you!' I said a blessing to her in Irish to show her that I knew her own language if she chose to use it. Immediately she turned back towards me and began her thanks again, this time with extraordinary profusion. 'That the blessing of God may be on you,' she said, 'on road and on ridgeway, on sea and on land, on flood and on mountain, in all the kingdoms of the world' – and so on, till I was too far off to hear what she was saying.

In a district like Spiddal one sees curious gradations of types, especially on Sundays and holidays, when everyone is dressed as their fancy leads them and as well as they can manage. As I watched the people coming from Mass the morning after we arrived this was curiously noticeable. The police and coastguards came first in their smartest uniforms; then the shopkeepers, dressed like the people of Dublin, but a little more, grotesquely; then the more well-to-do country folk, dressed only in the local clothes I have spoken of, but the best and newest kind, while the wearers themselves looked well-fed and healthy, and a few of them, especially the girls, magnificent built; then, last of all, one saw the destitute in still the same clothes, but this time patched and threadbare and ragged, the women mostly barefooted, and both sexes pinched with hunger and the fear of it. The class that one would be most interested to see increase is that of the typical well-to-do people, but except in a few districts it is not numerous, and is always aspiring after the dress of the shop-people or tending to sink down again among the paupers.

Later in the day we drove on another long stage to the west. As before, the country we passed through was not depressing, though stony and barren as a quarry. At every crossroads we passed groups of young, healthy looking boys and men amusing themselves with hurley or pitching, and further back on little heights, a small field's breadth from the road, there were many groups of girls sitting out by the hour, near enough to the road to see everything that was passing, yet far enough away to keep their shyness undisturbed. Their red dresses looked peculiarly beautiful among the fresh green of the grass and opening bracken, with a strip of sea behind them, and, far away, the grey cliffs of Clare. A little further on, some ten miles from Spiddal, inlets of the sea begin to run in towards the mountains, and the road turns north to avoid them across an expense of desolate bog far more dreary than the rocks of the coast. Here one sees a few wretched sheep nibbling in places among the turf, and occasionally a few ragged people walking rapidly by the roadside. Before we stopped for the night we had reached another bay coast-line, and were among stones again. Later in the evening we walked out round another small quay, with the usual little band of shabby hookers, and then along a road that rose in some places a few hundred feet above the sea; and as one looked down into the little fields that lay below it, they looked so small and rocky that

The Galway fish market photographed by John M. Synge

the very thought of tillage in them seemed like the freak of an eccentric. Yet in this particular place tiny cottages, some of them without windows, swarmed by the roadside and in the 'boreens,' or laneways, at either side, many of them built on a single sweep of stone with the naked living rock for their floor. A number of people were to be seen everywhere about them, the men loitering by the roadside and the women hurrying among the fields, feeding an odd calf or lamb, or driving in a few ducks before the night. In one place a few boys were playing pitch with trousers buttons, and a little farther on half-a-score of young men were making donkeys jump backwards and forwards over a low wall. As we came back we met two men who came and talked to us, one of them, by his hat and dress, plainly a man who had been away from Connemara. In a little while he told us that he had been in Gloucester and Bristol working on public works, but had wearied of it and came back to his country.

'Bristol,' he said, 'is the greatest town, I think, in all England, but the work in it is hard.'

I asked him about the fishing in the neigbourhood we were in. 'Ah,' he said, 'there's little fishing in it at all, for we have no good boats. There is no one asking for boats for this place, for the shopkeepers would rather have the people idle, so that they can get them for a shilling a day to go out in their old hookers and sell turf in Aran and on the coast of Clare.' Then we talked of Aran, and he told me of people I knew there who had died or got married since I had been on the islands and then they went on their way.

From *The Congested Districts under Ether*

B.N. Hedderman

1903

B.N. HEDDERMAN was born in County Clare and came to the Aran Islands in 1903 as one of the first Lady Dudley District Nurses, organized by the wife of the Lord Lieutenant. From 1903 to 1922 she served as district nurse on Inishmaan and Inishere, travelling between the islands and narrowly escaping being drowned on a few occasions when the currach she was travelling in capsized. Hedderman wrote a vivid account of her time on Aran which was published as *Glimpses of my Life in Aran* in 1917.

We had been two hours on the voyage, and I beheld for the first time the Aran group of islands rising up before us like real denizens of the ocean. How rugged, grey, and desolate they seemed, enveloped on all sides by a boundless sea, on whose breast I was today so lightly borne, and on whose bosom I would afterwards, as I thought with Ruskin, be so often tossed.

I shall long cherish a recollection of that first morning, when from the bridge of the steamer I could discern nothing more inviting than huge ridges of rock. Big, uneven boulders! Whole fields absolutely devoid of any shelter for herb or flower! At the same moment I beheld with reverence and admiration the 'Island Ruins,' links connecting us with a Celtic past, and an old castle standing almost at the water's edge, associated with the memory of the 'O'Briens of Ara.' They have come and gone, and this crumbling pile is the only monumental proof left to commemorate their sway.

As we approached the island of Inishere or South Island, I noticed tiny boats moving towards us with great rapidity, the boatmen plying their oars with wonderful dexterity.

As each crew drew nearer they arranged themselves beside the steamer, which seemed a leviathan in comparison. Confusion reigned for a moment, but with skill born of practice, each was quickly served and, in turn, extricated again with difficulty.

I confess that to an interested onlooker for the first time, this method of doing business was rather startling. Their Gaelic was simply beautiful, so soft and accurate, flowing from their lips in unaffected strains, 'the tongue of saints and sages.' . . .

I gazed as they chatted away, but unfortunately could not grasp much of what they were saying. The Captain, seeing my embarrassment, came to the rescue, acting as interpreter, explaining why I had come. This announcement sharpened the interest of one amongst them, who instantly became assertive, offering me to take me ashore in all the 'Bearla' (English language) he could command. He assisted me to alight, and called my attention to the little barque beneath, in which he had secured my passage. I descended without fear, though an involuntary chill got hold of me when I had to step in, sharing a berth with one of those already named – a rather boorish lad.

Battling with the oars, they sped o'er the waves with special speed, and to me, as to Coleridge's 'Ancient Mariner,'

> *Sweetly, sweetly, blew the breeze,*
> *On me alone it blew.*

We did not glide on, however, as quickly as the Ancient Mariner, for we were deeply freighted. There were tar, nets, straw, groceries, goods of all kinds, and fishing gear and curragh tackle around me; with a ballast representing Guinness & Co.; for I regret to say that, unlike the inhabitants of Tristan d'Acunha in the South Atlantic, some of these people do not use water as their only beverage.

It was a new experience, though not wholly a pleasant one, to find myself so soon hoisted on the surface of the waves. Though not fierce to-day, they lifted me sometimes to a considerable height, and I received occasional dashes of spray. This soaking with sea water, combined with jolting from side to side, wearied me, and I longed to rest.

My arrival on the beach created some little excitement. It was new to see a nurse; half the Island people had that day assembled there, waiting for those who had gone on board to fetch provisions ashore. A few girls were sitting on baskets, and others on the rocks, with their knitting. They watched me with keen curiosity, whispering amongst themselves. My chatelaine especially attracted them, and they appeared to concentrate a large share of attention on my hair, which I wore coiled. They asked if it were false. Shortly after landing it burst upon me that, after all, I was a stranger in a strange island . . .

There, is a little village in the Middle Island called 'The Moor,' and, because of its (comparatively) greater size, it is regarded by the islanders as most up-to-date and consequently as the capital. Indeed, those who reside there declare that they are never without dried fish – a distinction of quite an important nature, for too often a lack of this necessary article of food makes itself felt in bad weather when no boat can venture out.

It is also the proudest boast of 'The Moor' men that the tourist likes to linger there, though it is difficult to believe that its cobbled pathways and dreary appearance could appeal to anyone, and the general impression produced on the visitor must be one of dullness and desolation. It is called 'Blaithcliath' to denote its importance, because a Dublin student once stayed there.

The peaceful serenity of this old-world village was unexpectedly disturbed one mellow afternoon in the autumn when our gramophone arrived. It had been noticed that a box had been deposited with unusual care on the slip, so well secured that the boatmen who surveyed it exchanged glances, wondering what it could contain. I sometimes visit this landing-place, particularly on fine days, when there is a groundswell, to watch the difficulty experienced by the men in landing. On this particular occasion they called me forward, and I at once assumed wondrous importance as the person to whom this unusual package was addressed. As soon as it was announced that the box contained a gramophone the scene became one of excitement and wonder.

The news spread like prairie fire. A crowd gathered round peeping over each other's shoulders to see what was going on, and by the time the contents were unpacked fully a hundred people were squatting round, sitting on the bare ground, to witness the opening ceremony. The parts were carefully examined to see if we could arrange to piece them together. But, alas! we had no knowledge of the mechanism, nor was there any tradesman in the place who was any wiser. However, fortunately for us, there was a young graduate from Oxford visiting the islands, and he quickly consented to see what he could do. Eventually he succeeded, and suddenly the music started. The expression on the faces of the onlookers was indeed a sight to remember – the children in raptures, the old women en-chanted, the men hardly believing their ears, and for a few minutes all other thoughts were laid aside. The question no one could answer was, where were the men and women hiding whose voices sounded so sweetly? They could not be seen. One woman suggested the spirits of the Firbolgs – Pagan ancestors – which tradition associates with the Duns forts to be found in Inishmain. In the rush and general bustle going on, the men forgot to prepare the nets, and all work was temporarily suspended. They continued

John M. Synge photographed the landing of a curragh on the Aran Islands

exclaiming in Gaelic that 'somewhere there must be a person or there could not be a voice,' and the effect produced on them was really wonderful.

The day following a very pleasing incident occurred. A woman who had been ill with nervous trouble for many weeks previously heard of the mysterious music. She asked me to let her hear it. Of course I consented. It acted like a charm. The spell was instantaneous. She, too, forgot her trouble, and the sad, worn face, on which suffering had left its mark, at once lighted up with hope and pleasure. Often afterwards I invited her to come and hear the music, and her visits were invariably followed by happy results.

I had no idea before that the Islanders had such a passion for music and song. One evening all the old men had assembled at one of the cottages. Among the records was a hornpipe. Directly the first bar was played, six of the men stood up in a line some distance apart from each other; all somehow procured short sticks, and at the first note, feet, arms, and sticks commenced to keep time, each fellow swaying his body first to the right and then to the left. Scarcely any noise was heard, as they can move quite silently on the pampooties or cowhide shoes which they wear, the quiet being broken only by the clanking sound of the sticks as they clashed. Such a display was altogether foreign to me, but the motley

Emigrants at the Galway docks

crowd that looked on seemed in no way puzzled at the extraordinary motion of the performers. The pleasure of listening to the instrument, and the generosity of the donor, Mrs. Brian Wilson, are not likely to be quickly forgotten in the Island of Inishmain, for life in such a spot is indeed shorn of most of its joys.

From *Glimpses of My life in Aran*

James Joyce

1912

JAMES JOYCE (1882–1941) was born in Dublin, the eldest of a large family whose fortunes were in rapid decline. He was educated at Clongowes Wood College and by the Christian Brothers. In 1902, he graduated from University College Dublin and went to Paris to study medicine, but lack of funds forced him back to Dublin. In 1904, he met Nora Barnacle from Galway and a year later, they went to Trieste together and lived there until the 1920s, except for a short stay in Zurich during the First World War. In the early 1920s the Joyces moved to Paris and lived there until the Second World War, when they moved again to

Zurich, where Joyce died. In 1912, Joyce visited Galway to write several articles for a Trieste newspaper, *Piccola della Sera*.

4 Bowling Green, Galway. . . . Have just finished second article on Aran and will send. Send on at once twelve copies of P. de S. with 1st article. I went to Clifden on Monday to interview Marconi or see station. Could do neither and am waiting reply from Marconi House London. Wrote to Roberts 4 times and at last got enclosed. Have written a letter to Hone calling on him to see that I am acted loyally by. Immediately I hear will write. Call to the pharmacy and see that my letter to P – is forwarded at once. Tell Bartoli I have a lot of news *re* transatlantic scheme and to see my second article on Aran. I think since I have come so far I had better stay a little longer if possible. Nora's uncle feeds us in great style and I row and cycle and drive a good deal. I cycled to Oughterard on Sunday and visited the graveyard of *The Dead*. It is exactly as I imagined it and one of the headstones was to J. Joyce. . . .

From *Letters of James Joyce*

Augustus John
1915

ARTIST AUGUSTUS JOHN (1878–1961) was born in Tenby, England, and studied art at the Slade School with his sister Gwen. As a young man he was considered one of the outstanding artists of his day and won the Slade Prize in 1898. During The First World War John was sent to the Western Front as an artist but was sent back to England after a brawl. He used his friendship with Lord Beaverbrook to narrowly escape being court-martialled. Unable to travel to Europe during the war, John visited Galway and the Aran Islands. He attended the Versailles Conference as official artist and painted the portraits of many delegates.

With *what* excitement, on my part at any rate, did we cross over on the steamer *Dun Angus*, and step ashore at last on the quays of the western capital! Tall warehouses alternated with low whitewashed or pale coloured dwellings beside the wharves: across the harbour, the old Irish village of The Claddagh, a complex of thatched cabins, appeared to have sprung up in a fairy ring, like mushrooms from the ground: bevies of shawled, bare-footed girls passed, laughing, as we threaded the labyrinthine streets which resounded with the cries of fish-women: somewhere a voice, sweetened by distance, wailed nostalgically: 'Eileen allanah, Eileen asthore!' Black hookers lay along the quayside; among them Macnamara's newly rigged *Mary Ann*, 'a boon,' as Oliver Gogarty remarked with customary malice, 'to the local washer-women.' In Flaherty's little bar by the New Dock, where charming Kitty McGee presided, men of Aran awaited their passage to the islands; 'mountainy' women refreshed themselves with stout, and Welsh seamen, newly landed, celebrated the day in noggins of whisky. At dusk, dark forms could be espied, lurking among the fallen balks of the old timber-yard beyond, and women still lingered, murmuring, by the Spanish Gate – a face, or part of a face, blooming for an instant from shadowy veils and quickly averted. The Claddagh in the half-light begins to look unsubstantial and dream-like; the waters of Lough Corrib pour through the arches of the bridge, where salmon, massed in wavering rows, await the signal to ascend: more water gushes through the cavernous apertures of a dilapidated mill: in the main street stands Lynch's Castle, a rectangular tower of fine-cut stone: a tinker-girl, drunk and of a Raphaelesque beauty (in spite of a black eye), utters sweet bird-like sounds, while incessantly readjusting her shawl: Dick Innes's English accent, acquired at Llanelly, was becoming more marked: God knows how or whence he appeared, but we had certainly been, all three, to the Races, where we had found the tinker-girl and conveyed her back safely, her parcel of pig's-trotters and all. The fish-wives in the bar, ensconced with their stout, hand the pipe round as they pass derisory comments on current events: Winny Corcoran, my 'fond girl,' goes dodging by, on her way to the docks, and over Oranmore the pale sky darkens as Mr. Heard the D.I., taking a stroll, comes under the verbal fire of vainglorious patriots issuing from pubs: ridiculing them scornfully, he proceeds on his way, swaggering.

From *Chiaroscuro*

Arthur Whitten Brown

1919

ARTHUR WHITTEN BROWN (1886–1948) achieved fame with John Alcock as the first men to fly across the Atlantic. Brown was born in Glasgow and began his flying career before the First World War. During the war he was shot down over Germany and spent time as a prisoner of war. After the war Alcock and Brown entered the competition to be the first to fly across the Atlantic. Organized by *The Daily Mail* it had a prize of ten thousand pounds. During the flight they suffered many hazardous conditions, such as night flying and heavy fog, before they landed in Connemara.

From above the islands the mainland was visible, and we steered for the nearest point on it. The machine was still just underneath the clouds, and flying at two hundred and fifty feet; from which low height I saw plainly the white breakers foaming on to the shore. We crossed the coast of Ireland at 8.25 A.M.

I was then uncertain of our exact location, and suggested to Alcock that the best plan would be to find a railway line and follow it south. A few minutes later, however, the wireless masts at Clifden gave the key to our position. To attract attention, I fired red flares from the Very pistol; but as they seemed to be unnoticed from the ground, we circled over the village of Clifden, about two miles from the wireless station.

Although slightly off our course when we reached the coast, we were in the direct line of flight for Galway, at which place I had calculated to hit Ireland. Not far ahead we could see a cluster of hills, with their tops lost in low-lying clouds.

Here and elsewhere the danger of running into high ground hidden from sight by the mist would have been great, had we continued to fly across Ireland. Alcock, therefore, decided to land. . .

Having made up our minds to land at once, we searched below for a smooth stretch of ground. The most likely looking place in the neighborhood of Clifden was a field near the wireless station. With engines shut off, we glided towards it, heading into the wind.

Alcock flattened out at exactly the right moment. The machine sank gently, the wheels touched earth and began to run smoothly over the surface. Already I was indulging in the comforting reflection that the anxious flight had ended with a perfect landing. Then, so softly as not to be noticed at first, the front of the Vickers-Vimy tilted inexplicably, while the tail rose. Suddenly the craft stopped with an unpleasant squelch, tipped forward, shook itself, and remained poised on a slant, with its fore-end buried in the ground, as if trying to stand on its head.

I reached out a hand and arm just in time to save a nasty bump when the shock threw me forward. As it was, I only stopped a jarring collision with the help of my nose. Alcock had braced himself against the rudder control bar. The pressure he exerted against it to save himself from falling actually bent the straight bar, which was of hollow steel, almost into the shape of a horse-shoe.

Deceived by its smooth appearance, we had landed on top of a bog; which misfortune made the first non-stop transatlantic flight finish in a crash. It was pitiful to see the distorted shape of the aeroplane that had brought us from America, as it sprawled in ungainly manner over the sucking surface. The machine's nose and its lower wings were deep in the bog. The empty cockpit in front, used in a Vickers-Vimy bomber by the observer, was badly bent; but, being of steel, it did not collapse. Quite possibly we owe our lives to this fact. In passing, and while gripping firmly my wooden penholder (for the year is not yet over), I consider it extraordinary that no lives have been lost in the transatlantic flights of 1919.

The leading edge of the lower plane was bent in some places and smashed in others, the gasoline connections had snapped, and four of the propeller blades were buried in the ground, although none were broken. That about completed the record of the preliminary damage.

We had landed at 8:40 A.M., after being in the air for sixteen hours and twenty-eight minutes. The flight from coast to coast, on a straight course of one thousand six hundred and eighty nautical miles, lasted only fifteen hours and fifty-seven minutes, our average speed being one hundred and five to one hundred and six knots. For this relatively rapid performance, a strong following wind was largely responsible.

As a result of the burst connections from tank to carburetor, gasoline began to swill into the rear cockpit while we were still inside it. Very fortunately the liquid did not ignite. Alcock had taken care to switch off the current on the magnetos, as soon as he realized that a crash was imminent, so that the sparks should have no chance of starting a fire.

We scrambled out as best we could, and lost no time in salving the mailbag and our instruments. The gasoline rose rapidly, and it was impossible to withdraw my chart and the Baker navigating machine before they had been damaged.

I then fired two white Very flares, as a signal for help. Almost immediately a small party, composed of officers and men belonging to the military detachment at Clifden, approached from the wireless station.

'Anybody hurt?' – the usual inquiry when an aeroplane is crashed – was the first remark when they arrived within shouting distance.

'No.'

'Where you from?' – this when they had helped us clear the cockpit.

'America.'

Somebody laughed politely, as if in answer to an attempt at facetiousness that did not amount to much, but that ought to be taken notice of, anyhow, for the sake of courtesy. Quite evidently nobody received the statement seriously at first. Even a mention of our names meant nothing to them, and they remained unconvinced until Alcock showed them the mailbag from St. John's. Then they relieved their surprised feelings by spontaneous cheers and painful hand-shakes, and led us to the officers' mess for congratulations and hospitality.

The plane in which Alcock & Brown made the first Transatlantic flight

Burdened as we were with flying kit and heavy boots, the walk over the bog was a dragging discomfort. In addition, I suddenly discovered an intense sleepiness, and could easily have let myself lose consciousness while standing upright.

Arrived at the station, our first act was to send telegrams to the firm of Messers. Vickers, Ltd., which built the Vickers-Vimy, to the London *Daily Mail*, which promoted the transatlantic competition, and to the Royal Aero Club, which controlled it.

My memories of that day are dim and incomplete. I felt a keen sense of relief at being on land again; but this was coupled with a certain amount of dragging reaction from the tense mental concentration during the flight, so that my mind sagged. I was very sleepy, but not physically tired.

We lurched as we walked, owing to the stiffness that resulted from our having sat in the tiny cockpit for seventeen hours. Alcock, who during the whole period had kept his feet on the rudder bar and one hand on the control lever, would not confess to anything worse than a desire to stand up for the rest of his life – or at least until he could sit down painlessly. My hands were very unsteady. My mind was quite clear on matters pertaining to the flight, but hazy on extraneous subjects. After having listened so long to the loud-voiced hum of the Rolls-Royce motors, made louder than ever by the broken exhaust pipe on the starboard side, we were both very deaf, and our ears would not stop ringing.

Later in the day we motored to Galway with a representative of the London *Daily Mail*. It was a strange but very welcome change to see solid objects flashing past us, instead of miles upon monotonous miles of drifting, cloudy vapor.

Several times during that drive I lost the thread of connection with tangible surroundings, and lived again in near retrospect the fantastic happenings of the day, night and morning that had just passed. Subconsciously I still missed the rhythmic, relentless drone of the Rolls-Royce aero-engines. My eyes had not yet become accustomed to the absence of clouds around and below, and my mind felt somehow lost, now that it was no longer preoccupied with heavenly bodies, horizon, time, direction, charts, drift, tables of calculations, sextant, spirit level, compass, aneroid, altimeter, wireless receiver and the unexpected.

For a while, in fact, the immediate past seemed more prominent than the immediate present. Lassitude of mind, coupled with reaction from the long strain of tense and unbroken concentration on one supreme objective, made me lose my grip of normal continuity, so that I answered questions mechanically and wanted to avoid the effort of talk. The outstanding events and impressions of the flight – for example the long spin from four thousand to fifty feet, and the sudden sight of the white-capped ocean at the end of it – passed and repassed across my consciousness. I do not know whether Alcock underwent the same mental processes, but he remained very silent. Above all I felt the need of re-establishing normal balance by means of sleep.

The wayside gatherings seemed especially unreal – almost as if they had been scenes on the film. By some extraordinary method of news transmission the report of our arrival had spread all over the district, and in many districts between Clifden and Galway curious crowds had gathered. Near Galway we were stopped by another automobile, in which was Major Mays of the Royal Aero Club, whose duty it was to examine the seals on the Vickers-Vimy, thus making sure that we had not landed in Ireland in a machine other than that in which we left Newfoundland. A reception had been prepared at Galway; but our hosts, realizing how tired we must be, considerately made it a short and informal affair. Afterwards we slept – for the first time in over forty hours.

From *Flying the Atlantic in Sixteen Hours*

William Orpen

1920

WILLIAM ORPEN (1878–1931) was born in County Dublin and educated at the Metropolitan School of Art and at the Slade School in London. In 1901, he returned to Dublin to teach and became involved with the Royal Hibernian Academy. Orpen served as official war artist during the First World War and at the Versailles Peace Conference. In addition to painting, Orpen wrote several books, among them *An Onlooker in France* and *Outline of Art.*

I once attended an American wake 'way off in the wilds of Connemara, but it was the daughter of the house who was going this time to New York as a 'domestic.' And a great, fine, beautiful girl she was, with her red petticoats and her shapely legs and feet. Have you ever seen a western girl walking the roads, or jumping from stone to stone across a bog? It's a fine sight to see these girls swinging along, free and wild, with their white flesh coming out from under the shadows of their red petticoats.

This wake was held in her grandfather's cottage one night, to get to which one had to leave the road and pick one's way across the bog for about half a mile as

William Orpen

the crow flies. But it was a very zigzag business; one seemed quite near the cottage sometimes, and a few minutes afterwards one would find oneself far away from it. In the end I arrived about ten o'clock. The grandmother and grandfather sat in their places on each side of the fire, and benches were ranged round the walls, on which couples were seated. A few of the younger members of the family, including the girl herself, were busy handing round boiling hot tea and poteen. There was very little conversation; in fact, the silence was rather oppressive. Then suddenly the music man would play some sad air, and a few of the couples (there was not room for them all) would come to the middle of the room and dance very slowly, and in a weary, bored sort of way. When they had finished they would go back to their places on the bench. The man would sit down, and the lady would sit on his left knee; his left hand would hold her round the waist, leaving the right hand free for taking up boiling hot tea or poteen, or maybe a smoke. All the couples did exactly the same; they never changed partners, because each couple was going to be mated – their marriages had been 'arranged.' I watched them all the four hours or so I was there. Not a word did the man utter to his bride-to-be! Not a look did he give her! There was not even the twitch of a finger on the hand that held her waist; just the sad weary dance occasionally, and then silence. It seemed to me a strange way of courting, but I suppose it 'gets there just the same.' No matter what angle or point of view this great event, marriage, is approached, it works out to about the same finish, and this method was the custom of the country anyway.

At intervals some dark man would heave himself to his feet and recite a dirge about the sadness of the world, and Ireland in particular. When he finished these wailings, his voice broken with misery, there was always loud applause! The strange thing was, no one seemed to take the slightest interest in the beautiful girl who was going to leave her home in the dawn for the first time in her life, and who might never see it again or, alas! we her. I noticed that the few young men who were not 'arranged' for, never even threw her a side glance. So the night wore on: tea, music, poteen, dirge, tea, and so on. When it got to about two o'clock the rain came down in torrents, and I began to be nervous as to whether I could get back safely over the bog. Or should I have another glass of poteen and forget the world? However, I managed to get to my feet, and bade farewell to my hosts, and started off into the black, wet night. I had not gone a hundred yards before I heard the patter of bare feet running after me, and I heard a voice saying, 'Please, grandfather told me to see you safely over the bog.' It was the girl herself, and she took me by the hand and led me on till we got to the road. I then asked her what hour she was leaving in the morning. 'Six o'clock,' she said. So I told her that I would like to give her a little present, and explained where I was sleeping, and that I would leave the door open if she would come and wake me up; which she did, but no longer showing the beautiful white legs. No, she had high-heeled boots with 'brassy eyes' to them, such as Pegeen Mike (in the *Play-Boy of the Western World*) wished for, and the red petticoat was gone, and she had on a 'tailor made.'

Not one sign of nervousness did this girl show, and never before had she been farther than Maam Cross (about nine miles), which consists of a railway station, a pub, and about ten houses. That was the greatest town she had ever seen. And now she was off to New York; but she seemed to take it just as a matter of course.

From *Stories of Old Ireland and Myself*

Connemara Farmer

Signe Toksvig

1920

DANISH WRITER SIGNE TOKSVIG (1891–1983) emigrated to the
United States with her family at the age of fifteen. She won a scholar-
ship to Cornell University and graduated in 1916. Her first job was as a
writer at *Vogue* before she moved to the newly formed *New Republic*,
where she met and married the editor, Francis Hackett. They made
several trips to Ireland before eventually settling here in 1926. Ten years
later, when the Censorship Board banned novels by both of them, the
Hacketts left Ireland and moved to Denmark. A short visit to America
was prolonged due to the outbreak of the Second World War and the
Hacketts did not return permanently to Denmark until 1952.

To get from Dublin to Coole Park, the home of Lady Gregory, one
normally takes a train from Dublin to Athenry, and another from
Athenry to Gort, the village nearest to Coole. But times were not exactly
normal in Ireland when my husband and I visited it last summer, and
when we got to Athenry we were confronted by the blank fact that for

two months or so no trains had been running to Gort. Why? This was a rhetorical question. We knew very well that armed policemen must have been trying to travel on that train, and that the engineer had excused himself for an indefinite period, and that we had better find a Ford. We found one. It was very rickety and full of unwieldy first-aid-to-the-injured-auto things, but Gort was twenty miles away, and hope and beauty had long since left Athenry, and so we squeezed in and began to bump over stony Connaught.

It is very like stony New England, except for the important fact that the Pilgrim, after all, had a good-sized field when he had picked the stones off it and set them up as boundaries, whereas some of these 'fields' of Connaught were no larger than vegetable beds, it seemed to me, and yet the stones were piled high around them. Still, the sun shone a little, and in the pale light of rainy summer this gray-green landscape had its own wistful charm. Here and there, too, the madder-red of a Galway petticoat gleamed in a small yellow cornfield, and girls let their sickles fall to look at us. The country grew more lonely and more wild. The little fields choked under the stones. Sheep strayed about, and long-legged, ravenous pigs. No country estate was visible, and the sun was failing. Then we saw a long stretch of high gray stone wall and a mass of gloomy trees behind it. But this was Tillyra, we were told, and we knew it for the Norman retreat of Edward Martyn, famous in his own right as a playwright, and also as a large part of George Moore's *Ave ataque Vale*. We were later to visit him, with Lady Gregory, but now we thought only of Coole Park, and here suddenly it was – gray stone wall, venerable trees, and a quick, dark-haired woman to open the lodge gates. For what seemed to me a long while we drove through the park, still and lovely and darkening in the twilight. After another gate the thick leaves met overhead, and water dripped somewhere in a dim ravine. I had begun to feel that our car was violating Faery, when we drove into a great open meadowy place with haystacks on it, and in the centre, a tall, white, square, unromantic house.

Outside was a little black figure welcoming us. This was Lady Gregory, and as I had never seen her before, I noticed her fresh complexion, bright penetrating brown eyes, white hair black-veiled, slight tendency to stoutness, black mourning clothes and little black silk apron. She was most cordial, even to me, the unknown marital adjunct of a man whom she knew and liked, and we went into the tall white house.

Now there is one advantage of being young and unimportant and a marital adjunct, and this is that if one is silent, nobody notices. The conversation of the principals goes right on. And meanwhile one is left

Tuam Cathedral

free to make observations. This inestimable advantage I had most of the time I was at Coole Park, and it thrilled me. Seriously. In an otherwise drab college course on the 'drama,' the great discoveries had been Synge and Yeats and Lady Gregory, *Riders to the Sea*, *Cathleen ni Houlihan*, and *The Rising of the Moon*. And here I was free and alone to explore this house, the very hearth where Irish revival had warmed itself.

The drive had been cold, and I sat close to the fire while the principals exchanged comments on absent friends. Lady Gregory wanted to know about John Quinn, and probably she found out, but I looked at the dark, tall, rich room, lit by fluttering candles. Her beautiful warm voice and easy manner went well with this Library. The room had been accumulated in no frantic haste. One could imagine its growth from generation to generation until its present opulent age, – worn oriental rugs and curtains, walls of books in old gilt-leather bindings, solid furniture with the sheen of years, and fading red damask coverings. And paintings of frilled men, carvings, statuettes, miniatures, and a real lock of Napoleon's hair under his miniature next to the fireplace.

In the dining-room there was a splendid Zurbaran monk, and that was all I noticed until, candle in hand, Lady Gregory led me up the wide stairs to my room. The walls above the stairs were covered with sketches by Augustus John and Jack Yeats, and rows of eminent, engraved Englishmen who had been members of a famous breakfast club to which Sir William Gregory had belonged. They looked almost incredibly mild, dignified, and benevolent. Altogether different was an aggressive little sketch of Lady Gregory by Augustus John, far from flattering, but one which I could see represented something in her character – an angular fighting mood, which probably has carried her through many a storm at the Abbey Theatre. Not that I know that there ever have been any storms at the Abbey; this is only a supposition of mine, drawn from long observations of other small groups working together for the betterment, artistic or political, of their community.

Lady Gregory left me in my room with the casual remark that the Shaws (G. Bernard) always had this room, and that he might have been there at that very moment if he hadn't had to go to Parknasilla in Kerry. I think it was Parknasilla, but I felt with a reverential thrill that at least an epigram of his might still be lurking in the black shadows made blacker by my trembling candle. It was a cavernous room. I barely saw tapestried chairs and books and a huge white-frilled canopied bed. There were roses on a white dressing table. I went to open a window. It opened on the thickest, darkest, chilliest, quietist night that ever was since the creation of night. The darkness stole into the room and buried my candle, and the silence made my thoughts seem loud. I knew then why poets come to Coole.

From *Signe Toksvig's Irish Diaries*

Sean O'Casey

1925

DUBLIN-BORN PLAYWRIGHT Sean O'Casey (1884–1964) was self-educated. He started out as a labourer and became involved in the Labour Movement as a journalist and pamphleteer. He also served as Secretary of the Irish Citizen Army under James Connolly. After submitting many plays to the Abbey, *The Shadow of a Gunman* was finally produced in 1923. This was followed by *Juno and the Paycock* and *The Plough and the Stars*, which helped restore the Abbey as an artistic and a financial success. But when the Abbey turned down *The Silver Tassie* in 1928, O'Casey moved to England and lived there for the rest of his life.

*F*or the past few weeks my eyes have been a little troublesome, & I cannot write the letter I find my heart prompting me to write.

However, I cannot put off any longer the sending of my full and earnest appreciation of your great kindness to me during my stay in Beautiful Coole.

You will be glad to hear that I have given an absolute absolution to Gort, freeing it from all its sordid sins because of the loveliness of Coole. Besides, is it not written that, 'through much tribulation we shall enter the Kingdom of Heaven'?

I have long pondered over whether the beautiful pictures & statuary, the glorious books, or the wonderful woods, river & Lake of Coole deserve the apple of praise – for they are like the three

Sean O'Casey

competitors that stood before & showed their charms to Paris – but I think I must choose the woods, the Lake and the river. I am sending you a few thoughts builded on the delightful memories of Coole.

From *The Letters of Sean O'Casey*

Francis Stuart

1932

FRANCIS STUART (1902–2000) was born on a sheep farm in Australia to Ulster parents. When his father died three months later his mother brought him back to Ireland. Stuart was educated at Rugby and, at seventeen, married Iseult Gonne, the daughter of Maud Gonne MacBride. He started out writing poetry but turned to plays and novels. In 1939 he went to Germany and during the Second World War made broadcasts to Ireland. After the war he spent eight months in jail which was the inspiration for *Black List, Section H*. In this excerpt he describes a meeting with Liam O'Flaherty in Galway.

*O*ne autumn here in Glendalough I received a wire from Liam, whom I had not seen for a long time. 'Come and have dinner with me at the Station Hotel in Galway on Hallowe'en.'

Francis Stuart

I got out my car and drove the hundred and fifty miles. I had never been in Galway before and when I arrived it was just getting dusk. I went to the hotel, but Liam was not there, was not even expected. But I knew he would arrive from wherever it might be. I walked through the town and round the harbour. I went into a public-house and had a drink. How good it is waiting to meet a person one is fond of, whom one has not seen for a long time! All the things that have happened to one since then, all the things that, no doubt, have happened to the friend! Again that feeling of excitement, or expectancy before the veil has lifted.

I thought Galway the loveliest town I had seen in Ireland. Perhaps that is not saying much, but it had a glamour for me that evening that it has always kept.

I went back to the hotel and after a bit Liam walked in, with a suit-case following him, just off the boat from the Aran Islands. We shouted to each other and it was one of the best meetings I have ever had.

We went into the hotel bar to knock back a drink in celebration. Liam had just finished *Skerrett*.

'I've asked two girls to have dinner with us, Francis.'

'Splendid!'

Everything was splendid. We went on drinking at a great rate, without noticing, because there was so much to say.

After a bit we began to think it was a pity about the girls coming. We were much better off alone.

The girls arrived and we went in to dinner. They were very charming, but I think we must have been boring for them. We went on talking together and I had photographs of horses to show Liam and he had letters to show me and we sent out to have the town scoured for De Lacy, who was said to be around.

Finally we all drove out to a country house where some friends of one of the girls lived. Why we went I don't know. I don't remember very much more of that night except that I got into an argument about the breeding of some horse with the owner of the house and he took down books from the shelves to prove to me that I was wrong. I remember taking some volume on *Racing-up-to-Date* or the *Stud Book* into my hands and wondering where we were and hearing Liam knock over a whole suit of armour. I am afraid I behaved badly, and perhaps Liam did too. But I have heard since that the owner of that house was prompted to read one of my books by the whole business and liked it so much that he read others and ended by becoming an ardent admirer of my work. Perhaps that is not so, but I hope it is because it would be a slight atonement for my behaviour.

I had an invitation to lunch with Compton Mackenzie at a house beyond Dublin the next day. It was a hundred and thirty miles away, so I had asked to be called at eight. The hotel porter brought a cup of tea which I drank thirstily. In a moment he returned full of apologies. They had put salt into the tea instead of sugar. He brought more tea. I began to feel ill. I would have given a great deal to have been able to stay in bed that morning. But I had never met Compton Mackenzie and he had written so sympathetically about me in the *Daily Mail*, incidentally calling down upon himself endless abuse, that I felt I must go, no matter what. Liam came in while I was dressing and splashing cold water on my burning face.

'My God, how ill I feel.'

'You look feverish, Francis.'

'That's how I feel.'

'Well, good luck!'

'Good luck.'

Street Scene

I got into the car and left at nine. I have never had such a drive. After each bend in the road I had to stop and get out and be very ill. I thought I would pull up at some hotel on the way and go to bed. I kept on. At some point a farmer stopped me to give him a lift into Athlone. Above all I wanted to be alone. I asked him if it was far.

'Not in one of these machines,' he said. 'Why, we'll be there while I'm striking a match.' Like people unused to cars, he exaggerated their speed out of all reason. I had to listen to his talk about cattle and answer him for twelve miles.

From *Things to Live For*

Robert Flaherty

1934

OFTEN CALLED 'the father of the motion-picture documentary,' Robert Flaherty (1884–1951) was born in Iron Mountain, Michigan, to a prospecting family. He followed the family tradition and spent much of his youth prospecting for gold. Flaherty took his first moving pictures while working in the Hudson Bay area of northern Canada. He then persuaded investors to back another expedition which resulted in *Nanook of the North* in 1922. Paramount financed an expedition to the South Seas which resulted in the film *Moana* and, in 1934, he came to Ireland to make *Man of Aran*.

Robert Flaherty

*N*early three years ago, I was on my way across the Atlantic, in the *Berengaria* on my way from New York to Germany. I had just returned from the South Seas, where I had made my film *Moana*, and had no very definite plans for the future.

I met an Irish motor-engineer aboard the liner. He was travelling from America to the Co. Cork works of a great motor-car firm, and in the course of many conversations we had, this man told me something of the wild magnificence of the Aran Islands, and of the ceaseless struggle for the bare necessities of life carried on by the islanders. When the boat docked, I lost sight of him. I have never seen him since; I do not even know his name. But it was this chance-met Irishman who first gave me the idea of making a film in Aran. Had it not been for our shipboard talks, there would be no *Man of Aran* today.

I spent five months in Germany, and then, with my unknown friend's stories of the Aran Islands in mind, suggested to Mr. Michael Balcon, of Gaumont-British Picture Corporation, that I should go to Aran and spy out the land.

I travelled to Aran, and there, only fifteen hours from London, this is what I found. A bare rock, nine miles long and three wide at its broadest point. There is no shade and no shelter, for there are no trees; there are no trees *because there is no soil.* Tremendous seas, rolling in from the Atlantic, pound the island, sending their spray over the 500-feet-high cliffs, and sometimes blowing clean across the island, borne on savage gusts of wind. The island has no natural resources; the thirty-mile passage to Galway City is fraught with danger, a terror to sailors. Yet on this barren slab of rock nearly 1,200 souls have their existence.

The first islander I took care to find was Pat Mullin. Pat has had an adventurous life, travelling in America and other parts of the world, but now lives once again in his native Aran, and drives a jaunting-car on the island. I asked him how many people lived in the little seaport-village of Kilronan, for Pat knows everything and everybody on the island. He thought for a long time, and he answered, 'Two hundred and thirty.' He had been counting the inhabitants, cottage by cottage, in his head!

When a little while later, I returned with my three hand-cranked cameras and equipment, it was Pat who became my major-domo and casting manager. He found me my headquarters, near the only spring which would supply enough fresh water for our needs, and we settled here, in a six-roomed cottage belonging to an English-woman, in Kilmurvey, in the western part of the island. We converted an old stone lean-to shed into our laboratory, and installed a tiny petrol-engine, which developed enough electricity for the house-lighting, our film-lamps, and for the drying-machine and portable projector. I fancy that ours was the first 'foreign location' to do its own printing, developing and even cutting, on the spot.

Work started soon on the building of a small Irish cottage which I needed for interior scenes, and it was while we had workmen engaged in clearing the ground, levelling and building that I was able to study 'types' and make my first contacts with the islanders.

There was Old Patch Ruadh, who, as his Irish name implies, sports a huge red beard. There was little Michael Dillane, whom I first saw at an Irish dance in the village one night. He was only twelve years old, and Pat had the devil and all of a job to persuade Michael's parents to let the boy come and act for me. Maggie Dirrane, the 'Madonna' character of the film, came and worked in our house, so that we had plenty of opportunity to study her and get to know her. She was glad to act in the film, for it gave her the chance to earn a little extra money. This was precious to Maggie, for her husband had been crippled gathering seaweed in a storm, and was unable to work.

You will see this process of seaweed-gathering in the film. The islanders collect it in baskets. Then they scrape up what little grains of soft earth they can find hidden in crannies in the rock, mix it with boulders crushed to powder with blows from the heavy sledge-hammer, and perhaps add a little imported earth. They spread this compost in thin strips on the bare rock, manure it with seaweed, and in it plant their potatoes. A few yards treated in this way constitute a kitchen-garden; a quarter-acre is a farm! Potatoes, fish and bread are the islanders' main food. There is no other produce, except a few cattle, kept in artificially grassed pounds surrounded by stone walls. A man will, maybe, sell one yearling at Galway Market in a year, and that will pay his rent and rates. An old man is rich if he draws the 10s a week old age pension.

For the big storm-scenes in the picture, we had the services of Big Patcheen Conneely, Pat McDonough and Stephen Dirrane, the three most expert boatmen on the island. They took their frail curraghs – canoes made of tarred skins stretched over a wicker frame – to sea in weather in which you would have thought no boat could live. No man, indeed, but these three, knew the treacherous currents and narrow channels sufficiently to survive the storms they braved, and even so, the three canoemen went in peril of their lives for my storm-scenes.

These are terrible seas. They have snatched men from the very cliff-tops and dashed them to death on the rocks below. They have pounded the cottages themselves and laid them in ruins. One day we were shooting Maggie from above, as she gathered seaweed on a ledge fifty feet above the water. The sea was quite calm yet suddenly a great lazy swell loafed in from the ocean, and burst in a spatter of stones and spray which reached Maggie's ledge, and threw her down, bruised and battered, on the rock's edge. And I was told stories of how eight men in one family were 'taken by the sea' in one winter, and of curraghs, coming from Galway, reaching the island only to be driven by the furious waves clear back to Galway City again.

We spent nearly two years on the island, making our Gainsborough Picture, and the party was sad enough when we finally left. You cannot live two years with fine folk like the Aran Islanders without growing to love and know them, and we had worked with them, played with them in the evenings at billiards, at dancing; we had sat at their hearthsides, drinking potheen and telling tales. Great times we had had, and the women were weeping when we went down to the sea to go away back to England.

Later, nine of my Aran Island friends came to London. They had never been to England before; and, though they moved among wonders, they were calm and philosophical about it all. 'London's a great place,' they said, 'but not for us. We must go back to our Island.'

And I hope that when you see *Man of Aran* and recognize the thrill of the islanders' age-long battle with the rock, the sea and the storm, you will understand why.

From a press release.

Carrying seaweed for kelp

Sean O'Faolain

1939

JOHN WHELAN (1900–1991) was born in Cork and adopted the Irish version of his name soon after the 1916 Easter Rising. He was educated at Presentation College, Cork, at University College Cork and at Harvard. He taught in the United States for several years until he married fellow Corkonian Eileen Gould, and returned to Ireland. His *Midsummer Night Magic*, a collection of short stories, established him as a master of the genre. From 1940 to 1946 he edited the literary journal *The Bell*. In addition to short stories and novels, O'Faolain has written biographies on Daniel O'Connell and Constance Markiewicz.

*A*s you enter Denver, Colorado, you are met by an enormous scroll across the roadway which quotes Teddy Roosevelt as saying that the drive to Pike's Peak 'bankrupts the English language.' I feel that way about Galway. I must therefore compound, as Henry VIII did with his debts, by paying out light metal – a million words to the pound. What I really feel like doing is a wild dumb-show. I would model Galway's ruins, carve its arches, stir up its macaronic smells, which are chiefly porter, seaweed, and turf, spread out its grey sea, burrow its alleys, shake up its bones – and then scrape the dough off my fingers . . . in despair.

Galway is the most foreign town in Ireland – probably in Great Britain and Ireland: meaning thereby that it is barbarically native. It has no veneer, unless rust is a veneer, or the soot-skin of smoke, or the cake of sea-spray, or the common dirt of old age, stuck into every crevice like the years into an old man's skin. Neither sun, nor paint, nor chromium can alter Galway, or brighten it. Infinite variety cannot stale its custom. Like an old beauty under the enamel, the more she daubs the rouge the more does the antique face impress its power.

Galway is unpretendingly what it is, and (I feel) always wanted to be – a rank country town spreading out and out, hither and thither like spilt drink. The Normans founded it as a city – the famous Tribes of Galway reveal their origin in their names, D'Arcy, Blake, Joyce, Lynch, Skerret, Brown, Morris, Kirwan and so on. But after it had swaggered for its time like any Spanish don, imported its Spanish wines, built its square castles, sent out its ships, suffered its sieges, it soon relapsed into that Irish life-mode which has always been antipathetic to city-life, and decayed comfortably. It is now a precipitate of the hinterland of Connaught. If you ask any Galwayman to-day what the typical names are he will not reel off the tribes. Rather he will name the overlaying overlords – O'Flaherty, Flattery (a corruption), Laffey, Hines (supposed to be of the clan O'Heidhin which boasts descent from Con of the Hundred Battles), Lydon (said to be from Dutch Leyden), Lynskey, MacDonagh, and so forth. Galway has gone back to the bog. It is like that hinterland which feeds it. Is is dark, and weathered, and dusky. It is hell-raked by the wind at every corner (and comforted by pubs). It is sour, sweet and smelly as an empty barrel. It is a ship's bell on a wintry night – sonorous, vacant, moody. It is a Connemara pony out on grass, indifferent, wild-spirited, uncontrollable, shaggy. It is everything that rebels against the constriction of urbanization.

Compare it with a city like Kilkenny, a place which takes itself seriously – frugal, self-preserving, close, idealistic. But, then, that is a place with a county life behind it which bears as much likeness to County Galway as a cathedral close to a jungle. Compare it with Cork which has not one half of Galway's raciness, and has ten times its snobbery. Compare it with Limerick. Limerick regards Galway as early Christians must have regarded Nero. So, Galway continues to flourish – its population rose from 14,000 to 18,000 in the last ten years – and remains insistently rustic. Look at its Town Hall!

How near it is to the wild west, guess from the story of the sentry. He was a lad from Lettermullen, or somewhere like that – a place where they inflict bodily injury either with knives or lumps of rock. He saw a shadow moving towards him and cried, 'Halt!' The man ignored him and came on. 'Halt will you?' roared the boy from Lettermullen. The stranger still came on. 'Jaysus' moaned the sentry. 'But if I had a lump of rock I'd damn soon halt you!'

That story is Galway humour: derisive. I have a good friend in Galway, a Corkman, who, like all Corkmen, cannot sit still. From morning to night he is running and racing like a hare, involved in all sorts of schemes from Sport to Drama. The Galway people cannot understand him. Their natural reaction is to sit on the fence and jeer. They call him Lightning. A building-contractor became a father. 'Congratulations, Michael!' said a colleague warmly. And, then, over his shoulder, as he passed one, 'First contract the family ever delivered on time.' A would-be wit said to a man whose wife had never given him an heir, and patently never would, 'Congratulations, James!' James, inured to Galway 'wit,' said nothing, but smiled his thanks. The wit, not to be foiled, said, 'Whom do you suspect, James?' (Did I say Galway town had no veneer?)

I say town, because I know that nothing will ever make Galway anything but that. That is one third of its charm. You may sit in Williamsgate and have morning coffee, and see the clock opposite you permanently stopped; and if that is not one of Life's worst disadvantages removed, I do not want to hear of a worse. You may have a four-course lunch or a six-course dinner, if so minded, since the trans-Atlantic liners support a hotel otherwise comically, extragavantly, fantastically dispro-portionate. There is a University College whose roll is now larger than that of Cork University College, and whose professors have (with not more than a dishonourable exception or two) avoided producing any work of sufficient importance to bore anybody. There are two cinemas, more restaurants than Limerick, a Gaelic theatre which produces English plays, such as *Charley's Aunt* and *Journey's End*, a bookshop (where I could buy none of my own books), a port which must have cost half a million and chiefly gives shelter to hookers from Aran. It has more industries than one may wish to read about – the latest and most interesting being a hat factory, christened in French, *Les Modes Modernes*, and largely run by Austrians. It has the library which banned Shaw; indeed decided to burn all such objectionable books. It has a bus-service which runs one route. It is the only city I know which has raised a statue to an author – a charming little statue by the way – and none to a politician. That must be unique in Ireland. It has three newspapers, one hundred and three pubs, and one public lavatory. It has no museum, no art-gallery, no night-life, (unless you happen to know the password), no noise, no neon-lights, no Woolworth's, no salons, no highbrows, and no subways – but all the most interesting life is lived underground.

That is the second thing of importance about Galway. Like Gruyère it is burrowed, even as it smells like Gorgonzola. When a Galway man tells you a bit of gossip he hunches his shoulders, and makes eyes like a fish – both being the natural effects of long-life in a submarine. (With veracious wit a Corkman, whom I met in Galway this year, spoke of the local speak-easies as Davis Escape Chambers). Truly I never met such a place for scandalous gossip. If I were to believe a third of the stories I have heard there from time to time the whole of Galway leads a Jekyll and Hyde life. Hearing these yarns I thought that I would give five years of my life for a microphone to a Saturday-night confession-box at St. Nicholas' or St. Augustine's. Only – could I possibly believe them?

No man who wants his daughter to learn the truth about life could do better than send her for six months to Galway. With the relief of the actor whipping off a wig, they tell you story after story, in gushing delight at the vagaries of human nature, against their fellow-citizens: and it is all a taking aside of a mask accepted otherwise (that is to say for all public purposes) by all of them as human skin. Do not say –'Are the stories true?' Is any Irishman's story true? Always they are true, one feels, at bottom – somewhere down there among the fish, the skeletons, the pearls, the mermaids, the staved-in chests – stories that in this upper rarefied air of common-life have to be heightened to reproduce the effect of glaucous brilliance in the caverns where they were born. Yet, I think my daughter might well return from Galway and say to me, in an awed voice, 'My father, *is* that the truth?' I should have to say, 'My child, of course, it is not the truth. But it is life!' Galway is and lives a folk-tale.

This, from the point of view of the traveller is admirable, but from my point of view has one grave disadvantage. The best stories are those which might be indiscreet to repeat. It is one of the heartbreaking things about any Irish journey that the most racy aspects of Irish life had to become, always, the property of the folk-lorist; for these local stories go from mouth to mouth, gathering accretions as they go, rounding, swelling into veritable works of art, never to be recorded except out of the side of the mouth – with the eyes of the recorder glancing conspiratorially to his left as he releases his narrative joyously to his right. Visitors to Ireland rejoice in this, while they are with us, but they relapse into a painful scepticism when they leave us, and declare solemnly that nobody can believe an Irishman. We do not believe ourselves; not in the literal sense; we have no desire to; if we were all permitted to speak and print the common truth, there would be an end of this art of the folk-tale. Of Galway, then, I can only say, 'Go, and listen!' There the *shanachie* spits without rest. The bard is ever on the strum. Every living man is gasping to reveal to you a dead

The cover of
W.B. Yeats'
The Tower

secret. And should, in the murk of the wine-tavern, the Latona of all these oracles, some rustic Pythia speak in ambiguous, metaphorical, catalectic, hypermetrical, and generally macaronic hexameters, do not, as they of Delphos did, scorn the high-priest and declare that you cannot understand!' He probably doesn't understand himself! Why, if I got a penny for all the stories I have listened to, all stuttered with laughter, emphasized with glares, and nods, and nudges, and winks, but of which I admit that I finally understood not more than one-twentieth part . . .

I had one such night with a group of men in my hotel. They began by complaining bitterly that the screw was being turned on the local public-houses and that the Davis Escape Chambers, as my friend described the pubs which evade the licensing laws, were becoming fewer and fewer. Later in the night I was introduced to one of them. They led me down devious back, and black streets, until, suddenly halted and pressed into a doorway, I was savagely whispered at to keep quiet. We looked up and down the dark street. One of our number said, 'Hist!' Another found a secret bell-push, and pressed three times. It was as mysterious as the lanes of Paris. With a flutter no louder than a mouse somebody opened the door and we slipped into the darkness. Then when we were all in the black hall, Hey presto! – a curtain was drawn, and behold, there was revelry and brilliant lights and a goodly company of Galway's Public Enemies, as one might say, the King's Friends. Under the mellowing influence of John Jameson's Twelve Years in the Wood (like the Labour Party) I wondered how anybody, priest or policeman, could ever wish to curb such harmless joyousness.

I said so to a cheerful man with a Belfast accent, and he assured me, on his word of honour, as an Irishman, and a former teetotaller, and a Republican, and a lover of Galway, and a Knight of Columbanus, that the Church and the Law in Ireland, unlike the Church and the Law of Ireland, knows well that all these public pronouncements about temperance and so on and so forth are just so much eyewash: that everybody knows that there isn't a priest in Ireland but loves his drop as much as any layman; that he, actually, and as a matter of fact, and without exaggeration, and he saw it with his own two eyes, and it was no lie, knew a bishop, for a bet, to drink a pint of black velvet in Josie Mongan's hotel in Carna behind there in the back room 'the one behind the hall, do you know, in wan bloody draught!'

'I went up to him,' concluded this bard, 'and I shook him by the hand and I said, "My Lord," says I "It's epic!" He was as pleased as punch.'

The bard annotated his story by explaining that the reason the Church is not hard on drink is that it knows there is only one commandment to be taken seriously, and that is the sixth. But when I said, 'What about the ninth?' my friend grew haughty. He said that I should know that this was a Catholic country. And he hoped that we in Ireland know where to draw the line? I tried to appease him by telling the story of the curate I once met in the train to London, and asked what he was proposing to do there. For a moment my bard seemed to think I was about to tell an improper story. He thawed when I gave him the curate's answer.

'I come,' the little curate had said cheerfully, 'from a parish in the bogs, and I'm going to fill my lungs with enough petrol to last the winter in Tuam!'

From that the night grew warm with a discussion as to the morality of the I.R.A. during the fight for freedom.

'They left a thrail of schaming behind them, so they did,' said an elder. (What 'schaming' meant I could only guess).

'On the contrary,' said a young man who had been in the I.R.A., 'what was wrong with the I.R.A. it made all promotions depend on piety! A Holy Bloody War, that's what they made of it. A Holy Bloody War! Like O'Duffy's Angels of Monstarevan. Fightin' for Christ in Spain. And bringing back old Spanish customs with 'em to prove it!'

Cushlanakirk

At this a man who had fought with O'Duffy's Irish Brigade ('It was no nearer a Brigade than a Fire Brigade!' taunted the I.R.A. man) declared he had never heard Christ mentioned in Spain except as a swear-word. The I.R.A. man, now tactfully but maliciously pressed to prove his point about promotions and piety in the I.R.A. entered into a record of his own foiled amours, with such growing wrath in the recollection that he failed to observe the delight of the company. Thereby we entered obliquely into the inevitable political argument – this time as to whether we were better off or not under the British regime; and thereby the night went by in innocent fury of emotionalism, and the Davis Escape Chamber did its useful work.

By the way the favorite Galway drink is a Patent, i.e. half a pint of porter and a bottle of Guinness in it. In Cork this is called a Predom. I have also heard it called a System, and a Half-in-Half.

The two typical characters I offer for Galway are Padraic O'Conaire, the novelist, whose statue peeps at you elfishly through Browne's arch at the top of Eyre Square, and Martin MacDonagh, the local capitalist. Padraic was an original. He was born in Galway, learned Irish in Rosmuck, went to the Civil Service in London, left in 1917 to evade conscription, and came to Ireland; there he began to write his stories, in Gaelic, and wandered all over the west with a little ass and cart. Drink was his chief, but not only, weakness. He had the makings of a genius in him. He was the first Gaelic writer who knew his Maupassant and the only one in the European literary tradition. Towards the end of his days the poor little man fell into the clutches of respectability, and it was sad to see him – so low had he fallen – refuse a drink. Happily, he recovered in time, and died a vagabond. I take my hat off to Galway for putting up that statue to Padraic. Only one other town that I know in Ireland did as much for a writer – Doneraile, in County Cork; the writer there, at a very far remove from Padraic O'Conaire, being Canon Patrick Sheehan.

Martin MacDonagh is an equally polar contrast: the son of a poor man who got a foothold in business and left Martin with a chance to make good. Martin did so well that before he passed on he had become a T.D., was chairman of various local councils, owned a saw-mill, a fishing-fleet, a flour-mill, a chemical-works, thriving shops, more or less owned the Galway Steam-Shipping Company, was a Director of the Gas Company, a coal-importer, kept a stud of racehorses, had his own electric power years before the Shannon scheme, owned house-property, including the old Claddagh, and lived on Corrib Island. The business still flourishes, run by a son who rejoices in the name of The Trout.

The small, or big town, magnates have tremendous influence, and can do a great deal to build up the life of the countryside. William of Tullamore, MacDonagh of Galway, Mongan of Carna, Dillon of Ballaghadereen, Gallacher of Strabane, Lyons of Sligo, Vickery of Bantry, MacEllin of Balla, the Bourkes of Castlebar, J.J. O'Malley of Westport, the Brennans of Bandon, Governey of Carlow, so on and so on – these are the men who now have Ireland in their hands, from whom leadership may be expected, who can raise standards in politics, culture and social manners, and impress them on Ireland for the next hundred years – if they so will.

Some people hate that the old Claddagh fishing village in Galway has gone – that hamlet inside a city, which snuggled down so flat-bellied on the beach from which it took its name. It was, indeed, a lovely haphazard collection of thatched cottages, which had all the natural beauty of the Irish lime-washed cottage – grace of moulding, soft sensuous waves of bellying lime to catch the sun – no mortar, three inches of lime laid on the stone–crafty skill in the thatching, lovely iridescent colours in the wall, matt colour on the roof of straw, an almost inevitable beauty of proportion inside. But, oh! – how inadequate for our large Irish families, and if inevitably lovely so inevitably verminous, and a consolidation of low standards of living; so that I have never met anybody who regretted the loss of the Claddagh who would have willingly lived there. Its loss is symbolic. The picturesque Ireland will likewise vanish bit by bit, but, like Galway city its real character will not alter. Those business-men who have already begun to replace the influence of the Big House may or may not be men of culture, or of creative power socially. They are the natural growth. We must accept them as the material of the final structure just as we do the rise of the new Claddagh.

The great time to visit Galway is in the week prior to August Bank Holiday – for the Galway Races on Wednesday and Thursday. It is a ritual to go from there to the Limerick Junction races, thence to the Dublin Horse Show, and thence back to the country for shooting and fishing. Galway and the west are so well known to sportsmen that there is no need to do more than mention the Galway Blazers, or the East Galways, and for the rest remember that the cheapest fishing in the world is to be had in Connemara – free almost everywhere. The town itself supports over a score of Soccer, Rugby, Gaelic football, and Hurley Clubs. In summer there is tennis, boating, swimming, handball, and as for the winter I warn the chance visitor that he had better take lessons before playing cards within twenty miles of Galway city.

From *An Irish Journey*

Ethel Mannin

1940

ETHEL MANNIN (1900–1984) was born in London to a family with roots in the West of Ireland. She started her writing career as an advertising copywriter and went on to write almost 100 books. In January 1940, she bought a small cottage near Mannin Bay in Connemara but had to leave within months due to her mother's illness. She did not return to Ireland again until the end of the Second World War. After the death of her second husband in 1958, Mannin travelled in Africa, Asia and Russia and wrote books about her journeys. She was a close friend of W.B. Yeats and her *Connemara Journal* was dedicated to Maud Gonne MacBride.

On a sunny morning in April, 1940, I closed the shutters of a three-roomed whitewashed cabin in Connemara, and at the garden gate waved good-bye to Patrick who was making what he called 'a little road' across the rough, uneven stretch of grass to the pine wood. I had an

The blessing of the Claddagh fleet

English ambition to make that bouldery, boggy bit of ground into a garden. I did not, then, understand why the local people just scythed the grass in the summer (or turned the cows loose and left it to them), put in, perhaps, a clump or two of pampas grass for decoration, and let it go at that. It puzzled me that they called any rough bit of field with a few furze bushes in it a 'garden' – even when it was not attached to any house; just as they called any stretch of rock-strewn rising ground 'mountain.' 'Mountain' for me meant something at least three thousand feet high; I would not even call the Twelve Pins mountains. 'Garden' for me meant flower-beds and roses and herbaceous borders. At the very edge of the sea, out at Mannin Bay some five miles away, an English friend, in the course of years, had made a most wonderful garden; it is true that she had erected screens of thin plaited wood against the Atlantic gales, and that she had two gardeners – whereas I had only Patrick whose services were erratic. (When he would bring the milk in the morning, at about eleven, after the milking, I would enquire, 'Are you going to work for me today, Patrick?' He would push his ragged cap to the back of his head and look wildly round as though rocks and stones and grass would give him the Yea or Nay, and he would answer, 'Ah, I don't know, ma'am, I'm sure!' Sometimes he would and sometimes he wouldn't). Nevertheless, I sent to Dublin for rose-bushes and hydrangeas, and Patrick brought a wheelbarrow load of manure from his place higher up the boreen, and we put the bushes and shrubs in. We dug a few flower-beds and a friend from here and there gave me a plant or two. The friend at Mannin Bay gave some slips of white fuchsia. Patrick brought from his place some fearsome-looking plants with great leaves like the blades of swords and we planted them along the stream where the land drained down. An Englishman came and looked at the place and waved an arm over the wet slope and urged me to 'pack it with rhododendrons.' I smiled and made no comment, for rhododendrons are a guinea a piece and more, and this Englishman and I had different values, different standards. (He told me once that on the housekeeper's night out, when one was left to fend for oneself, there was nothing nicer than half a bottle of champagne and a small pot of caviar; one could manage very well on that, he assured me, and recommended it) . . .

It was January when Patrick and I began to make the garden. We dug up quantities of daffodil and narcissus bulbs from the grounds of a big old house falling into ruins nearby. The gardens there are terraced, and their beauty, when the house was inhabited, has become a legend in these parts. Now the sheep and cattle graze on the grass-grown terraces, and the ground-floor rooms of the house itself are filled with hay and serve as barns. The lady of quality who made those gardens even had daffodils planted out on the tiny island in the lake at the foot of her demesne. This cottage also overlooks that lake, where it flows out to the Atlantic. At the other side of it the 'mountain' rises up in a long low stony ridge, bare and brown, you would think there was no grass at all on the mountain, yet the small black local cattle graze there and thrive – though they are later sent up to the midlands for fattening.

Sand and fine shingle were brought in a donkeycart from the sea shore to make a 'drive' up to the front door – the previous tenant, it seems, years ago, had been content to pick a muddy way over the grass. I collected stones from the wilderness and set them at either side of this broad sandy path and white washed them, and Patrick and I white washed the house itself, and distempered it yellow within, and I painted the front door a bright blue, and a girl from the town inquired, 'Are you going to leave it that colour?' . . . I painted the gates of the drive green, in a howling bitter wind, and Patrick's mother hobbled down the boreen and came into the house and tapped at everything with her stick, and roared with laughter because the dresser was so small – though it seemed a normal size to me – and was filled with wonder at the settee which converts into a bed, exclaiming at the wonder of it, and that there wouldn't be the like of it anyway in these parts . . .

'We all thought ye'd be different,' said Patrick's mother.

'How different?' I inquired, puzzled. They all knew I was the mad English writer who had taken a cottage in the wilds of Connemara, was known to have had two husbands and was reputed, God help me, to have had nine. (Why nine, I have always wondered. It seems such an insult to one's intelligence, somehow).

'We thought ye'd be more grand – more of a grand lady,' she explained. 'But here ye are workin' with Patrick like a common workman!' She nudged me in the ribs, and smiled. 'Ah, but I like ye for it!' she added. I thought I had never received a compliment I liked more.

The daffodils flourished; I cut bunches of them and put them about on window-sills in jugs, and the house 'came to itself,' as they say here after standing empty, and the worse for it, for years. Patrick hacked back trees and shrubs to expose the view of lake and mountain, and people who had passed up and down the boreen without being aware of the house suddenly saw it, quite startlingly white, and 'outlandish' with its bright blue front door, and it became the talk of the place, so that people strolled out from the town two miles or so away on Sunday evenings – there is no afternoon here; after mid-day it is 'evening'– to look at the strange new sight.

I began work on a book, *Christianity or Chaos*: a Re-statement of Religion. I worked on it at nights, despite the physical exhaustion of the manual labour of the day, and wrote several chapters. The spirit of Catholic Ireland blew with the smoke of turf fires across the pages. In months of solitude in that lonely Connemara cottage I discovered, in a kind of slow spiritual revelation, how God could be, for a devout Catholic people, 'nearer than the door.'

That year the palm and shamrock met – that is to say St. Patrick's Day fell on Palm Sunday, and it has been said that when that happens that year Ireland would become a unity of thirty-two counties; unfortunately the superstition was given the lie.

When I left in April it was suddenly, in response to a telegram of family bad news. I expected to be back quite soon. I was so confident that it would be merely a matter of weeks, months at most, that I left a silk dressing-gown hanging on a peg, a rubber hot-water bottle on a hook. That was April 1940. I tried every year, but did not get back till

November, 1945. Other English people got back, came and went, but they had business of 'national importance,' whereas I had none, and was not prepared to contrive any . . .

I left everything, but I mention the dressing-gown and hot-water bottle specifically because they are symbolic of changing values, changing standards. The dressing-gown was then just an old thing, good enough to slip on in the mornings for bringing in the turf; as to the hot-water bottle there were plenty more where that one came from . . . So little did we dream in the spring of 1940 of the shape of things to come. Five and a half years later I took the dressing-gown down from its rusty peg and gazed at it almost in awe – for I had nothing back in England as good now, nor even given the coupons could I buy anything as good, for this is silk – real silk, not rayon; this was acquired before the synthetic became a necessary cult. How little, in those far-off days, did we value the things which, because they were so abundant, we so easily acquired! And how could we dream that the time would come when to procure a rubber hot-water bottle it would first be necessary to get a doctor's certificate, and that even then it would take months? Eagerly in November 1945 I seized upon the hot-water bottle, but of course it had perished long ago . . . like the tins of good soup, sweet corn, spaghetti, in the dresser cupboard.

And Patrick's little road is no more, the grass and weeds have long ago grown over it; and Patrick himself is no more, but lies under the grass in the little churchyard beside the lake. And the trees he cut back have grown up again and obscured the view, and the roses failed, whether from lack of attention, poorness of soil, or the Atlantic gales, who shall say; from all three most probably. Only the morello cherry which Patrick planted on the north wall after I had gone seems to like its bleak position, and the sword-blade plants have grown to a jungle hugeness and are more ferocious-looking than ever, and there is some enormous jungly-looking stuff like an overgrown rhubarb; and the fuchsia slips have become flourishing bushes.

It is all a garden still in the Connemara sense, for the grass has been kept down and the wild rhododendrons beside the drive cut back, and clumps of cotoneaster near the house trimmed to a round shape, but it is no longer even the beginnings of a garden in the English sense. Today it has rained very heavily, and the rosebeds are full of water deep enough for ducks to swim in; the ground is completely water-logged and can soak up no more, and the water lies on the shingly drive. It is clear that in the summer the red-hot pokers made a brave show, but there is no evidence of any other flower, though there is gorse in bloom, and there is still fuchsia in flower – white, from the lovely garden out at Mannin Bay, (but the friend who made it lives there no more, nor even in this country) and

Going to Market

the common red. There are a few faded hydrangeas – rather beautifully and decoratively faded, and there are a great many bulrushes . . .

It is strange and confusing coming back to a place one has only lived in for a few months after five-and-a-half years. Many things, like kettles and oil-cans, have rusted into disuse, and what the rust did not get the moth did. A house un-lived-in for a long time gets a kind of sickness, like an unloved person. It needs warmth and care to bring it to itself again. The unrelieved damp has caused distemper to flake, paint to crack. In the little entrance-hall – the 'porch' they call it here – there is actually green moss on the walls. There are bad patches where the plaster has come away in slabs. With more intelligent care-taking – windows opened regularly – it need not have been so bad; on the other hand it could have been worse perhaps. Five and a half years is a long time. One is both disheartened and relieved; part of oneself could weep with sheer exasperation, disappointment in human nature, undefined depression – that vague *je ne sais quoi* which has to do with a sense of futility and disillusion – whilst another part of oneself says what-the-hell, and what-did-you-expect-quoth-she . . . There is this confused reaction, this conflict of feeling. The big moments invariably elude one; they burn themselves out before realization, in a too intense anticipation. For the really big moments and hours there is no anticipation; they are fire from on high and burn themselves directly into us.

From *Connemara Journal*

Oliver St. John Gogarty

1949

OLIVER ST. JOHN GOGARTY (1878–1957), a friend of James Joyce, was the inspiration for 'stately plump Buck Mulligan' in *Ulysses*. Born in Dublin, he was educated at Clongowes Wood College, Trinity College Dublin and Oxford University. He built up a large medical practice and a reputation as a sometimes controversial wit. His Free State sympathies caused him to be captured by the Republicans during the Civil War but he escaped by swimming the Liffey. He presented two swans to the river in gratitude. His house in Renvyle, Connemara, was burnt down during the Civil War, but he rebuilt it as a hotel, with Edward Lutyens as architect. After losing a libel suit Gogarty moved to England and then, in 1939, to New York.

*W*hy should anyone want to go farther than Galway? Why indeed? Galway is the gossip capital of Ireland. It is not without significance that the statue in its principal square should be that of a shanachie or story-teller. The citizens know (sometimes beforehand) what is happening in every county, and lack of information neither limits nor diminishes the tale. Therefore it came as no surprise to me to hear that I was welcome until I realized that that was but a figure of speech, an exordium indispensable to conversation.

You do not altogether leave Dublin by crossing the island to its western side, but you leave a great deal of bitterness and acrimony behind. Personalities take the place of politics in Galway. The first citizen of Galway was Morty Mor – Big Martin – who died a little while ago. Never did the Gaelic language record a death more majestically in three fateful words,

Morty Mor Morb

It had the language of Rome behind it, in which each word can fall like a stroke of fate. It is not as unbecoming as it would seem to talk of a dead man in a town where there are so many living persons about, because in

Galway, as in China, the dead are more important than the living, so that a friendly reminiscence is enough to recall them from oblivion.

Morty Mor McDonough was big-headed and very tall. He dressed in black, for, since clergymen wear it, black commands respect; and as the greatest employer in the town, respect was his due. His character was as great as his power; he could talk up to the other men in black, and there was no cowing him. His rheumy eyes gazed slowly at you as he made up his mind. He was loyal to Galway town, the City of the Tribes, so loyal that he resented the visit of two missioners from Meath who came to collect for what they called the Maynooth Mission to China. They were astonished to find themselves refused. Conscious of power, they became insistent and brusque. Morty Mor spoke.

'I will not subscribe to a Maynooth Mission to China; but *I will subscribe* to a Chinese Mission to Maynooth to teach you manners.'

It was a new conception: a Chinese Mission to the great theological college of Maynooth or anywhere at all! The Chinese do not send missions to proselytise 'foreign devils.' That is why it came as an original suggestion from Morty Mor. Suppose that the suggestion were to be adopted. How wonderful it would be if a sampan from China were to berth in the Liffey and its cargo of bonzes to come ashore and to proceed in a barge up the quiet waters of the Royal Canal to Maynooth! If they were not first subjected to a reception by the President and an urine analysis, their progress would be one serene procession in their reconditioned barge or houseboat. With what dignity would they acknowledge the salutations of the aborigines who would wave them on with cheers of encouragement on their unprecedented journey. With what gravity would they await, with hands hidden in their robes, the inrush of water that would raise them up to higher levels in the locks until, at last, the mule, garlanded and with harness decorated, would draw them westward through the long reach to the wall of Maynooth. How they would admire that wall, impassively comparing it with the wall of the Forbidden City that held the Old Buddha before the rising of the Boxers undid her. And then the reception in the *aula maxima* in Maynooth: yellow and purple; bonze, bishop and acolytes in one glory of double imperial dyes; the Imperial yellow of the Middle Empire and the purple of Imperial Rome!

Those introductions: 'T'as Yuan Ming from the Temple of the Haunted Dragon by the Peak of the Celestial Pool meet Dr. Cod, Bishop of Ferns.' 'Ma Tu Fang from the Pavilion of Shining Truth by the River of White Jade – Dr. Scanlan.' (Afar off, voices singing, 'Hurry to bless the hands that play.')

It was so convincing, albeit a vision, that I began to detect a Chinese influence in the deportment of the Galway divines: a sedateness and weight, an *embonpoint* and amplitude, that endowed them with a ceremonious courtesy that had something in it of the Middle Kingdom.

I did not come to Galway to dream of China; and far be it from me to teach manners or anything else. I will turn my face to the South when the time comes, comforted by the thought that I never had a pupil.

What a town Galway is, beside its rippling, abundant river, swan-laden, salmon-full! The Corrib must be one of the largest rivers in the world for its length, which cannot be more than a mile or two. It used to turn many a mill. Its canalised waterways are there to-day, green-haired with weeds and overgrown; but as crystal clear as when they first rushed to the sea from Lough Corrib and Lough Mask.

If the mayor had any taste he would cut the weeds from the river-banks and let even wild roses, that ask for no gardener, take their place; and he would strictly forbid plastering with cement the faces of houses that owe their proportions to the influence of Spain, houses of cut stone that had large, oblong windows centuries before England emerged from half-timbered, casement-lit cottages. The few remains of historical houses owe their preservation to a priest who cherished history in stone. Now the stones are painted over and any travelling circus can hire Eyre Square.

All my wishes are fulfilled; but if I had one more wish it would be that I might be mayor of Galway even for one year – Galway, a cleaner Venice, with living water in place of the brackish, stagnant canals! The men who built those Galway houses with gardens giving on the mill-races felt the beauty that water has and its power to inspire. The sides of the mill-races now are filled with whatever rubbish lies out of reach of the stream. You need not be a landscape-gardener to see what a town of enchantment Galway could be made were its many water-courses to be lined with lilac, laburnum, woodbine and hawthorn; especially hawthorn, which is exempt from vandalism because it is unlucky to bring it into a house. These bushes would cost nothing or next to nothing to plant; and they would have a double bloom in the long Spring, a bloom above and a bloom reflected. The streets are clean; why should the banks of the clear streams be left as witnesses to the tolerance for ruin which seems to lie in the character of the Irish nowadays?

What has obsessed the Irishman with thanatophilia – this love of death, decadence and decay? The toleration of eyesores is its outward sign. Even the farmer, when he has prospered and moves to a larger house, leaves the old sheiling to rot and deface the landscape with its gable angles rising against the sky.

Spanish Arch must have been the sea-gate of Galway town. It abuts the river. Beyond it lies nothing but a few nondescript cottages and the

The Chancel Arch at Tuam Cathedral

empty dock. Its watch-tower is half gone, but the arch and one closed-up beside it are still strong.

So Clare Sheridan, the sculptor, has bought the arch and the houses next to it. She plans to have a hanging garden on the top of the arch overlooking the rushing water. Her niece, Shane Leslie's only daughter, Anita, is restoring, not far away, the strong castle of Oranmore, the fortress that guarded the approach by 'the Great Shore' to Galway from the south.

This is not the first of the old XIVth-century castles to rescued from utter dilapidation in Galway. Yeats restored the castle at Ballylee close to Coole Park. He called the keep Thor Ballylee, because he thought that 'castle' was somewhat ostentatious, although every large dwelling of stone built in Ireland before Cromwell came with his bible and his Black and Tans was called a castle.

Yeats was well aware of this toleration of ruin in the heart of the native. He knew that they would preserve nothing if left to themselves. He knew that out of their perpetual preoccupation with the past came a desire to make all grandeur portion and parcel of that Past. Therefore he composed the lines to be engraved on a stone of the door of his tower, praying,

May these characters remain
When all is ruin once again.

So why all this pother about ornamenting a town? The answer is obvious. In it lies the difference between beauty and ugliness, between grandeur and meanness, between cleanliness and dirt. A beautiful place engenders sentiments of pride and affection in the hearts of those who inhabit it. This gives rise to stability and to patriotism. Conversely, they who dwell in squalor, deprived of beauty, have nothing in their souls but a reflex of that squalor, discontent and hatred for all things lovely and pleasant. In this tragedy lies, and the road to rebellion until Squalor sits enthroned: all this in Ireland, the wealthiest country in the world.

Into Oranmore Castle builders are bringing baths and basins and hot and cold water. Electric power and light are already laid on. Great cisterns collect water from the slightly domed roof. Walls are being plastered and panelled. Even the dungeon or prison on the third floor which took a small boy weeks to clear of rubbish, in which a baby's skeleton was found, is being repaired.

Maybe this and other restorations are the result of the scarcity of houses. Whatever be the cause, it is something to be grateful for that people of taste are giving an example of what can be done in a town that has the enviable endowment of ancient walls and waters running beneath them – everything for its inhabitants but the eye to see.

I took tea with some friends. I soon discovered that there was much that I had missed in Galway. Apparently I had been thinking only of its natural advantages that could make it one of the loveliest towns on earth. Little did I realise that already it was a Cytherea, a shrine where Venus was worshipped. I thought that I knew the history of Galway. I had read Hardiman and studied the report of the Commissioners who were appointed to preserve its archives. But the enactments touching Venus only referred to fines for those citizens who permitted their houses to become houses of assignation for friars. It was all so long ago that I discounted it as accurate history. But though the friars who dealt in such real estate were long dead, from what I was now told I judged that the reign of an obscure Venus was flourishing still. At last I exclaimed:

'But if such things go on, how does society hold together in the daytime?'

I did not intend to expostulate or to appear incredulous. I merely wondered how such things could be kept clandestine in such a small town. I had often wondered how Anne Boleyn, Shakespeare, Mistress Fitton, Kit Marlowe, Ben and the rest of the boys 'got away with it,' so to speak, where the houses were half-timbered and everyone knew the neighbour's business. The answer was now apparent: they didn't get away with anything. There were always intelligent observers about. So the beauty that I longed to see by the canals and river is hidden in the boudoirs of the town. It was a consolation in a way, but a way that was questionable.

While I was occupied with such thoughts as these, my hostess asked:

'Did I hear about the retreat for women?'

The Cathedral of Clonfert

And I had been thinking that, by her account, their bedrooms were their retreats. But I was wrong! 'Retreat,' in the sense in which the word was used, meant a religious meeting to hear sermons, to examine conscience, and to pray.

'I heard nothing about the Retreat.'

How could I? I was only just arrived.

'Oh, you must hear it. It was advertised for weeks: "*Women only*. On the 4th there will be a retreat for women; and sermons on the Sacrament of Matrimony."'

'Weren't all the men aching with curiosity to find out what the sermons would be like?'

She smiled complacently; then she went on:

'Well the great day, or rather evening, came round at last. Every woman, including Mrs. Dunne, that could get out, was there to hear a Franciscan father preaching. Now, Mrs. Dunne came from the Claddagh, and she had eight children, including ones that she was nursing, so it was no easy matter for her to leave the house. Anyway, she took the baby under her shawl and off with her to the Retreat. She was a bit late when she arrived and the sermon was in full blast. God help me! I shouldn't say that. But you know what I mean. The preacher had got himself worked up.'

The lady laughed so much at this point that my curiosity, inert for the most part about Retreats, was aroused. At last she was able to continue.

'Well, Mrs Dunne got in and found a place by the door. She listened for a minute to the sermon on Holy Matrimony and then said fervently as she turned to go: "I wish to God I knew as little about it as that fellow."'

I thought of the white swans stemming the Corrib and waiting for a word from the Franciscans of comfort to the birds.

With such things to concern them indoors, is it any wonder that there is apathy among the citizens regarding the appearance of their town?

From *Rolling Down the Lea*

Frank O'Connor

1950

FRANK O'CONNOR (1903–1966) was the pen name of Michael O'Donovan. He was born in Cork and educated locally by the Christian Brothers. He worked for the Cork County Library, becoming County Librarian. He adopted his pen name because he was still a civil servant when he started writing. O'Connor's first collection of stories, *Guests of the Nation*, explored the relationships between the English and Irish and established his reputation. In addition to short stories and novels, O'Connor also wrote two volumes of autobiography, *An Only Child* and *My Father's Son*.

The architectural vagaries and delights of Clare continue along the Galway border. In Corcomroe, in the extreme north of Clare, by the coast, is a Cistercian abbey with the tomb of Conor O'Brien. At a place called Drumacoo, across the border, and a little off the main Galway road, is a queer little tenth-century church with a trabeated west door looking like something from an Egyptian temple and an inserted Early Gothic door on the south side which transports you at once to the Cotswolds.

Inland there is the remains of the Celtic monastery of Kilmacduagh: the usual amorphous clutter of cathedral, round tower and ruined chapels which you see all over the country in hundreds of places, but which also has the remains of a striking Transitional chapel at the foot of the field. It is known as 'Hynes' Chapel' and has the usual Transitional coign-shafts, a beautiful deeply splayed east window, and very tall, slender chancel pillars, from which the archstones have dropped. Kilmacduagh is worth a visit if for nothing but its picturesque setting on the hillside with the bushy slopes of Slieve Aughty behind.

Architecturally both Galway and Mayo well repay study. With the election of Giolla Mac Liaigh ('Gelasius') as Primate in place of St. Malachy, Connacht conformed to the Roman obedience, and there are a number of interesting Late Romanesque and Transitional churches. In the beginning of the thirteenth century Cahal O'Connor Redhand, who, like his brother-in-law, Donough O'Brien, seems to have been a man of great taste, built a number of monasteries, all of which are good.

In Tuam, for instance, there was at one time a small, highly decorated Romanesque cathedral, supposed by Petrie to have been built by Turlough O'Connor early in the twelfth century, though the date seems to me impossible. It probably belongs to the last quarter of the century, and is the work of either Rory or Cahal Redhand. The builder who erected the new Gothic cathedral did not like to destroy it entirely, and took in the chancel arch as a west porch. Then a nineteenth-century architect reversed the process and built a horrid church *in front* of the old chancel, restoring it to its original function and leaving the Gothic cathedral as a chapter-house. It must be one of the oddest architectural vagaries in the whole of Western Europe. The chancel arch, and particularly the east window, are very beautiful and most elaborately decorated.

About seven miles out of Tuam, at a place called Knockmoy, is the ruin of a Cistercian abbey, of which a great deal remains and which is very interesting. This was founded by Redhand, we are told, to celebrate his victory over the Normans in 1189, and he is supposed to be buried in the founder's tomb (Curtis' *Mediaeval Ireland* buries him in the Franciscan monastery he founded at Athlone, but, as there were no Franciscans in Ireland during his reign, it is hard to see how he achieved that). There is another monastery at a desolate spot on the edge of the Lake at Annaghdown, which has a decorated window and the remains of a decorated doorway of the Midland type – very Late Romanesque, I fancy.

But the architectural gem of the county is Clonfert cathedral, about nine miles east of Ballinasloe and seven west of Banagher – the devil of a place to get to, but well worth it when you do get there.

It is one of those 'cathedrals' established, not because they were suitable sites for a diocesan see, but because the spot had been sanctified by the cell of some hermit saint. It could be conveniently lost in any respectable English parish church. The doorway, a tall, gabled porch, extravagantly and exquisitely decorated in every conceivable pattern of Romanesque, is twelfth century except for the inner order, which belongs to a fifteenth-century restoration that also added the chancel arch with its delightful and absurd decorations and the little tower which stands on the west front, with no other apparent means of subsistence. The original inner order of decorated chevrons has been built into the wall inside the door. The date of the beautiful east window is disputed, but it seems to me to be thirteenth-century work. It resembles the window in one of the Clonmacnois churches and that in Hynes' Chapel in Kilmacduagh. All are good; everything in this little church is good, but the doorway and east window are of remarkable beauty.

It is one of the peculiarities of literary history that, for no apparent reason, a literary movement will centre round some particular region. In Cork, for instance, you have a group of story-tellers like Dr. Edith Somerville, Elizabeth Bowen, Daniel Corkery and Seán O'Faolain, while in these western counties the Irish dramatic movement produced Lady Gregory and Edward Martyn of Galway, George Moore of Mayo, Yeats of Sligo. Unfortunately, Lady Gregory's house in Coole, the headquarters of the Irish Literary Theatre, was sold by Mr. De Valera's Government to a Galway builder for £500 and torn down for scrap. Merely as a literary museum its value to the nation was almost incalculable; one feels that they should at least have held out for £600.

The old lady was a holy terror; that is the only way I can describe her. On the first evening that I called at Yeats' I also met her. She came into the drawing-room in her mantilla, and, while I warmed to Yeats, she struck cold terror into my heart. In my embarrassment I told the story of

Ruins at Kilmacduagh

an unfortunate Gaelic teacher I knew in Cork, whose only hope of collecting his salary was to put on a concert or a play, and who would have got no salary at all if he produced a play which required the payment of royalties. He produced her *Workhouse Ward* under the title of *Crime and Punishment*, translated from the *original* Russian by Fyodor Dostoievsky. The old lady looked at me bleakly. 'And didn't he know it was wrong?' she asked in her flat, charwoman's voice – a comment which deserves to go down to history with 'We are not amused.'

For the rest of my life I nourished something like an inferiority complex about the old lady until long after Yeats' death. Mrs. Yeats revealed to me that he was as terrified of her as I was. She had always treated him as a talented but naughty child. When at last he married and took his young wife to Coole, he felt the time had come for him to assert his manhood. No animals were permitted in Coole – which, considering what most Irish country houses are like, seems to me to be kindness to Christians – and Yeats was fond of his cat. Now that he was a married man, a mature man, a famous man, he was surely entitled to his cat. So Pangur was duly bundled up and brought to Gort. But as the outside car drove up the avenue of Coole the married, mature, famous man grew panic-stricken at the thought of the old lady's forbidding countenance. He bade the jarvey drive him first to the stables. There Pangur was deposited until, everyone having gone to bed, Yeats crept out in his slippers and brought him up to the bedroom. Yet till the day she died he secretly nursed the hope of being able to treat her as an equal. Nobody who had not been squelched by her could realize the relief with which I heard this.

From *Leinster, Munster & Connacht*

Olivia Manning

1950

BORN IN PORTSMOUTH, England, into a naval family, Olivia Manning (1911–1980) was raised partly in Ireland. After art school she went to London and eked out a living doing menial tasks until her first novel, *The Wind Changes* was published in 1937. Just before the outbreak of the Second World War, Manning married Reginald Donald Smith and moved with him to Bucharest. Her experiences there and later in Egypt and the Middle East were the inspiration for her novels. Manning and Smith moved to Greece and were evacuated to Egypt just two days before the Nazis raised the swastika over the Acropolis.

There could have been no more perfect day for entering Galway – 'the city of Strangers.' The narrow streeets were crowded with people, many of them visitors. Probably Galway is the most visited town in the west, for it has not only its charm of old streets and water-ways but the modern seaside suburb of Salthill, and an ancient harbour from which the little steamship *Dun Aengus* sets out for the Aran Islands that lie across the mouth of the bay.

All the girls were in their summer dresses. While I waited to be served in a haberdashery shop, three country girls were examining the rolls of dress material that had been heaped on the counter for them. The choice at last was between the red and the blue, and the girl who was buying held each piece in turn to her face and gave rise to a great discussion of its merits.

'Now how much would I be needing?' she asked the young, very shy male assistant, forcing him into the excitement of the purchase.

'You'd need mebbe three yards, now – mebbe three and a half.'

'Would that be enough for the New Look?'

Renvyle Castle

'The New Look!' echoed the youth as though that were something sacred and too mysteriously feminine for him. 'I wouldn't know that.'

'Why, haven't you seen the New Look?' squealed the girls, inspired by the warm, bright weather into dreams of dresses of Mediterranean brilliance. When, in a country of endless rain and wind, would the New Look or any other Look get much of a chance? But every heat-wave is eternal until it stops.

The excitement of the girls filled not only the shop but the streets. The pavements were packed. Young men, brown, bearded, dressed like Aran islanders, seemed to be everywhere – handsome and romantic: yachtsmen perhaps, students or artists; and the loveliest girls.

If only the weather would last.

Galway, Irish enough today, was founded by a foreigner. It developed as a foreign city with little part in the mists and legends of the Celtic west. For centuries the main interest of its citizens was commerce. Galway became a thriving port – Port-na-gall, the Harbour of Strangers, or Merchants; the two words mean the same in Gaelic so foreign is commerce to the Irish nature. The strangers became wealthy, built for themselves fine houses in the Spanish style, imported wines and foodstuffs, silks, brocades and furs. To travellers this city must have seemed an oasis of diligence on this remote shore, and it might have survived as such, a rival to Belfast, had the ruling families not chosen to remain faithful to the Church of Rome.

The site of Galway is an ancient one. Some say its name does not derive from *Port-na-gall*, but commemorates Gailleamh, daughter of Breasail, who was drowned in the Corrib in ancient times. Others think it derives from *galmbraith* – a rocky, barren country. Galway Bay is mentioned by Ptolemy and named Ausoba on his map. At one time there was nothing here but a small fishing village like the Claddagh. In 1230 Richard de Burgh conquered the district from the O'Conors and built his Norman fortress round which the city of Galway grew, an isolated outpost of Anglo-Norman enterprise. De Burgh brought over twelve families to develop this promising site: the Welsh families of Athy, Jones (later called Joyce), Martin and Morris; and the Anglo-Norman families of Blake, Bodkin, Browne, D'Arcy, Diane, Ffont, Ffrench, Lynch and Skerrett. These, known as the Twelve Tribes of Galway, were joined in 1488 by a thirteenth – the Kirwans. The name of the de Burgh family in time took on the Gaelic form of Burke and when Richard de Burke took the status of Rí-mor his tenantry became known as Clann Rickard. Thus the earldom of Clanrickarde came into existence.

The Galway tribes took to commerce and grew rich. They had no great love of the English; they held aloof from and distrusted the native Irish; their chief trade was with Spain. At one time the Corporation decreed that the O's and Mac's should not be permitted to swagger in the streets of Galway, and over one of the city's gates were the words: 'From the Ferocious O'Flaherties, Good Lord Deliver Us.'

Sir Henry Sydney, when Lord Deputy of Ireland, was delighted to find among the wild unfriendly Irish, the civilised Galway citizens and described them as 'the most refined and enlightened people to be found anywhere.'

All the tribes had wealth and power but the Lynches seem to have been dominant from the first. The lynx crest, from which the family name derived, can be seen everywhere today on tombs and buildings, and the Lynch mansion, built about 1600, still stands on the main shopping street. In 1485 Percy Lynch was elected first mayor of Galway; he was followed by Dominick Lynch and then in 1493 by the celebrated James Lynch who condemned his own son to death and hanged him when no one else would carry out the sentence. Lynch Law, usually a very different process, has been unjustly named after this example of unbending justice.

The story of James Lynch and his son Walter has the quality of Elizabethan tragedy. The father went in 1492 on a business trip to Cadiz where he was entertained by the wealthy Gomez family. In return for this hospitality he brought back as a guest to his own home a very handsome boy, the young son of Gomez. He promised to return the boy safely on his next trip to Spain. Lynch's son, Walter, was about the same age as the Spanish youth, was equally good looking, and noted in Galway for his high spirits, charm and sweetness of temperament. (Only its ultimate tragedy can have kept Hollywood away from this story). The two boys liked one another from the start. Their friendship would have been perfect but for the fact that Walter was absorbed by his love for Agnes, the girl to whom he was promised in marriage. One day he imagined he saw Agnes smile invitingly at Gomez and, furiously jealous, he accused her of preferring the Spaniard. She told him not to be ridiculous; they quarrelled and parted. It so happened that that very evening Agnes's father, who was proud of his knowledge of the Spanish language, invited Gomez to dine and converse with him. Walter, who was hanging miserably round the house, saw Gomez leave it at some late hour and jumped to the conclusion that he had been secretly visiting Agnes. Gomez, not knowing the town well, took the wrong turning and, with Walter following him, wandered down to the dockside. There, in the darkness, Walter seized him, stabbed him through the breast and threw his body into the water. Next morning the body was washed ashore with the dagger still in it – but there was no need to find and accuse the murderer. Walter, his jealousy gone, in a state of stupefied remorse, had been wandering about all night. As soon as he saw his father carrying the body back on horseback to the house, he rushed forward to confess his guilt.

The crime of murder was serious enough but much worse was the violation of the laws of hospitality. Lynch could find no excuse for his son. Three days later, sitting in judgement upon him, he condemned him to death. Walter expected and asked nothing better, but the townspeople, who had been touched by the boy's terrible remorse, were horrified by what seemed to them an inhuman sentence. They felt that Walter's grief had been punishment enough. The women of the Lynch family felt this even more strongly and his mother and sister, with Agnes who now, of course, loved him more than ever, went together to beg Walter's life from his father and judge. Nothing would move Lynch. He was determined that the sentence should be carried out.

The mother, a member of the powerful Blake family, was equally determined to save her son. She went to her father and brothers and begged them to save their young kinsman from this shameful death by hanging. The Blakes were roused and, with the townsfolk behind them, set out for the Lynch mansion to rescue Walter. Walter, recovering now from his first self-condemnation and realising that death would separate him for ever from Agnes, was not unwilling to be rescued.

James Lynch was told that the Blakes were on their way to the house. He ordered the execution to take place at once, but no one would act as

Galway street scene showing Lynch's Castle

executioner. Nothing had been done by the time the crowd reached Lynch's Castle and started hammering upon the doors. James Lynch, fighting down his own desire to forgive his son, ordered Walter to prepare himself for death. With the house echoing the uproar outside it, Lynch led Walter up a back stairway to the top floor and there with his own hands hanged the boy from a window. This window overlooked the churchyard of St. Nicholas and can still be seen preserved in the churchyard wall in Market Street. James Lynch spent the rest of his life in perpetual mourning, never leaving his house or seeing any person who was not a member of his own family. Agnes died of grief.

The Church of St. Nicholas has changed very little since that day when Walter Lynch looked out on it for the last time. It is built of blue limestone, a bleak and enduring stone that tends to give a sombre appearance to the whole town. Since the victories of William of Orange, St. Nicholas's has been a Protestant church with a handful of worshippers, but before that time it was the chief church of the city. It is almost as old as Galway itself and the history of one is close linked with the history of the other.

The foundation stone of St. Nicholas was laid in 1320, some ninety years after the arrival of Richard de Burgh. Before that date a small chapel of the Knights Templars stood on the spot; this was demolished when the Order was disbanded but a fragment of its structure can still be seen covering the tomb of a crusader, a de Burgh, who died in 1250. The new church was built to commemorate the victory of another Richard de Burgh, 'the Red Earl,' who defeated Edward Bruce at Athenry, a victory made the more satisfactory by the fact Bruce had defeated Richard at Connor in 1315. It was dedicated, like most sea-port churches, to the patron saint of sailors, children and thieves. This first small church, of the Second Pointed or Decorated period, was added to and enriched as the Galway tribes prospered and became a secure and cultivated local aristocracy. Toward the end of the fifteenth century they had reason to petition the Pope. Describing themselves as 'a modest and civil people' and the native Irish as 'a savage race, unpolished and illiterate,' they asked that they should be granted an absolute local control of the church, its clergy and of all civil matters.

The early days of the Reformation passed over them lightly. When in 1537, Lord deputy Grey ordered the citizens to renounce allegiance to the Pope and acknowledge the supremacy of Henry VIII, they prudently took the oath. This did not prevent Grey from confiscating a vast quantity of church 'jewels, ornaments, crosses and images': of which only 40 shillings' worth reached the king's treasury. The power of the tribes was not only unaffected by these changing times but continued to grow. They became so exclusive that the de Burghs (or de Burke as their name became on Irish tongues), now Earls of Clanrickarde, who had intermarried with the Irish and were fast becoming Irish themselves, were felt by the Galway bourgeoisie to be no longer respectable; their rights in the city were brought up and, like the O's and the Mac's, they were excluded from its gates. A by-law forbad any inhabitant of Galway to invite to his home for Christmas or Easter the Burkes or their kinspeople the MacWilliams, or any similar sept.

This old enmity between the settlers and the Irish faded at last. During the sixteenth century Galway was famed for a classical school kept by Alexander Lynch. Among the 1,200 scholars were two brilliant boys, close friends – one was Alexander's own son, John, who later became Archdeacon of Tuam and author of *Cambrensis Eversus*; the other, future author of *Oxygia*, a ferocious O'Flaherty. John Lynch (1599–1673), the most famous scholar of his day, fled to France when Galway was taken by the Cromwellians . . .

When Cromwell descended on Galway, the tribes took to the hills. Ulick de Burke, who had led the Irish against the Commonwealth, was permitted to keep his lands but ordered to retire to one of his estates. The wild Galway highlands became filled with Blakes, Martins and Lynches who now lived side by side with the O's and the Mac's and the ferocious O'Flaherties of Iar Connaught. One of the loveliest and most remote areas of Galway is known as Joyce's Country. The Martins went to Connemara; the Blakes to share Renvyle with the old sea-faring clan of O'Malley.

In 1656 the Commissioners of Ireland, offering for sale the forfeited Galway mansions and lands, were describing the port with an auctioneer's enthusiasm as one of the most considerable in the British Islands. By then Galway was already in decline. The citizens had taken Henry's oath but, to all intents and purposes, had remained Catholic. Every new restriction placed on the Irish Catholics was a blow that helped kill Galway's trade. Its downfall was completed in 1741 when a great plague swept the city and the famous Galway races had to be held in Tuam.

Six years later the Governor of Galway reported that he could not find enough Protestants to fill the offices of the corporation. Almost any ruffian who claimed to be Protestant was put into office while the old Catholic families who had made Galway's greatness lived in exile in the hills. The few Catholics who remained in the town, deprived as they were of the right to trade legitimately, took to smuggling. When, at the end of the eighteenth century, the anti-Catholic laws began to relax, the trade of the port was lost. The docks were deserted; grass grew in the streets; the city walls and fortifications were in ruins. After the Catholic Bill of 1793, life began slowly to return to Galway's streets but even today they have something of the ravaged look of a man whom sickness has brought to the point of death.

The fabled misfortune of the Gael, having at last overtaken the rich City of the Strangers, seems never to have left it. At one time during the Blessing of the Sea that heralds the herring season, two hundred fishing boats or more would follow the decorated boat that carried the priests and acolytes out into the bay; a remnant of these remain. For one reason or another the mills and jute factory closed down. In the early nineteenth century an attempt was made to establish a line of steam packets, but one vessel was burnt after it had crossed the Atlantic, another ran upon a rock in the bay and rumours of sabotage at last bankrupted the owners. The stone buildings in Eyre Square is all that remains of the company.

Before the Second World War Galway had become a port of call for Cunard, Hamburg-Amerika and Norddeutscher Lloyd transatlantic liners, but the war ended all that and the quays are again idle. Galway's main hope now lies in the growing tourist trade which is filling the town and the residential area of Salthill with new life. The sea front mansions that, ten years ago, were empty and falling into decay, are now prosperous hotels gazing out upon the Salthill sands and beyond to the beautiful expanse of Galway Bay with its lighthouse chalk-white against the dark hills of Clare and the Aran Islands lying like whales on the distant horizon.

From *The Dreaming Shore*

V.S. Pritchett

1950

VICTOR SAWDON PRITCHETT (1900–1997) was born at Ipswich, Suffolk. When his father lost the family's money, Victor had to leave school at sixteen and was apprenticed to the leather industry. After five years in the tannery he went to Paris and, a few years later, found his first literary work as a journalist with the *Christian Science Monitor*. In 1924, Pritchett was assigned to Dublin, where he married his first wife, Evelyn Maude Vigors. Pritchett had a long association with *The New Statesman*, serving both as fiction critic and literary editor. In 1974, Pritchett was elected President of PEN and was knighted a year later.

V.S. Pritchett

After Athlone the country begins to get milder, the trees scarcer and bent over by the wind. Families of tinkers are camped along the stone walls – the wildest looking people in Ireland, though occasionally a noble-looking figure stands out. The land gets rocky, Lough Corrib burns blue, the salmon fishermen are out, and in Galway you see those lordly fish lined up like small submarines in the shallow water, worshiped by the crowd looking over the walls. This superb city, on a bay, that is unequaled in the west of Ireland, is thriving; and it has one of the best restaurants in the country. I forget how many liners call at Galway but the people are proud of the port, and one realizes, as one hears Limerick or Cork pulled to pieces and hears 'Cork men' and 'Limerick men' spoken of as rival clans, that there is a sort of underground and very masculine war of character between the Irish cities and that it is passionately waged.

Galway is a rich place. In the evenings, at the best hotel, the survivors of the old upper-class life turn up – remarkably dressed women of a certain age, horsy, sporting, excitable in the Irish fashion. There is an easygoing dash in their appearance, and a marked eccentricity if one compares them with their more stolid opposite numbers in Cheltenham or Bath, knitting or sleeping over their novels. There is a touch of outrageous gaiety. You hear flattering phrases – the first duty of man and woman is to charm, and to hell with the rest. The feeling for amusement and for the sparkle of pleasure goes deep. Life is dull, but luck may change it. And even if you know there is 'nothing in luck,' you'd lose a lot of the pleasure of life if you didn't kid yourself that you believed in it. You can't live without excitement. With rich and poor it is the same – though there are misanthropists about too.

I used to sit on a wall with an old peasant in the mountainy country near Clifden while he let his greyhound off to put up a hare. If it came off, he would be shouting with excitement: 'He has him! He has *not*! He has him! He has *not*! He has him beat. He has him destroyed in the corner. He has *not*, he's away over the wall.' And so on. An afternoon came pelting to life for a poor man living alone with his rags, his whiskey bottle and his dog.

From *At Home and Abroad*

Diana Mosley

1951

DIANA MITFORD was born in 1910, one of the famous Mitford sisters that included Nancy, Jessica and Unity. At eighteen she married Bryan Guinness of the brewing family but left him a few years later for Oswald Mosley, the leader of British fascists. She was on close terms with the top Nazis and she knew both Hitler and Churchill well. During the Second World War the Mosleys were detained under the Defence Regulations Act and she spent ten months in Holloway Prison. In the early fifties, the Mosleys bought and renovated the old bishop's palace at Clonfert.

The same year, 1951, as we went to live in France at the Orsay Temple we bought an old house, formerly a bishop's palace, at Clonfert in

Co. Galway. It was less than a mile west of the Shannon, a broad river which regularly overflowed its banks in winter causing widespread floods. The name Clonfert means 'an island' in Gaelic, and the house itself was never flooded. It stood in flat country on the edge of the bog. In the garden there were great beech trees and an avenue of age-old yews called the Nun's Walk which had been used by our predecessor for exercising his hunters when there was frost. There was a carpet of needles under the yews that remained soft in even the hardest winter.

It was George McVeagh who told us about Clonfert. He was our Dublin solicitor to whom we had been introduced by Derek and Pam, a delightful man, whose passion was snipe shooting. He often shot over the bog near Clonfert, so he knew it was for sale.

We put in bathrooms and electric light and central heating, and while the work was going on at Clonfert the boys and Mr. Leigh Williams and I stayed with Pam at Tullamaine. The drive over, which I did every day, was never easy. Either there was frost and I slithered on black ice, or else there were deluges of rain; once for a week there was snow. It was lovely to get back after a dreary cold day standing about in rubble to Tullamaine and Pam's delicious dinner. Clonfert Palace was in parts so ancient and its walls were so thick that piercing them for heating pipes was a far harder job than anyone had anticipated. It seemed to take forever. There was hardly a single window of which the sash cord was not broken. The French call sash windows *fenêtres* guillotines and these really were guillotines; one might very well have been beheaded by a Clonfert window. While Harry Conniffe and his son Paddy put the garden in order I measured the windows for curtains and tried to decide where the electric light points must go. Of all the many houses I have done up in my life the hardest work was Clonfert. Fortunately I could not peer into the future and see how vain our labours were to prove. Our furniture and books had been stored in Cork, and had arrived in very poor shape. We got curtains and covers made in Dublin and by degrees the house became comfortable and pretty. We did not install a telephone; it seemed to us wonderfully peaceful to be without, but we lived to regret it.

The house faced south and just across the lawn was Clonfert Cathedral, a large and ancient church with a curiously-carved Norman west doorway. As is usual in Ireland, this old church was the place of worship of a small handful of Protestants. The vast majority of the people were Catholics and they filled their little modern church to the brim. To any outsider it seemed crazy that of the two sects of Christians it should be the few belonging to the reformed church who made up the tiny congregation in the old cathedral, built centuries before reform was ever

Clifden

dreamed of. Not only few in numbers, they were also lax in attendance compared with the Catholics. They could easily have fitted into a minuscule chapel.

To the newcomer Clonfert did not at first sight give the impression of being a village at all, but in fact there were dozens of people living here and there in well-hidden little old cottages. One realized how numerous they were when they came out of church on Sunday or a saint's day, or when there was a hunt on the bog.

The East Galway hounds hunted a big country and there were always a couple of meets a week within reach of Clonfert. Max adored hunting. We had brought our Crowood ponies to Ireland and it so happened that Max's pony, Johnny, was a star. He enjoyed hunting every bit as much as did Max himself. When they were standing while a covert was drawn and the huntsman blew 'gone away' on his horn, Johnny in his excitement before galloping off to the first fence would give a great sigh. 'He sounds just like a train when it leaves a station in the Paris metro,' said Max. He could jump fences and walls bigger than himself.

The hunt could never cross the bog, which was treacherous and dangerous for the horses, therefore sometimes on winter Sundays after church the village men and boys would hunt there on foot. Everyone brought his dog, one saw mongrel, puppy, whelp and hound and curs of low degree just as in Goldsmith's day. One Sunday they were out and Max was feeding Johnny in his stable and just preparing to run off and join the hunt when a man was heard to holla quite near at hand. Max told me: 'There was a great thumping noise; it was Johnny's heart beating.' The pony knew that a holla meant someone had seen the fox and he was dying to be off. As Max ran out of the stable without him he heard Johnny give a furious squeal. The holla at Clonfert also reminded one of how little Ireland has changed since the eighteenth century, for the bog echoed with wild cries of 'Ya-hoo.' Jonathan Swift, 'the great dane' as the Irish call him, had stayed with the Bishop in our house, which was old even in his day. Max thought it must have been here that he conceived his idea of Houyhnhnms and Yahoos.

When we went to Ireland Max was eleven and Alexander twelve. They took their tutor with them; there was no hateful boarding school to interfere with their lives, but Alexander bitterly regretted Crowood and Ramsbury and the old familiar faces. He suffered as we had when we left Asthall, and as Debo had when Farve sold Swinbrook. Like us, he gets deeply attached to places. He never cared for hunting; he buried himself in books. At gymkhanas in the summer he was to be seen kindly holding two horses for Max, the reins hitched over his arms, reading, oblivious of his surroundings.

There is no doubt that round Clonfert the people were exceptionally kind and welcoming. We quickly became very fond of the place. My room looked over the bog, and through the open windows delicious scents wafted in from the sweet smelling wild flowers which covered it in spring, and sounds of curlews, snipe and water-fowl of all kinds. Sometimes one heard the curious dry sound of wild geese flying in formation to Norway or wherever it is they go. At Clonfert I regretted knowing so little about birds . . .

We had only been in Clonfert for two and a half years when a disaster happened. M. and I were in London and about to return to Ireland, but I put off my journey for a day because Farve was coming south and it was a good chance to see him. I dined with him and flew to Dublin next morning. When I got through the customs I was surprised to see M. standing in the crowd, I had not expected him to meet me. As I approached I noticed he was unshaven. He took my hand and said gently: 'Sit down here on this seat. Everything is all right. Nobody is hurt.'

'*Hurt*!' I said, and my heart missed a beat. 'Why, has something terrible happened?'

He told me that in the night there had been a great fire at Clonfert. He and Alexander and two French people we had with us and the horses and dogs were all safe, but most of the house and furniture and pictures had been destroyed. Madeleine, our French cook, had run up to her room on the second floor to fetch something when she was supposed to be sitting out on the lawn, safe. Cut off by the flames, she had had to jump into a blanket held by M. and Alexander. She was bruised but no bones were broken. During the time it took to persuade her to jump the dining-room ceiling fell in; had it not been for her, M. and Alexander could easily have got the pictures out. My bedroom was the very centre of the furnace, nothing remained. All that was found amongst the cinders on the ground floor beneath were the blackened springs from the mattress of my four-post bed; a pretty bed with slender carved mahogany posts and a canopy of blue taffeta. The dining-room also was completely burnt; it was full of pictures of M.'s forbears, and it had a charming French table of about 1840 inlaid with roses and ribbons, all destroyed.

It had happened in the middle of a bitter December night. M. sent the car to telephone for help, but by the time the fire brigades from Ballinasloe and Birr got to Clonfert it was too late; the damage was done. The firemen were brave and efficient but what saved the west end of the house, the drawing room and the library, was that the wind changed. The fire began in the chimney of the maids' sitting-room where peat and wood were burnt winter and summer. An old beam in the chimney, dried no doubt by our central heating, had smouldered and finally blazed up, and the whole chimney was found to be coated with a deposit of inflammable tar-like substance, said to be the result of mixing peat and wood on the hearth.

At the back of the house there was a farm; Mrs. Blake Kelly was wakened by the persistent neighing and whinnying of her horses. Reluctant to stir out of bed, for it was bitterly cold, she finally got up, looked out of the window and saw the blaze. She called her son: 'The palace is on fire!' He ran round to the front of the house, he knew where Alexander slept and threw pebbles at his window until he woke up. But for the horses and their terror of flames there might have a tragedy.

To make matters worse great floods rose so that the Dublin road became impassable and Clonfert was cut off. A few days later when I was able to go and I saw the blackened ruin I felt not only sad but guilty. It seemed as if we had come to a centuries-old house that slumbered peacefully near the bog for ages until we pulled it about, put in heating, dried it unnaturally, and now it was ruined. A curious thing happened: when I heard about the fire, and for many days afterwards, my hand trembled so that I could hardly hold a pen to write a letter.

From *A Life of Contrasts*

Paul Henry

1952

BELFAST-BORN ARTIST Paul Henry (1876–1958) studied at the Belfast School of Art before enrolling in the Academie Julian in Paris. He studied with James McNeill Whistler and became one of the best-known Irish artists in Paris at the end of the nineteenth century. Henry moved to Dublin and became active on the local art scene, becoming one of the founding members of the Society of Dublin Painters. In the twenties he moved to Achill Island off County Mayo and his landscapes of the west of Ireland made him famous.

One of the most extraordinary distinctions possessed by the West of Ireland is the unique spell it exerts – a subtle and powerful spirit of attractiveness to which even the most lethargic and sophisticated traveller invariably succumbs. This is the more extraordinary, and says not a little for the general receptivity of mankind to the subtler things of the spirit, as Ireland's most enduring and attractive qualities are not of the obvious kind which lie on, or close to, the surface and reveal themselves at a glance or a first casual encounter. This alluring charm has been felt by most people who have penetrated west of the Shannon; but it is in Connemara – that small choice district of West Galway – one seems to get closest to the secret source of this current attractiveness.

Into this strip of the seaboard of a county have been collected many things of interest for all types of mind, and many interesting and beautiful things which are seldom found in combination, but when found have the happy faculty of producing a harmony at once singularly satisfying and delightful. The scenery, the people, the sense of 'colour' in which the district is steeped – all charming things in themselves and all of them of an unusual quality – act and react, blend and separate to form new combinations against what for want of a more precise word we call the 'background' of Connemara. This is her intimate, essential spirit, her air of remoteness, her aloofness, her unexpectedness. This 'background,' though an attraction of the less obvious kind, is the fairy cord that binds one, the invisible mesh of the enchanted net which falls over one in this delectable land.

Connemara is, roughly speaking, the district bounded on the south by Galway City – 'the Citie of the Tribes' – and on the north by Leenane. Lapped all along her eastern border by the waters of the romantic Lough Corrib; on the west the long rollers of the Atlantic sweep into a series of fascinating bays and mysterious silent fiords. The country is broken up by

A curragh off Barna

mountains and lakes and busy brown rivers; and the little scattered groups of cottages and isolated queer villages add a final grace of intimacy to a landscape of exceptional charm.

To leave the train at Galway City with the idea of working up through the country to rejoin the railway at Westport gives one the opportunity of exploring this most romantic of Irish cities. The traveller will here find himself in an atmosphere subtle and pervading which more nearly approaches that of the eighteenth century than any other place in Ireland. No one can deny the insidious magic of the old, grey, crumbling town. It was John Lynch, the author of *Cambrensis Eversus* and a fugitive from Cromwellian ferocity, who sang in his exile, '*As Jerusalem seemed to the Prophet Jeremiah the princess of provinces, the beauty of Israel, so thou, O Galway, dost to me appear of perfect beauty.*' And the city of John Lynch's rhapsody is the very largely in essential atmosphere the city of to-day.

Looking upon Galway as one of the gates to the extreme west, one has a choice of two routes. One may either follow the coastline, which is more truly and intimately Connemara, or travel up the sinuous river into Lough Corrib – famous in spring for its 'dapping' and in winter for its countless wildfowl, as far as Maam, within easy reach of Recess, the core and centre of Connemara. Another way is to enter at Westport. Passing either down the Eriff Valley – a magnificent glen – or through Louisburgh and the fine Delphi Pass, one emerges at the head of the superb fiord of Killary with Mweelrea – the highest mountain in Connaught – guarding its entrance. From this point through the 'Twelve Pins' and their foothills and past numberless lakes we enter Connemara.

Here, from the summit of one of her higher mountains, the eye travels over the peerless country, dotted with innumerable little loughs beloved of the fisherman, over the gracious lines of her cloud-dappled hills, and the valleys where the purple shadows linger; over the scattered 'clachans' – little handfuls of whitewashed toy houses – tucked away in the sheltered folds of the hills, to the coastline, bitten into with sandy bays guarded by islets of porphyry set in an opal and azure sea. Out of the sou'west a wisp of mist – a grey veil trailing from a grey cloud floating in the blue – passes over the hills. Where it catches on a height it breaks in showers on the toy houses and passes on leaving the wet, sparkling eyes of the cottages laughing back to the sun.

At a turn of a lonely road among the mountains – far from village or house – a woman comes down a rough track from the higher hills. Dressed in geranium-red homespun and with an orange head-shawl, the turbulence of her colour flames against the encircling mountains. She hangs on her foot for a second as she returns your salute. A wild grace is in the carriage of her head, the beautiful softness of her voice, soft as the rains of her native hills, wraps you round like a caress. Her grey eyes, soft and kindly, hold yet a smouldering fire; the brooding mystery of her race is round her like an aura. She passes by, coming from the mountain solitudes and going apparently into them again, a rare, aloof, dignified figure.

Here in Connemara on a day when the wind blows from the west, the pale rose morning light turns to silver as the tumultuous high-flying clouds race over the mountains, their indigo shadows hurrying across the green of the uplands and the gold of the ripening harvest towards the distant plum-coloured hills. As the sun ascends the clouds scurry faster, and their shadows beat a quicker measure towards the horizon. The colour flames and burns among the hills; and the deep tarns set in a hundred corries – the surface of their waters curled over by the wind and reflecting the deep blue of the sky – glow like enamels, azure shot through with gold. The big clouds, typical of 'The West,' grow listless as the day declines. They come up slower still and more majestic, gathering colour from the descending sun till as it dips beyond the sea they seem hardly to move, piling themselves up into airy cloud-built palaces glowing with reflected fire. The cool purple dusk creeps over the hills, while far in the west the day dies in a deep mauve seen through a shower of dust of gold.

From *Ireland of the Welcomes*

Brendan Behan

1957

DUBLINER BRENDAN BEHAN (1923–1964) was born into a Republican family. He joined the IRA at fifteen and two years later he was arrested in Liverpool for carrying explosives. He spent three years in Borstal, the reformatory which was to be the inspiration for his best-known work, *Borstal Boy*. In 1941, he was deported to Ireland and immediately sentenced to fourteen years for shooting a policemen with intent to kill. Released on amnesty after serving three years, Behan began writing while working as a housepainter. The London production of *The Quare Fellow* established him as a major playwright.

*G*alway City – It's really a town – is a hard place to explain, but if I tell you that I was once sold sixty acres of land there at a fair in the town itself, you'll probably begin to have some idea that it is an unusual place. Nowadays, it's a haunt of commercial travelers relaxing at weekends, a few Aran Islanders over to sign some stupid forms, and farmers who come in there to buy potatoes from Michael Joe Burke who was wounded in some boating accident in the Mediterranean during the war. Michael insists that he doesn't remember it, that he was too drunk – he was in the British Navy and he has a pension; they don't apparently care about people being drunk in the Navy which is uncommon civil of them and to their lasting credit.

One of my best friends always was the late Monsignor Pádraig de Brún, who was President of University College, Galway until he retired and became Chairman of the Irish Arts Council until his death a couple of years ago. A man of great learning and, what is more important, charity, he was a mathematician who translated the whole of Dante's *Divine Comedy* into Irish as well as many ancient Greek plays. His brother is the Master-General of the Dominican Order and was the confessor of the late Pope Pius XII, and now has been made Cardinal.

The people of Galway are very proud of being from Galway though, personally, I think that it is silly enough being proud of being from anywhere in particular. You get all sorts from everywhere, as the Old Etonian said to the Wykehamist, both being con-men. But proud and all as the Galwegians are, there are pubs where they won't be admitted. I know one where they are hardly admitted at all because they're not respectable enough – I suppose in dress (they don't go in very much for the black tie and that) while there's another pub where they're not admitted for more puritanical reasons—the proprietor thinks they shouldn't be drinking. The centre of social life in Galway, however, is a pub called 'The Old Malt House' where everybody goes about nine o'clock of an evening. It's a warm-hearted place owned by Ned Walsh whose father was murdered in 1920, by the Black and Tans – they were the British Mau Mau of the time (oaths, mutilations and all, they had) . . .

The peace anywhere along the shores of Galway Bay is something that would make you wish that all this cruelty would stop. There's no more wonderful feeling than swimming there out in the Atlantic Ocean – in a good year it's far better than Cannes or anywhere else on the Mediterranean. At Cannes or one of those places, you're surrounded by millions of people, the beaches are leased out and you can't even be sure of getting a place where you can take off your clothes in private. Not that I'm against people taking off their clothes before each other but, as you can see at Cannes, it becomes less attractive after the age of thirty. I don't like this at all and there should be something done about it – maybe the United Nations could pass a resolution against it. There are two things on which the Americans and the Russians might well join forces – first, to make people know as much at eighteen as they do at thirty-eight; and second, to make people as attractive-looking at thirty-eight or forty-eight as they were at eighteen – but I suppose the brewers would be against it. All else, though, is waste and nobody should be impressed by the Sputnik or the Bluenik or any other nick.

I often think of things like that lying on the flat of my back on the rocks at Carraroe. It's a tourist place, Irish-speaking – the tourists are good for the locality from the money point of view but not very good for the people, really. It's a place to be, though, – you can eat fresh lobster for every meal with lovely griddle-bread and porter. The only thing to avoid there is the boys that have recently arrived back from England – they're inclined to be full of Edgware Road English – they're not very co-operative, you might say.

An old friend of mine that lives there is Patrick Griffin. He's a man now about ninety, if he's still alive when this book appears. His wife Máire doesn't speak any English but she has the sweetest Irish I ever heard. Patrick, long ago, was reputed to be the best potheen maker in the district. I remember talking to a son of his, who came home from America where he had been drafted into the Army, and I asked him what it was like.

'It was very good,' he said, 'and I found the Irish a great help to me.'

'How was that,' I said, 'in the American Army?'

'Because,' he said, 'a lot of the recruits are from South Boston and a great number from Connemara and from the Aran Islands and,' he said, 'we could speak Irish among ourselves and the N.C.O.s and officers didn't know what we were saying.'

I remember, too, meeting in Patrick Griffin's house an old lady who told me that she had been twenty years in America and she came back with hardly a word of English. Beside Patrick's house live the kindly O'Nuallain family. Many's the good swim I had with Diarmuid, the eldest son. He has recently been ordained and is now away with the missions in Nigeria.

Patrick's house stands on a little bay and the Atlantic comes in right beside it. In a graveyard just at the back is buried the author, Maurice O'Sullivan, whose book *Twenty Years A-Growing* is published in Penguins and in the World's Classics series by the Oxford University Press.

Another good friend of mine in Carraroe is Stiofán O Fláithbheartaigh. He said to me after I came back from America, '*Cead fáilte sa bhaile romhat, A Bhreandáin*: a hundred welcomes home to you, Brendan!'

'*Cead* mile *fáilte*,' I said, 'surely, Stiofán: a hundred *thousand* welcomes!'

'*Muise*, isn't a hundred welcomes enough for any man?' said Stiofán.

A lot of well-known people beside myself go to Carraroe in the summer. Up to some years ago, a regular visitor was Freddie Boland, Ireland's Representative at the United Nations, who was President of that show last year. I think he's the only diplomat I've ever been photographed with, for when he was Ambassador in London, he came to the first night of *The Quare Fellow* and himself, my wife and myself, were all snapped talking together in the foyer. Siobhán MacKenna, her husband, Dennis O'Dea and her son are in Carraroe frequently – Siobhán, of course, grew up in Galway and started her acting career there in the Gaelic Theatre. In fact, you can say nearly anybody that's anyway prominent in Irish life finds his way to Carraroe at some time.

Except for the money that the visitors leave behind them, the whole of the Galway sea-board is a poor enough place. With the young people leaving for Kilburn and Clapham, the number of Irish-speakers is going down. The only way in which the native language could possibly be preserved there is by some form of economic socialism, but the Government are willing to do anything in their power to save the language, except adopt the radical solution of organizing a state fishing industry along the coast. If it's economic for trawlers to come from France and Spain to fish off Galway, it ought to be possible for the Government at home, to take the fishing industry out of the hands of private enterprise, organize it on a nationalized basis and send the fishermen out into the Atlantic – but their conservatism is stronger than their Gaelicism.

The people themselves catch fish, of course, but mostly on a very small scale for they haven't the proper equipment. It's in the interests of the big fishing firms in Dublin to keep things as they are – they prefer to sell a

The gate of the Franciscan convent

few fish dear than a lot of fish cheap. A couple of years ago, Peadar O'Donnell was trying to negotiate with East Germany for the sale of salted herrings, and some members of the Dail who are living quite comfortably themselves said that the curse of God would fall upon any dealings with the Communists. But these people who were so free with their admonitions were all living in Dublin suburban villas, and they weren't out at the crack of dawn digging up little patches of land. For with the few fish they catch, the people of Connemara cultivate infinitesimal patches of ground – they break up the rocks and gather seaweed to try and fertilize the miserable clay to get a few potatoes and vegetables.

And the women have to work hard, too – usually they try to raise a few turkeys for which they get about a shilling a pound from the Dublin dealers, who then sell them for about four to five shillings But with the expansion of the battery-fed turkey industry, I'm glad to say that the Dublin dealers' profits won't be so high. But I think that the women in the West will still be able to get about the same amount of money for their turkeys.

Let nobody tell you otherwise – the industry of the people of Connemara (and the poor people in the other parts of the country as well) is marvellous. They work very hard for the little bit of money they manage to scrape together and it's a great pity they're not helped more.

But in other ways they're comfortable enough and I give the Government credit for that – the idea that Connemara is a rocky wilderness dotted with broken-down cabins in which the people exist, is all nonsense. There are no cabins in Connemara. Housing all over rural Ireland is extremely good. The people live in slated, electric, four-and-five-roomed houses, with running water and good sanitation and the Government provided those houses over the list thirty years.

Nevertheless, though I like the old Gaelic civilization as it was, I wouldn't be adverse to seeing a few large chimney stacks around Connemara. One industry was introduced by the Government some years ago – the growing of tomatoes in greenhouses. The tomatoes are, maybe, a bit more expensive than the Dutch ones, but they have a finer flavour and, as production increases, they will grow cheaper – or they ought to.

One piece of advice I give freely to anyone visiting the West, is to keep away from potheen. No matter what anyone tells you about the fine old drop of 'Mountain Dew,' it stands to common sense that a few old men, sitting up in the back of a haggard in the mountains with milk churns and all sorts of improvised utensils, cannot hope to make good spirits, when most modern distilleries, equipped with every device that science can provide, can't find it easy to produce decent whiskey. Potheen is just murder – it's the end and you can take it from me, for I have a wide enough experience of it.

I once knew an old man who drank potheen at the rate of about a couple of pints a day for a fortnight, when he finally wasn't able to drink any more and he got so ill that he was on his back for another fortnight before he recovered.

I asked him, 'Why,' I said, 'if it makes you so sick, do you continue to drink it? Do you not remember the terrible hangovers you had?' 'Well, no,' he said, 'because, to tell you the truth, when I've been off it for about a fortnight, I feel so good that I just have to go out and celebrate.'

From *Brendan Behan's Ireland*

John Huston

1962

WRITER AND DIRECTOR John Huston (1908–1987), the son of actor Walter Huston, was born in Missouri and made his stage debut at the age of three. He first went to Hollywood as a writer in 1932 but abandoned it to travel. He returned to Hollywood in 1938 and soon became one of its most successful directors, making his name with such films as *The Maltese Falcon*, *The Treasure of the Sierra Madre*, *The Asphalt Jungle*, *The African Queen*, *Beat the Devil*, *Wise Blood* and *The Dead*. For many years Huston maintained a home at St. Clerans in County Galway and hunted with the Galway Blazers.

From Courtown I used to drive out to Galway, Limerick and Cork with my horse in a trailer, for short tours of hunting. On one of these hunts – in Galway – we were crossing a field and I saw a house in the distance behind a ruined tower. I asked about it, and was told that its name was St. Clerans.

Some months later Ricki went out to stay with Derek Trench and his wife, Pat, for the Galway Race Meeting. Only in Dublin do you go to a hotel. Everyone knows everyone else in Ireland, and wherever you go you're someone's guest. The Old South in the United States must have been something like that. If you want to bring your horse for the hunt, both you and your horse are put up.

When Ricki came back, she mentioned having seen a beautiful, old place named St. Clerans that was now vacant and for sale. I went right down to get a good look at it. St. Clerans was located near Galway City between Loughrea and Craughwell in Ireland's western coastal region. The house was in utter disrepair. The roof was leaking and the flooring gone, but the stonework was beautiful and the proportions were classic. It was a fine example of a Georgian manor house. The estate itself consisted of 100 Irish acres (about 110 U.S. acres), and the setting was extraordinary. There was an enormous vegetable garden and a great walled tree garden. Irish captains of sailing ships used to bring back trees from around the world, and at St. Clerans one of them had created a tree garden full of exotic species, bordered by flowers. I fell in love with the place instantly and decided to buy it.

St. Clerans was then owned by the Land Commission, and we purchased it at an auction. It cost very little to buy, but a small fortune and the better part of two years to restore.

The estate was in two sections, with the manor house to the fore. You walked down a gravel path through the trees and across a trout stream to get to the other section, where there were a thirteenth-century tower, the groom's quarters, stables and a lovely little steward's cottage. This cottage was the first building to be redone, and became Ricki's domain. It was here that she raised the children. Even after the big house was restored she still preferred the little house and spent most of her time there with the nurse, Tony and Anjelica. In this section, above the garages and stables, there were two spacious lofts, one of which I used for my studio. My assistant, Gladys Hill, lived in the other . . .

The church of St. Kenannach

Even before the restoration of St. Clerans was finished I began to collect things wherever I went around the world. From Japan I had an entire Japanese bath, with shoji doors and mats, sent over and installed. The bath accommodated up to six bathers, and was wonderful for after hunting. I saw a Kenzo screen in Japan which had a flowering stump with a bird on it – beautifully simple – and I asked a printmaker to reproduce it, which he did by means of the largest woodblocks ever made in Japan. We compared them with the original, and they were exact copies. You couldn't tell the difference except that the prints were signed by the maker. We used them for wallpaper in the dining room. In the drawing room there were silk curtains especially woven from an ancient Chinese pattern.

St. Clerans had three stories. The main entrance was on the second floor. The lower floor had a stone-and-concrete moat – a surround – that permitted full windows and plenty of light. It was here that I had the Japanese bath. I also installed a gallery for pre-Columbian art. There was an office for the estate manager, a storeroom, the wine cellar, an apartment for members of the staff and a lovely room we called the TV room. We only visited the TV room to see world soccer, horseracing, boxing matches, events we'd watch in groups, betting fiercely with one another.

The front part of the main floor had been added in 1820. There was a spacious entrance hall paved in Galway marble – a marble with the imprint of oyster and other fossil shells and plants – white against black. I put that in. The dining room and the drawing room were long and wide, identical in size, with bow windows. There was a large inner hall with a bar and the main staircase. The study was on one side of the inner hallway and the kitchen on the other. Off the kitchen were the pantry, the staff room and maids' rooms.

In the third-floor hallway two Chinese porcelain drum-stools flanked the Red Sitting Room – so-called from the color of its silk wallcoverings – in which there were beautiful Venetian cupboards. There were Chinese porcelain; Etruscan, Magna Grecia and Arezzo ceramics; and paintings by Juan Gris and Morris Graves. Also on this floor was the Gray Room – a woman's bedroom, muted in color. In it there were Japanese screens and a collection of Japanese 'fan paintings' – paintings made to be copied on fans. On the wall of the Gray Room, above the headboard (a Mexican colonial altarpiece), hung a fourteenth-century Sicilian carved wooden crucifix.

Another bedroom (there were five on this floor, all told) was called the Napoleon Room because of its canopied Empire bed. A Bhutan Room contained bronzes and fabrics from that little-known country. The fourth bedroom was the Gold Room – again because of its color – furnished with a charming old Irish bed of brass and painted porcelain, Georgian wardrobe and Georgian sofa table.

My room had a big, canopied four-poster Florentine matrimonial bed, carved with doves and flowers, two Louis XIV leather chairs with brass studs, a thirteenth-century Greek ikon and a chest of drawers which had originally been used for vestments in a French cathedral. All the bedrooms were large, and all had fireplaces. Even the bathrooms had fireplaces.

I had old tiles imported from Mexico for the kitchen and all the bathrooms. The library-study featured mostly primitive art – African, Sepik River – and a few pieces of pre-Columbian. There were no paintings in the dining room—only the Japanese woodblocks. The table was a thirteen-foot mahogany Georgian three-pod, with chairs of the same period.

The drawing room was predominantly Louis XV, punctuated by artifacts: a Greek marble horse's head, Japanese screens from the Momoyama period, a Gandhara head, Egyptian eighteenth-dynasty pieces and a 'Water Lily' painting by Monet.

I like to mix good art. The fact that pieces are not of the same period and culture doesn't mean that they will not go together. On the contrary, I think it is very interesting to mix periods, races and cultures. The very contrasts tend to show off the various pieces to better advantage.

As the years rolled by, we kept adding and changing. Gottfried Reinhardt gave me a Meissen chandelier from his father's castle in Salzburg; Ricki found a great marble-topped French table; Giacomo Manzu made me a gift of one of his bronze chairs with vegetables . . . the list is too long!

The main entrance to the manor house was flanked by medieval stone lions I'd found in County Cork; in the courtyard there was a cast-iron figure of Punchinello which I discovered in the Paris Flea Market. St. Clerans has been described as one of the most beautiful homes in the world. For me it was all of that and more.

I remember with nostalgia the lovely countryside, the horses and the people–those wonderful Irish people who were my neighbors. I had a constant stream of visitors with famous names – motion-picture stars, writers, musicians and painters – but my neighbors hadn't any idea who these people were. When they did, they were not in the least impressed. For them the only truly important thing in the world was the hunt. Hunting was enough.

From *An Open Book*

Micheál MacLiammóir

1966

MICHEÁL MACLIAMMÓIR. (1899–1978) was born either in Cork or England and was formerly known as Michael Wilmore. He made his debut on the London Stage at the of twelve and in 1915 began studying art at the Slade Art School in London. In 1927 MacLiammóir returned to Ireland to join Anew MacMaster's Shakespearean touring company. He was one of the founders of the Galway Gaelic Theatre, and in 1928, with Hilton Edwards, the Gate Theatre. He gained an international reputation as an actor with roles in several Orson Welles films. He achieved fame in the sixties with dramatic monologues such as *The Importance of Being Oscar.*

There is in Irish mythology a region in the depths of the Land of the Young, the Celtic Valhalla, that is known as *Ioldathach*, the Many Coloured Land, and the visible Ireland in which we live and work and talk with our friends seems, at times, to be but the reflection of that visionary place. I am writing these words in a little town in Connemara, and when I look out the window I see, above the thatched and slated roofs, April driving wild, dappled clouds across the sky, brightening or darkening the waters of a score of still, small lakes and running streams, alternately veiling and revealing the faint mountains far away, filling at one moment the grey of the craggy hillside with shadow or blurring the gold furze-blossom with light. The rainbow's arc is poised above thin, floating vapours, a flight of swallows passes, a black-and-white cat, misleadingly demure, sits at the door of a house whose walls are daubed with light blue. And everywhere the airs are coloured, multitudinous and ever-changing, as subtle and fleeting as the noise of water running among stones. The green, of course, is everywhere, but for the most part you will find it in brief and unexpected moments of intensity: in a handful of little fields huddled between low, ragged walls of loose stones that appear at times in the tricky light like strings of broken pearls; in ridges of coarse grass by the roadside; in rings and knolls that grow over the raths, the burial places of the ancients – it is, I think, never the predominant note, even in the fat pasture lands of Meath or Dublin. Still less is it all-pervading in those regions in the west or south where, in my eyes, the country reveals her ultimate secrets among rocks and mountains and glens and the dense purplish-brown of bogs riddled with glittering water and darkened by thorn-trees twisted by the Atlantic winds. Here, if there be any basic colour note at all, it is silver or grey or gold, according to the weather's capricious fancy, and on certain rare summer evenings, unless you are staring directly into the west in search of some fiery magic, the earth and sky and the water slowly wrap themselves in a mantle of blue so dimly profound you feel you could hold it in your arms.

From *Ireland*

Michael York

1968

BORN IN FULMER, Buckinghamshire, in 1942, Michael York-Johnson was educated at Oxford University. He began his acting career with the National Youth Theatre and with the Oxford University Dramatic Society, and made his film debut as Lucentio in *The Taming of the Shrew*. Since then York has appeared in almost 80 films with roles varying from Shakespeare to comedy to swashbuckling adventures, and he has performed on Broadway and on television. In 1968, he married Patricia McCallum and their first home together was a rented castle in County Galway.

R eturning to London, I bought a new MGC sports car to speed us to the west of Ireland, where *Alfred* was to be filmed. In this remote, unchanged corner of furthest Europe it seemed natural that castles should be available for rent. We leased Creggana Castle near Galway, an ancient turret set amidst green fields and their patchwork of grey stone walls, that had been restored by a French architect with every modern comfort. Meals, however, were still spit-roasted over an open peat fire in the huge stone living room and were often more burnt than King Alfred's legendary cakes! None the less, we delighted in this first romantic 'home.'

David Hemmings, playing the legendary English king, had rented the even more impressive Oranmore Castle and flew the banner of Wessex from its sea-girt battlements. Not to be outdone, I raised King Guthrum's Danish standard over mine. One night there was a furious pounding at our massive front door which opened to reveal a posse of locals with faces and accents out of Synge and O'Casey. 'T'wouldn't be the English flag you're after flying there?' one gnarled countenance demanded querulously. Reassured, they shambled off into the moonlight, reminding me that the bigotry and hostility that had killed Behan's hostage were still very much alive . . .

Alfred was filmed either out of doors amidst the local bogs, brays and hills or in a studio complex erected in a local field that looked like an Anglo-Saxon theme park with its ancient buildings and modern facilities. It was here that we raped, pillaged and plundered, carrying on exactly as those shocked chroniclers had described to me in the hushed quiet of an Oxford library. In one thrilling sequence we used the River Shannon as the Viking 'swan-road' over which their longships came swooping ashore. Exact replicas of the Gokkstadt ship, they were immensely seaworthy. Indeed, some hardy fool was planning to sail one to America as a publicity stunt – presumably using the Vinland map for guidance! We also employed a contingent of the Irish army as extras so that, in the quaint ways of this singular nation, many had their first taste of warfare using spears and battleaxes. Most spent their time lolling on sword and sward, blond wigs outrageously askew, looking for all the world like drag queens on a day trip.

It was a magnificent summer, the best since 1922 according to the locals. So instead of the wild, windblown skies the film-makers had hoped for, we had an interrupted Mediterranean blue. Later I was able to confirm a correlation between Pat's and my presence and the weather. I hardly dare tempt providence by saying so, but fine weather seems to follow us wherever we go. I even became an adept horseman, although my enthusiasm remained as skin-deep as the bruises sustained from being involuntarily catapulted over stones walls in mid-gallop.

From *Travelling Player*

James Plunkett

1972

JAMES PLUNKETT KELLY was born in Dublin in 1920 and educated at the Synge Street Christian Brothers College. In 1955, he joined Radio Éireann as Assistant Programme Head and later transferred to Telefís Éireann as producer. Plunkett has written scripts for radio, television and film as well as a play, *The Risen People.* He has also written two collections of short stories, *The Trusting and the Maimed* and *Collected Stories,* and several novels, the best-known being *Strumpet City* and *Farewell Companions.* He lives in Dublin and is a member of Aosdána.

*W*hen I think of Galway city two pictures come automatically to mind. One is Albert Power's statue of the Gaelic writer Padraig O Conaire in Eyre Square, a dimunitive figure with an abstracted air, his head bent as though he were listening to the band. Padraig wrote in a style which made concessions to modern concepts of form, a thing which was not approved at all by the more ardent language enthusiasts, certainly not any one of my own teachers, who set us a question on our favorite writer in Irish. When I wrote in honestly that mine was Padraig O Conaire (I think he was the only one I could read and understand) I was told to find another quick, because Padraig was anglicised.

The other picture is Galway in race week some years ago, with the gaily painted caravans of the tinkers everywhere, followed by their strings of ponies and tribes of goats, the pedlars, the fruit sellers, the tipsters, the thimble riggers and the three card trick men. When I was young there was a three card trick man who operated every Sunday morning (weather, as they say, permitting) on the north quays of Dublin, opposite the Ha'penny Bridge. I got to know his line of guff practically by heart, so if I say that the three card trick men operating at Galway races were deplorable amateurs, I can claim to know what I am talking about.

The great weakness of the three card trick profession is that it has become surrounded by ritual. First there is the three card trick man himself, whose sleight of hand, coupled to his superior intellectual equipment, marks him off at once as the leader. He is entrusted with the properties; a small, collapsible table (designed to fold into invisibility at the approach of the Law), three cards of which one is a picture card and, of course, the money.

Next come his touts, already provided with money by the three card trick man himself, whose business it is, by their apparent success as gamblers, to arouse cupidity in the onlookers and persuade them to plunge . . . .

It is a time worn formula, interwoven with variations so unsubtle that the wonder is there are still people who are ignorant of it. At Galway races, instead of changing touts as he changed his pitch, the three card man kept the same two all the time, apparently oblivious of the fact that people at race meetings, including the potential lambs, are not planted firmly in the same piece of soil like a tree, but wander at will and are likely to remark the singularity of two people so dedicated to the person of the three card trick man that they stick to him like glue. To raise suspicion further, there was another remarkable factor. The three card trick man in question had fair hair and wore a blue suit with a brown shirt and a red tie. The tout who did most of the business of encouraging the Lambs by turning up the corner of the picture card when the three card trick man's attention was distracted had fair hair too. There was a remarkable family resemblance. Instead of trying to disguise it, however, he went out of his way to acknowledge it. He, too, wore a blue suit, a brown shirt and a red tie. It underlines the need for an association of some sort, to enforce standards of competence. Otherwise the profession will get a bad name.

Galway, wedged between the sea and the great stretch of Lough Corrib, is the gateway to Connemara. In season, from the Weir Bridge spanning the Corrib river, hundreds of salmon can be seen lying on the bed of the river, waiting for the rain which will raise the levels so that they can pass up to their spawning grounds in the rivers and lakes which cover that scenically beautiful stretch of country. It begins properly when you cross the bridge beyond the village of Oughterard on the long and lovely journey to Clifden. Bogland with pools to reflect the sky, clumps of heather, lakes, brown streams, and blue mountains fill mile after mile. In a public house at Maam Cross I first heard Irish spoken as an everyday language by Herds who had been attending to their small Connemara sheep. At Cleggan, where you can buy your fish at the quayside straight from the boats, the best fish I have ever tasted. I saw the dolphins coming into the bay to play all day within a few yards of the shore. I remarked their scatterbrained antics to a fisherman and thought they were amusing, but he said they were unlucky and brought bad weather. They did. For a week after their arrival it blew a storm and poured rain. In a way it had its compensations. As the flooded rivers began to subside at last there were trout to be caught in plenty, trout with delicate pink flesh as well as the white variety, and salmon were being sold in Letterfrack and Clifden for half nothing.

From *The Gems She Wore*

Tim Robinson

1972

MAPMAKER TIM ROBINSON was born in Yorkshire in 1935. After completing his national service in Malaya, he went on to study at Cambridge University. Robinson lived in London, Istanbul, and Vienna before coming to the west of Ireland in 1972 to make a map of the Aran Islands. He has been making maps of and writing about the west of Ireland ever since and makes his home in Connemara. His books include *Mapping South Connemara, Mementos of Mortality, Stones of Aran, Connemara* and an autobiography *My Time in Space*.

For some years I have spent a few weeks of each spring and autumn walking the southern coast of Connemara. It is a strange region. Granite, harsh-edged, glittering, shows its teeth everywhere in the heathery wastes and ridged potato fields, and even between the houses of the shapeless villages. The peaty, acidic soil is burdened with countless boulders left by glaciers that came down from the mountains immediately to the north during the last Ice Age. The land has been scrubbed raw, by the ice, by the Atlantic gales, by poverty.

South Connemara was very sparsely peopled in early times, judging by the fewness of its archaeological sites. To the merchants of mediaeval Galway it was a lair of pirates, of the 'Ferocious O'Flaherties.' Some of those dispossessed of better lands by the Cromwellians in 1650 or hunted out of Ulster by the Orangemen in 1795 settled in this unenviable quarter. By the nineteenth century a teeming and periodically starving population was crowded into a narrow coastal strip, fishing, gathering molluscs on the shore, growing potatoes in tiny plots of black waterlogged soil which they fertilized with seaweed, and cutting turf, the only fuel this treeless land affords, from the vast bogs that made the interior almost impassable and otherwise sterile. The sea's deeply penetrating inlets were their lanes of communication and bore the trade they depended on, the export of turf to the stony and fuelless Aran Islands, the Burren in County Clare, and to Galway city. By the beginning of this century the bogland near the coast had been stripped to bare rock.

Modern times have introduced other resources – tourism, some light industry, the teaching of Irish in summer schools, the dole – but the pattern set by that old coastal folklife, a human tidemark between the two sustaining desolations of the sea and the bog, has not been obliterated. From the little mounds of shells left by Neolithic winkle-pickers, to the newest bungalow, a daydream of California's blessed clime, sprouting between two knolls of wet rock and already weatherstained, the dense record of life has been scribbled in the margin of the sea. Only the very shoreline itself, now that the main roads passing by half a mile or so inland have drawn habitation away from it, has been left a lonely place, a long graveyard for the black skeletons of the wooden boats that used to throng the waterways.

This shoreline is of incredible complexity. The two little fishing villages of Ros a' Mhíl and Roundstone are only about twenty miles apart, but, even estimating from a small-scale map and ignoring the fifty or more sizeable islands in the bays and off the headlands, there are at least two hundred and fifty miles of coast between them. It was this strange geography, like a rope of closely interwoven strands flung down in twists and coils across an otherwise bare surface, that brought me to the region; I had a conception filling my head of the correspondingly strange map I could make of it, in which all the density of reference would cluster along one line between two almost blank zones, and that line so convoluted as to visit every square inch of the sheet. And having selected this particular stretch of coast because its near unmappability perversely suggested the possibility of mapping it, I had felt the idea of walking its entire length impose itself like a duty, a ritual of deep if obscure significance through which I would be made adequate to the task of creating an image of the terrain.

In the first month of days of walking I covered perhaps a quarter of the way; the going is not easy. At that stage I wrote some pages which I have now looked over, as I pause between the end of walking and the beginning of drawing, and try to recall those first steps towards the heart of Connemara.

I carry with me on this tangled tightrope of a journey the dozen sheets of the six-inch Ordnance Survey map that cover the area, on which to note my finds – a few rare plants, a number of archaelogical sites, endless hundreds of tiny landing-stages, and above all the Irish placenames I collect from the people of the region. As these maps were last revised eighty years ago I also have to mark in new buildings and paths, which sometimes involves compass-work and the pacing-out of distances. But on the whole the mensurational side of cartography is not my concern; in my efforts to see a little farther into this terrain I stand, if not on the shoulders of giants, then on those of an army, for the original Survey, made in the 1830s, was carried out in the style and with the manpower of a military operation, which in various of its aspects is just what it was. This horde of men who tramped over the countryside with theodolites and chains so adequately measured its lengths, breadths and heights that I am free to concentrate on that mysterious and neglected fourth dimension of cartography which extends deep into the self of the cartographer. My task is to establish a network of lines involving this dimension, along which the landscape can enter my mind, unfragmented and undistorted, to be projected into a map that will be faithful to more than the measurable.

The principles of this subjective triangulation of the world are only now beginning to become expressible for me as I work on this, my third, map. I can throw a glancing light on them by saying that the base-triangle of the system is that formed by the three churchtowers of Proust's Martinville, and for the discovery of its other significant points I have to rely on the sort of magical illumination that produces sometimes poetry and sometimes jokes – but when I use the word 'magical' of my procedures it is only as a blank to hold a space open until I find some more penetrating adjective.

Magic is a tool more easily mislaid than a compass. In my anxiety to miss no tricks on the exactly scientific level, I sometimes go out overburdened with the desire to find classifiable elements of the scene, which I can post off in the form of neat lists to the helpful experts who advise me on archaeology, botany, geology, placenames and so on; and then I merely succeed in blurring for myself the location of those more elusive places, the rivetholes through which I will be able to fasten my experience of the territory to my expression of it on paper, that are only spotted through a mobile reposefulness of mind. In fact after the first week of tramping arduous miles of solitude, with a very thin file of reports to show for the effort, having forgotten the ritual element in this endless walking and come to regard it as merely a means, which was proving inefficient, of finding curiosities, I was almost ready to admit that this wearisome muddle of land and sea was unmappable by my pedestrian methods. Worse still, the inner recesses of these bays, which from the various hilltops I climbed to get a conspectus of the country looked like the roots of a marvellous silver tree winding far into the rich darkness of the hinterland, had, when investigated in detail, slimy shores of black mud tidemarked by gigantic heaps of khaki seaweed, which seemed to multiply the miles by the accusation of insanity.

But by degrees, under the hypnosis of repetitive days, my perceptions changed, and all that had seemed to stand between me and my object – the steep rocky promontories, the ankle-turning shinglebacks, the slithery penetralia of the inlets – became instead part of what I was there for, the shore itself. Then the various incidental difficulties such as the field-walls and drainage ditches that came right down to the water's edge, and even the banks of seaweed, no longer impeded me psychologically, and my body ceased to notice them as physical obstacles. I saw with interest how the walls were continued onto the foreshore by little ramparts of piled boulders linking outcrops of rock, to stop the cattle wandering at low tide. I heard the drainage channels beginning to murmur as an exceptional tide of the autumn equinox, silently brimming and gleaming along the land's edge like the rim of water about an over-filled glass, reached into them and perturbed their stagnation. And the incredible bulk of seaweed itself took on an explanatory role as I realized the influence it has had on the fine structure of the coastline – for in the old days it was the only fertilizer used on this sour land, and there is a spot corresponding to each cottage and in places to each field where boatloads of it used to be landed, so that long stretches of the coast have been remodelled in ways so slight they eluded my eye at first, by the removal of a few stones here to make a navigable passage to high-water mark and the piling up of a few stones there to make a tiny quay.

Thus, in this region commonly said to be bare of archaeological interest, the shore revealed itself as a human construct, the work of numberless generations, in which it was tempting to discern the superimposition and entanglement of evolutionary sequences. There are landing-places even more primaeval-looking than those little hummocks of boulders at the field's edge, for where the thick blanket-bog of the interior comes down to sea level it ends in strange soft black cliffs which collapse here and there to form little muddy harbours, out of the walls of which the gnarled roots of long-buried forests protrude as weird but handy bollards. Farther up the scale are substantial dry-stone jetties built by energetic families, and the handsome masonry piers, famine-relief work of the last century, some of which have been given a twentieth-century topping or cladding, and finally the huge and precisely geometrical concrete acreage of the new EEC-grant-aided harbour works at Ros a' Mhíl, which has probably come into existence over the centuries by progressive improvement of some little alignment of boulders or a twisted bog-oak root now reburied deep in its foundations.

But beyond all these fascinating explanations of itself, the shore drew me on by the mesmeric glittering of its waters; the days of walking became a drug, until I felt I was abandoning myself to the pursuit of this glittering for its own sake, that I welcomed every conceivable complexity of inter-play between land and sea. I devoured distances, although I was working in finer and finer detail. Such a labour of mind and body is at first crushingly exhausting, rises to bliss as the activity fuels its own source of vigour, and then a point of satiety is reached rather suddenly, it is time to break off, go home, and lie for a spell under waves of tiredness.

From *Setting Foot on the Shores of Connemara*

Benedict Kiely

1978

BORN IN OMAGH, County Tyrone, in 1919, Benedict Kiely received his early education from the Christian Brothers before entering a Jesuit novitiate. An illness a year later resulted in an extended stay in a Dublin hospital, and Kiely abandoned his vocation on his recovery. He enrolled in University College Dublin and, after graduation, he pursued a career in journalism before turning to fiction. Kiely spent several years in the United States, lecturing and writing for *The New Yorker* and other publications. In 1980 Kiely received the Irish Academy of Letters Award for Literature.

Elisa Johanna is not alone. Close beside her the *Hurnay* from Lubeck is loading timber; and the *Naomh Eanna* that joins Ireland to the Aran Islands, and the *Galway Bay*, are still enjoying the morning slumber that's made all the more sweet by the knowledge that somebody else is awake and working; and the monstrous *Egee* from Caen is sucking in black ore from the mines of Tynagh. The ore is stored on the quayside in a crazy sort of structure that at a distance looks like an oriental pavilion. There are, I know, various views about the value to Ireland of the present mode of exporting a portion of her bowels to far foreign fields yet it does make for activity in Galway harbour in the early morning.

It's a good fifteen years since I last walked in Galway city or around the harbour, or any closer to them than Paddy Burke's Oyster House at Clarinbridge when Paddy, God rest him, was there to give the full warmth of a Galway welcome. Why it should be fifteen years, or why one should be as close as Clarinbridge without coming on to Galway, I can't exactly say. But my journeys in these parts in those years always seemed to be from Clare to Dublin or Dublin to Clare by the high exciting road along the ridge of Slieve Auchty where you strain your eyes all the time for the first glimmer of Loch Graney or Loch Cutra; or by a detour to view Black Head and the white stony Burren of North Clare and to meditate on the ancient ruins of Corcomroe Abbey and on Yeat's vision of Dermot and Dervorgilla.

It helps a great deal to appreciate the strange moonscape of the Burren – the name means Big Rock – if you read those descriptive lines at the beginning of Yeats's *The Dreaming of the Bones*:

> *Somewhere among great rocks, on the scarce grass,*
> *Birds cry, they cry their loneliness.*
> *Even the sunlight can be lonely here,*
> *Even hot noon is lonely.*

Then if you found yourself in the Burren and wanted to get back to Dublin, it was hardly a detour and always a delight to call to see Paddy Burke, particularly if you had known him long before the English Royal family and John Huston started to visit his place; and if you had feasted well with Paddy, on black velvet, on bread and smoked salmon or Galway oysters, then it seemed the part of a wise man to slink back to the comparative safety of Dublin and leave Galway city until the next time round.

For, drunk or sober, a man may stay in Galway city at least a day more than he meant to.

The last time and the time before that I was at Galway harbour at this hour of the morning I was on my way from the Castle hotel in Lower Abbeygate Street to the Aran Islands. The Castle hotel is to the Aran Islands as Hong Kong is, or was, to the British empire, a foothold and trading post on the mainland. In days of more uninhibited roistering the older people on the islands used to say about the behaviour of the younger people: 'We don't know where the devil is by day, but by night he's in the Castle hotel in Lower Abbeygate Street.'

On no previous morning, though, in Galway harbour did I see so much business afoot. This may be a sign of the Irish economic revival, about which we have read, and a good thing, too, we suppose, and long overdue. But to get away from the noise and dust of it I do, more or less, what George Moore, the novelist, did, about 70 years ago and walk on and out as far as I can go with the living rugged Corrib and the crazy gulls to my right, and the bay, grey with white splurges, and the sullen hills of Clare ahead of me.

There was a *feis*, or Gaelic cultural festival, to be held in Galway city and a Gaelic League secretary in Dublin had told Mr. Moore that his musical cousin, Mr. Edward Martyn of Tulira Castle which is over there by the town of Gort and now the residence of Lord Hemphill, would be there to judge the traditional singing. Lady Gregory and Mr. Yeats would be there also. Mr. Moore who, on his own whimsical admission, couldn't bear to be left out of anything, took off for Galway. Seventy or so years ago.

Cousin Edward is there, as endearingly comic as Cousin George always made him seem to be. Mr. Yeats is made to talk as, indeed, he may then have talked. The walk that the three of them had around Galway makes some of the best reading to be found in the three volumes of Moore's *Hail and Farewell* . . .

Oh, what gentlemanly melancholy, what a dying fall, and Marius the Epicurean meditating on the morning of the sun-warmed stones of the decayed, ancestral villa. All bullshit, Mr. Moore!

But what would Moore in his pose as Marius have had to say about the black guts of the Tynagh mines sailing off, as he did himself, to gallant

France? Or of that stout wench from Groningen scattering her fertilising dust in the dacent eyes of Irishmen?

From the point of this wharf Moore saw some laughing Galway girls wading in the salt pools. One of them was so brazen and so daring that she hoisted her kirtle right up to her waist. George seemed to think that her performance was for his benefit. It may well have been – although he was a little bit given to self-gratulatory whimsies of that sort. Didn't he think, or pretend to, that every young nun he met anywhere was mutely appealing to him to be rescued?

But what, I wonder as I head back for the Spanish Arch, would Mr. Moore think of Salthill nowadays on a Sunday in the summer or of the men at the swimming pool there who complained in letters to the papers that their privacy was being shattered by young women in bikinis?

Women, we all know, can be a nuisance at times, particularly in pubs, if there are any pubs left. But women sober and young and by salt sea pools and in bikinis might have moved Mr. Moore of Moore Hall to talk not only about mermaids but even about Aphrodite, not in Aulis but in the cold Galway sea. He would have given the matter serious thought – and brought Cousin Edward along to embarrass his modesty by the sights – nor would the letter he wrote to the papers have been one of complaint.

Galway is the city or town in Ireland most possessed by water: living water, wild water, clean water, sea-water, river-water, lake-water, but not water in the whiskey except you add it yourself.

The restless bay at my back, I walk under the Spanish Arch and over the roaring Corrib, and along by the canal which is the most restless canal I've ever seen. It never seems able to make up its mind, to rest content with its lot in life and stay where it is. It always seems as if it had half a notion to go back with a rush, engulfing all before it, to the tumult of the original stream.

Then when I pass the crowded friendly university college and the vast cathedral – empty at this hour of the day, except for the Lord himself and two whispering nuns, and myself with my audibly creaking knees – I am assaulted by all the wild airs and memories of Connacht. It doesn't seem to matter there which way the winds are blowing. They all come at you from the long chain of lakes, Corrib and Mask and Carra and Conn, when you stand on the big bridge at the fringe of Galway city and look northwards in the general direction of Cong.

It's the most exciting bridge in Ireland, making a man want to be young again, and a boatman or a hunter or a spearer of salmon, or a character in a novel by that good man, the late Walter Macken who couldn't be totally happy anywhere except in the west.

The crowded friendly college: for like all our colleges, and like most colleges elsewhere it's crowded and not so long ago the students were

Galway women painted by Michaél MacLiammóir

making their protest for what the Germans euphemistically used to call elbow-room. It is a friendly college, which may be because it partakes of the character of the city. The group of students that I lectured to there one evening leave a pleasant impression on the memory, particularly a young man in whose father's house I once was, not far from the town of Boyle in County Roscommon and close to the grave of Carolan, the blind harper and composer whose eighteenth-century music is splendidly played today by Paddy Moloney, the piper, and the Chieftains: and close to the grave of the mythological god and cyclopean monster, Balor of the Evil Eye.

This young man says to me at the end of the night that most of his fellow students read nobody except John McGahern and Edna O'Brien. This gives me matter for thought long after the young people have gone and I am sitting alone, sipping and reading, in the only hotel in the world in which I was ever introduced to a live lobster.

This day long ago I was in the bar and a man came in with a bag and put the complicated splendidly-designed creature on the counter. He was still the dull colour of the Galway rocks that hadn't protected him well enough. The red radiance would come later on, for the delight of men, and of women too, he would be boiled alive. The man who brought him in solemnly introduced him to everybody in the bar. There was much laughter and extending of hands in mock salutation. Let it be said, in some slight extenuation, that we were all half tipsy. But nobody was tipsy enough to reach the hand too far forward. The mechanism of the creature fascinated me. His eyes were out, as Mrs Mulligan used to say, like organ stops. He saw us, for sure. What he thought of us we will never know.

John McGahern went to University College Galway so that it's reasonable that students at Galway would want to read him. But there's a lot more to it than that. The centre of the truth may be that until Edna O'Brien and John McGahern came along no Irish writer that I can think of ever really spoke to the young. In terms of patriotism, yes, and the rising of the moon, and 'did that play of mine send out certain men the English shot.' But not about domestic matters, like masturbation, around which adults and the ages have built a mythology and a theodicy, or about the passing or failing of examinations, or the domination of a strong father, or a mother dying slowly of a dread disease; or about young girls wondering what it was all about and being determined to find out. Most of us seem to have been born with minds as matured, to put it nicely, as that of the changeling in the cradle who speaks with the voice of an old man, or that of 'the eagle cock that blinks and blinks on Ballygawley Hill.' and is, according to the Sligo poet, the oldest thing under the moon.

When I describe McGahern as the Frank Sinatra of the Irish novel I mean no denigration – if the word is permissible. Sinatra fans will wonder why I bother to hedge the remark. When Sinatra first set his audiences screaming he did so because he appealed to young people who had problems that they thought a scream might solve.

All this, of course, may be just a special quality of our time, and here I give up theorising and look from the most exciting bridge in Ireland at the white wonder of a shower gathering high in the air above the Corrib. There's a lot of quite audible screaming in the world we live in.

From *All the Way to Bantry Bay*

Pete McCarthy

1996

EXPLORER AND comedian Pete McCarthy was born in Warrington, England, and spent most of his childhood summers with his grandparents in Ireland. He has worked as a radio and television presenter of such shows as *Travelog*, *Desperateley Seeking Something*, *Breakaway* and *Country Tracks*. While researching his book *McCarthy's Bar*, he travelled the length and breadth of Ireland – at all times obeying the simple rule 'Never Pass a Bar That Has Your Name On It'. Published in 2000, the book became a number-one bestseller in Ireland, the U.K. and Australia. It also won the British Book Awards' Newcomer of the Year and the Thomas Cook Travel Writing Award.

*T*here's a roundabout of such consummate ugliness on the Galway ring road that it would have been refused planning permission in New Jersey. You'd never dream you were within a mile of one of the loveliest city centres in the country. A tawdry mall of video boutiques and foam-backed carpet emporia festers beneath the golden arch of the giant 'M.' Christ, you think, get me out of this place before I see the cut-price exhaust centre, or World of Leather.

But the most astonishing feature of this depressing landscape is the fact that by the side of the road, in every direction, women in tracksuits—stiff-backed, high-elbowed, bums out, in twos and threes or by themselves, in headphones or neck towels or smoking fags – are power walking. Perhaps it's a virus that's drifted across on a freakishly warm breeze from America. I wonder if the Unionists know about it? They wouldn't want this sort of caper catching on in Portadown or Ballymena as a result of some subversive cross-border initiative. Imagine if the Orangemen all started walking like that. They'd look ridiculous.

It's unseasonably hot as I drive into the city, and the place is seething with people. I head straight for the B&B I've booked in advance on the strength of the street name: Nuns' Island. It turns out to be a splendid old house built in the 1730s with stone walls two feet thick. The river flows past the end of the back garden on its way to the salmon weir, and the sea is just a few hundred yards away. There's a sign in my bathroom that says: 'No Smoking (on Sundays and Holy Days).'

Like every B&B landlady I have encountered so far, Mrs O'Flaherty is an honours graduate of the course in Celtic Hospitality. Studies entitled 'Be True To Your Most Eccentric Instincts.' She's a big woman in a tweed skirt and what I eventually conclude, having eliminated all other possibilities, must be a turquoise mohair cape. A small jowly dog, coughing and wheezing like a Romanian asbestos miner who's taken early retirement, peeps out from beneath a prodigious armpit. She never puts it down, and I have to concede the possibility it may be surgically attached.

'I've lived all my life here,' she tells me. 'The city has a wonderful history. Did you know there was once a sign over the west gate of the town? It said "From the Ferocious O'Flahertys, Good Lord, Deliver Us."'

She raises her eyebrows as if to say, 'Well there you are then,' and gives me a potty but endearing smile.

'The city was once ruled by fourteen English families called the Tribes of Galway. Did you know that? And do you know about the Lynch Stone?'

'No,' I say, but I bet I soon will.

In 1493 James Lynch FitzStephen, the mayor of Galway, went on a business trip to Spain. To thank his hosts for their hospitality, he took their only son back to Galway for a holiday. But FitzStephen had an only son of his own, who was involved in a passionate love affair. Fearing the Spaniard might be a rival, he accused him of trying to steal his girlfriend. The Spaniard, baffled, insisted he was only here for the oysters and the stout. This cut no ice with young Lynch, who stabbed him dead, then confessed to his father.

The mayor did what any father in his position would have done: he arrested and tried his son, found him guilty, and sentenced him to death. When an executioner couldn't be found because the lad was so popular, he strung him up himself from an upstairs window of his house, in front of a fascinated but unenthusiastic crowd.

'So is that where the expression 'to lynch someone' comes from? I ask.

'Do you know,' says Mrs O'Flaherty, 'I haven't a bleddy clue.'

From *McCarthy's Bar*

Sources

Giraldus Cambrensis   Giraldus Cambrensis, *The first version of the Topography of Ireland*, trans. John J. O'Meara: Dundalk, Dundalgan Press, 1951. Reprinted by permission of Dundalgan Press.

Fynes Moryson   *The Field Day Anthology of Irish Writing*: Derry, Field Day Publications, 1991

Oliver St. John   Edmund Hogan, *The Description of Ireland*: Dublin, M.H. Gill, 1878

John Speed   *An Epitome of Mr. John Speed's Theatre of the Empire of Great Britain*: London, Thomas Bosset, 1676

Ann Fanshawe   Ann Fanshawe, *The Memoirs of Ann, Lady Fanshawe:* London, John Lane The Bodley Head, 1907

Edmund Ludlow   Edmund Ludlow, *Memoirs of Edmund Ludlow*: Vivay (Switzerland) 1689

John Dunton   Edward MacLysaght, *Irish Life in the Seventeenth Century:* Cork, Cork University Press, 1950

Edward Lhuyd   R.T. Gunther, *Early Science in Oxford*. Oxford, R.T. Gunther, 1945

Samuel Molyneux   Thomas Molyneux, *The Journey to Connaught:* Dublin, Irish Archaeological Society, 1846

John Wesley   *The Journal of John Wesley*: Oxford, Oxford University Press, 1987

Arthur Young   *Arthur Young's Tour in Ireland:* London, George Bell & sons, 1892

Daniel Beaufort   The journals of Daniel Beaufort at Trinity College Dublin (Catalogue number 4035). Reprinted by permission of the Trustees of Trinity College Dublin

Mary Beaufort   From 'Journal of our tour to inspect the Charter Schools: 1808' at Trinity College Dublin (Catalogue number 4035). Reprinted by permission of the Trustees of Trinity College Dublin

George Petrie   William Stokes, *The Life and Labours in Art and Archaeology of George Petrie:* London, Longmans, Green, & company, 1868

Martha Louisa Blake   *Letters from the Irish Highlands of Connemara:* London, John Murray, 1825

Hermann von Pückler-Muskau   Hermann von Pückler-Muskau, *Tour in England, Ireland and France:* Philadelphia, Carey, Lea & Blanchard, 1833

Maria Edgeworth   Maria Edgeworth, *Tour in Connemara:* London, Constable & company, 1950

Alexis de Tocqueville   *Alexis de Tocqueville's Journey in Ireland*: Washington DC, Catholic University of America Press, 1990. Reprinted by permission of Catholic University of America Press

Caesar Otway   Caesar Otway, *A Tour in Connaught:* Dublin, William Curry Junior and company, 1839

John O'Donovan   P.A. Ó Síocháin, *Aran:Islands of Legend:* Dublin, Foilsiúcháin Eireann, 1962

Anthony Trollope   Anthony Trollope, *Autobiography of Anthony Trollope:* New York, G. Munro, 1883

William Makepeace Thackeray   William Makepeace Thackeray, *The Irish Sketchbook:* Belfast, The Blackstaff Press, 1843

Asenath Nicholson   Asenath Nicholson, *The Bible in Ireland:* New York, The John Day Company, 1927

Thomas Carlyle   Thomas Carlyle, *Reminiscences of my Irish journey in 1849:* London, S. Low, Marston, Searle, & Rivington, 1882

Harriet Martineau   Harriet Martineau, *Letters from Ireland:* London, J. Chapman, 1852

Thomas Colville Scott   Thomas Colville Scott, *Connemara after the Famine*, ed. Tim Robinson: Dublin, The Lilliput Press, 1995. Reprinted by permission of the Lilliput Press and Tim Robinson.

Samuel Ferguson   *The Dublin University Magazine:* Dublin, William Curry, Junior & company

Martin Haverty   *The Aran Isles; or a Report of the Excursion of the Ethnological Section of the British Association from Dublin to the Western Islands of Aran in September 1857:* Dublin, University Press, 1859

William Wilde   *Wilde's Lough Corrib:* Dublin, At the Sign of the Three Candles, 1938

Wilfrid Scawen Blunt   Wilfrid Scawen Blunt, *My Diaries:* London, M. Secker, 1920

Edith Somerville   Edith Somerville, *Through Connemara in a Governess Cart:* London, W.H. Allen & company, Ltd., 1893

Arthur Symons   Arthur Symons, *Cities and Seacoasts and Islands:* London, W. Collins sons & company, 1918

William Butler Yeats   William Butler Yeats, *Autobiographies:* London, Macmillan and company Ltd., 1926. Reprinted by permission of AP Watt on behalf of Estate William Butler Yeats

Maud Gonne MacBride   Maud Gonne MacBride, *A Servant of the Queen: Reminiscences by Maud Gonne MacBride:* London, V. Gollancz, 1938

George Moore   George Moore, *Hail and Farewell:* New York, D. Appleton and company, 1925

John Millington Synge   John M. Synge, *In Wicklow, West Kerry, The Congetsed Districts, Under Ether:* Boston, John W. Luce & company, 1912

B.N. Hedderman   B.N. Hedderman, *Glimpses of my Life in Aran:* Bristol, Wright, 1917

James Joyce   *Letters of James Joyce Volumes II & III* ed. Richard Ellman: New York, The Viking Press, 1957. © 1966, 1975 by F. Lionel Munro, as Administrator of the Estate of James Joyce. Reprinted by permission of Viking Penguin, a division of Penguin Putnam Inc.

Augustus John   Augustus John, *Chiaroscuro:* London, Jonathan Cape, 1952

Arthur Whitten Brown   Arthur Whitten Brown, *Flying the Atlantic in Sixteen Hour:* New York, Frederick A. Stokes Company, 1920

William Orpen   William Orpen, *Stories of Old Ireland & Myself:* New York, Henry Holt and company, 1925

Signe Toksvig   From *Signe Toksvig's Irish Diaries,* 1926-1937, ed. Lis Pihl: Dublin, the Lilliput Press, 1994. Reprinted by permission of the Lilliput Press and Lis Pihl

Sean O'Casey   Sean O'Casey, *The Letters of Sean O'Casey 1910-1941:* New York: the Macmillan company, 1975-92

Francis Stuart   Francis Stuart, *Things to Live For:* New York, the Macmillan Company, 1935

Robert Flaherty   A press release from the Gaumont-British Picture Company

Sean O'Faolain   Sean O'Faolain, *An Irish Journey:* London, Longmans, Green & company.(© 1940 Sean O'Faolain.) Reproduced by permission of the Estate of Sean O'Faolain c/o Rogers, Coleridge & White Ltd., 20 Powis Mews, London W11 1JN

Ethel Mannin   Ethel Mannin, *A Connemara Journal:* London, Westhouse, 1947

Oliver St. John Gogarty   Oliver St. John Gogarty, *Rolling Down the Lea:* London, Constable, 1950

Frank O'Connor   Frank O'Connor, *Leinster, Munster and Connaught:* London, Robert Hale Limited, 1950. (© Frank O'Connor: as printed in the original volume). Reprinted by permission of PFD on behalf of Estate of Frank O'Connor.

Olivia Manning   Olivia Manning, *The Dreaming Shore:* London, Evans Brothers, 1950

V. S. Pritchett   V. S. Pritchett, *At Home and Abroad:* San Francisco, North Point Press, 1989. (© V S Pritchett 1990). Reproduced by permission of PFD on behalf of the Estate of V S Pritchett.

Diana Mosley   Diana Mosley, *A Life of Contrasts:* London, Hamish Hamilton, 1977

Church on Inchaguile in Lough Corrib drawn by George Petrie

Paul Henry   From *Ireland of the Welcomes*

Brendan Behan   *Brendan Behan's Island:* London, Hutchinson, 1962. Reprinted by permission of the Random House Group Ltd.

John Huston   John Huston, *An Open Book:* London, Macmillan, 1980. (© 1980 by John Huston). Reprinted by permission of Alfred A. Knopf, a division of Random House, Inc.

Micheál MacLiammóir   *Ireland,* Edwin Smith: London, Thames & Hudson, 1966. ©1966 Thames & Hudson

Michael York   Michael York, *Travelling Player:* London, Headline, 1991. Reprinted by permission of Headline Book Publishing Ltd.

James Plunkett   James Plunkett, *The Gems She Wore*: London, Hutchinson, 1972. Copyright © James Plunkett 1972. Reprinted by permission of PFD on behalf of James Plunkett

Tim Robinson   Tim Robinson, *Setting Foot on the Shores of Connemara:* Dublin, the Lilliput Press, 1996. Reprinted by permission of the Lilliput Press and Tim Robinson

Benedict Kiely   Benedict Kiely, *All the way to Bantry Bay:* London, Victor Gollancz, 1978. Reprinted by permission of A.P. Watt Ltd., on behalf of Michael B. Yeats

Pete McCarthy   Pete McCarthy, *McCarthy's Bar:* London, Hodder & Stoughton Limited, 1996. Reprinted by permission of Hodder and Stoughton Ltd.

Picture Credits

John Millington Synge photographs of the Galway Fish Market, Aran Island spinners and landing a curragh, courtesy of the Trustees of Trinity College Dublin

Portraits of George Petrie and Samuel Ferguson, and William Wakeman's Kilcannanagh church courtesy of the Royal Irish Academy

W.B. Yeats portrait by John Butler Yeats, John Millington Synge portrait by Harold Oakley courtesy of the Hugh Lane Municipal Gallery

Sean O'Casey portrait by Patrick Tuohy courtesy Dr. John O'Brien and the Hugh Lane Municipal Gallery

Francis Stuart portrait by Edward McGuire courtesy of Sally McGuire and the Hugh Lane Municipal Gallery

Portrait of George Moore by Eduord Manet.

Photographs from the Lawrence Collection on pages x, 14, 82, 89, 95, 117, 227 courtesy the National Photographic Archive

Photograph of Alcock & Brown's Vimy plane courtesy the Hulton Getty Picture Archive

Pictures on the pages listed are from the following books:

24, *The Antiquities of Ireland*, Daniel Grose: Dublin, Irish Architectural Archive, 1991

119, 159, *The Aran Islands*, J.M. Synge: Dublin, Maunsel, 1907

109, *The Beauties of Ireland*, JN Brewer: London, Sherwood Jones 1825

219, *Crossroads in Ireland*, Padraic Colum: New York, Macmillan, 1930

10, *Down by the Claddagh*, Peadar O'Dowd: Galway, Kennys Bookshop & Art Gallery, 1993

26, 105, 176, 206, *The Ecclesiastical Architecture of Ireland*, George Petrie: Dublin, Hodges & Smith, 1845

17, 64, 84, 93, 97, *The History of the Town and Country of Galway*, James Hardiman: Dublin, W. Folds, 1820

108, *In Vinculis*, W. S. Blunt: London, Kegan Paul, Trench & Co., 1889

168, 172, 199, *Irish Pictures*, Richard Lovett: London, Religious Tract Soc 1888

45, *Life in the West of Ireland*, Jack Yeats: Dublin, Maunsel & Co., 1912

8, *Memoirs of Edmund Ludlow*, Edmund Ludlow: Vivay, 1689

vii, 30, 33, 47, 75, 76, 86, 151, 189, *Picturesque Ireland*, John Savage: New York, T. Kelly, 1878

165, 178, 182, *Picturesque Views of the Antiquities of Ireland*, R.O. Newenham: London, T&W Boone, 1830

9, 59, *Select Views of Lough Derg and the River Shannon*, Paul Gauci: London Wm, Spooner, 1831

60, 143, 193, 219, *The West of Ireland*, Henry Coulter: Dublin, Hodges & Smith, 1862

113, *Through Connemara in a Governess Cart*, Edith Somerville: London, W.H. Allen & Co, 1893

vi, x, 2, 7, 27, 29, 37, 54, 140, 146, 155, 184, 203, *The Tourists Handbook*: illus. James Mahony: London, W. Smith and Sons, Strand. Dublin: M'Glashan & Gill, Sackville Street, 1853

40, 72, 75, 79, *Three Months' Tour in Ireland*, Marie-Ann de Bovet: London, Chapman & Hall, 1891

125, 163, *Yeats' Ireland*, Benedict Kiely: London, Aurum, 1989

Acknowledgements

St. Nicholas Church in the early twentieth century. (Lawrence Collection R784)

I gratefully acknowledge the co-operation of the copyright owners. I'd also like to thank the following institutions and people who have helped in the compilation of this book:

American Irish Historical Society, Boole Library at University College Cork, Galway County Library, James Hardiman Library, Galway, National Library of Ireland, New-York Historical Society, New York Public Library, Pepys Library, Magdalene College Cambridge, Manuscripts Department at Trinity College Dublin, Royal Irish Academy, and the Hugh-Lane Municipal Gallery

Jennifer Barnet, Marie Boran, Don Chase, Joseph Coencas, Bernard Devaney, Penelope Durell, Aude Fitzsimons, Margaret Flannery, Liz Foster, Anissa Fox, Marylin Gaughan, Sharon Greenwald, James Hart, Kieran Hoare, Patrick Kelly, Delia Kelly, Mary Kelly, Des Kenny, Tom Kenny, Bill Kopert, Sabine Lacaze, Jennifer Lewis, Maureen Moran, Elizabeth MacDonagh, Pat McMahon, Reet Neelis, Peadar O'Dowd, Dónall Ó Luanaigh, Siobháin O'Rafferty, Sarah Pollard, Norbert Schering, Kerry Stevens, Flicka Small, Margaret Twomey, Jenny Wright.

Index